LARS ENARSON

THE JOY OF THE WHOLE EARTH

JERUSALEM

AND THE

FUTURE OF THE WORLD

ARIEL MEDIA   ARIELMEDIA.SE

Published by Ariel Media (*arielmedia.se*)
An imprint of The Watchman International, Inc. (*thewatchman.org*)
PO Box 94, Lake Mills, IA 50450, USA

Design: John Enarson
Cover Photo: Kobby Dagan / Shutterstock.com
Inside Flap Photo: Jostein Skevik / Shofar Media

First Edition
Printed in the United States of America
ISBN 978-0-9763217-2-9

To my beloved wife Harriet.
You always believed in me!

CONTENTS

FOREWORD

Was the Garden of Eden located where Jerusalem is today? Is it possible to know? Abraham, Moses, and David, the apostles, prophets, and Jesus Himself knew of the future destiny of Jerusalem. Do you know what is about to happen? What will the Messiah do when he comes back to Jerusalem? And where will you be?

There are a variety of Christian, Jewish, and secular books on the subject of Jerusalem—from the classic, historical *O Jerusalem*, to prophetic titles, like *Jerusalem Countdown*. However, I do not think there is another book like *The Joy of the Whole Earth: Jerusalem and the Future of the World*.

It might be unusual for a wife to write the foreword to her husband's book, but since I know Lars better than anyone, I feel I can also better share what he wishes to convey through his book.

We moved with our family to Israel in 1997, and have lived here most of the time since. I believe that God gave Lars a calling to Israel and the Jewish people already as a small boy when an old Jewish man put his hands on him and blessed him. This experience made a deep impression on my husband and he remembers it vividly to this day.

God has given Lars a zeal to prepare the way for Messiah's return to His city and to prepare His people to be ready when He comes. *The Joy of the Whole Earth* wishes to give you knowledge and insight into the complete vision of Jerusalem, from past to future—the city where God has chosen to make His name dwell for eternity. It wants to equip you to be part of God's wonderful plan for this earth and His kingdom.

This book represents a seismic shift in Christian thinking, a reorientation, a shift of focus. Many are not used to the concept of holy space, or holy places, and the biblical testimony about Jerusalem may very well challenge you. I encourage you to let the Scriptures open your eyes.

For you as a reader to get the most out of this book about Jerusalem, you must be a lover of God's Word. I don't know of any Bible teacher that uses as much Scripture when he teaches, as Lars. As a young boy, he was mentored to memorize Scripture daily, and thanks to that, he has an enormous foundation of the Word of God in his heart.

Throughout the years, I have seen Lars study about Israel and Jerusalem, hour upon hour, day and night. He is a man who seeks the truth, no matter how long it takes, or how difficult it may be. This book is a result of specifically the last seven years of study, with the goal to convey the awesome reality of what the Scriptures show us about Jerusalem—the city of our great King!

Lars has also discovered the rich treasure of wisdom and commentary on the Scriptures found among the Jewish people. From this treasure chest, he draws illustrations that parallel the Gospels in a beautiful way, just like Jesus taught regarding the learned scribes, *"Therefore every scribe who has become a disciple of the kingdom of heaven is like a head of a household, who brings out of his treasure things new and old."* (NASB)

Part of the revelation in *The Joy of the Whole Earth* is also Lars' own journey to discover, more than ever, the reality of what the Bible teaches. Messiah will be back in Jerusalem—probably sooner than any of us realize—and His kingdom will be real and tangible, and will have consequences for each and every one of us.

Lars and I want to thank our son John, who has done a remarkable job in helping us edit this book, as well as doing all the layout. Without his God-given talents and insight... *Oy vey!* A huge "thank you" also goes to Amy Muckelstone for proofreading and correcting the grammar. Any remaining flaws are our own and not that of Amy's remarkable talent and generous dedication.

We have tried to make important facts approachable and understandable with maps and illustrations. This book will gradually reveal to you—from Genesis to Revelation—why Jerusalem is so important, and why a tiny piece of real estate in the heart of the city is at the center of world upheaval. The end time conflict is upon us! It is a battle over God's throne on earth, where His anointed King will reign!

As you read *The Joy of the Whole Earth*, I pray that you will study and absorb God's Word, so that you will be grounded in truth, ready for what is ahead. I pray that you will get a revelation in your heart that will never leave you, a revelation of the most beautiful of all cities—Jerusalem—her history and her future. It is our future and yours, if you love her!

God bless you as you begin your journey to discover Jerusalem!

Harriet E. Enarson
Israel, April 2015

> *"If I forget thee, O Jerusalem, let my right hand forget her cunning. Let my tongue cleave to the roof of my mouth, if I remember thee not; if I set not Jerusalem above my chiefest joy."* (Ps 137:5–6 KJV)

1

THE GARDEN OF EDEN

*"A glorious throne set on high from the beginning
is the place of our sanctuary." —Jeremiah 17:12*

This book is about God's city—Jerusalem. Even though *"The earth is the LORD's and the fullness thereof,"* (Ps 24:1) there is one city in the world that God specifically calls His own. This makes Jerusalem different than all other places on earth. King Cyrus wrote in his famous decree:

> *"Any of you who are his people may go to Jerusalem in Judah to rebuild this Temple of the Lord, the God of Israel, who lives in Jerusalem."* (Ezr 1:3 NLT)

The Creator of heaven and earth is the God who lives in Jerusalem. It is His city. Every year, the postal services in Jerusalem receive letters from people that are simply just addressed, "To God." They are always forwarded to the Chief Rabbi at the Western Wall in Jerusalem's Old City and placed between the stones in the wall.

In the Book of Zechariah, God calls Zion *"the apple of his eye."* (Zec 2:8) God looks at the world through the lens of Jerusalem.

"Thus says the Lord GOD: This is Jerusalem. I have set her in the center of the nations, with countries all around her." (Eze 5:5)

From God's point of view, Jerusalem is the center of the earth. To be more specific, the Temple Mount is the center. And if you want to be even more specific than that, it is the stone that is located under the golden cupola of the present day Dome of the Rock that is the **absolute** center.

The Dutch archaeological architect Leen Ritmeyer, has in his fascinating book *The Quest* convincingly proven that this stone was located in the Most Holy Place, in both the First and Second Temples.[1] It was on this stone that the Ark of the Covenant, with the mercy seat overshadowed by the cherubim of glory, stood. It is where God's presence dwelt and where no man, except the high priest, once a year, was allowed to enter.

In Jewish tradition, this stone is called *Even HaShtiya,* the "Foundation Stone," and it was from the dust in this place that God created Adam. The Garden of Eden was also situated here.

The Rivers

Through the centuries, many have speculated about where the Garden of Eden was located. There is some interesting biblical support for the Jewish tradition that connects Eden with Jerusalem. Let us begin by looking at the rivers that flowed from the garden. We read about Eden in the Book of Genesis:

"And the LORD God planted a garden in Eden, in the east, and there he put the man whom he had formed. And out of the ground the LORD God made to spring up every tree that

---

1   Leen Ritmeyer, *The Quest: Revealing the Temple Mount in Jerusalem* (Jerusalem: Carta, 2012).

is pleasant to the sight and good for food. The tree of life was in the midst of the garden, and the tree of the knowledge of good and evil. A river flowed out of Eden to water the garden, and there it divided and became four rivers. The name of the first is the Pishon. It is the one that flowed around the whole land of Havilah, where there is gold. And the gold of that land is good; bdellium and onyx stone are there. The name of the second river is the Gihon. It is the one that flowed around the whole land of Cush. And the name of the third river is the Tigris, which flows east of Assyria. And the fourth river is the Euphrates." (Gen 2:8–14)

Tigris and Euphrates

It says here, *"A river flowed out of Eden to water the garden, and there it divided and became four rivers."* (Gen 2:10) The last two of these four rivers, the Tigris, *"which flows east of Assyria,"* (Gen 2:14) and the Euphrates, are known to this day with the same names and are therefore easy to find on a map. This has caused some to believe that the Garden of Eden was located in the area where Iraq is today. However, this is where these rivers finish their course, in the Persian Gulf, not where they begin. The Garden of Eden was located where all these rivers **began**. The headwaters of both the Tigris and Euphrates are today situated in southern Turkey. Let us keep this in mind as we continue.

Gihon

The first two rivers that flowed from the Garden of Eden, the Pishon and the Gihon, are not known today. But the Bible gives us some clues to where they were located. It says about the Gihon River, *"It is the one that flowed around the whole land of Cush."* (Gen 2:13) Cush is the biblical name of the region of Ethiopia and Southern Sudan. From this we can deduct that Eden must have been located somewhere in the Middle East between Iraq/Turkey and Ethiopia/Sudan.

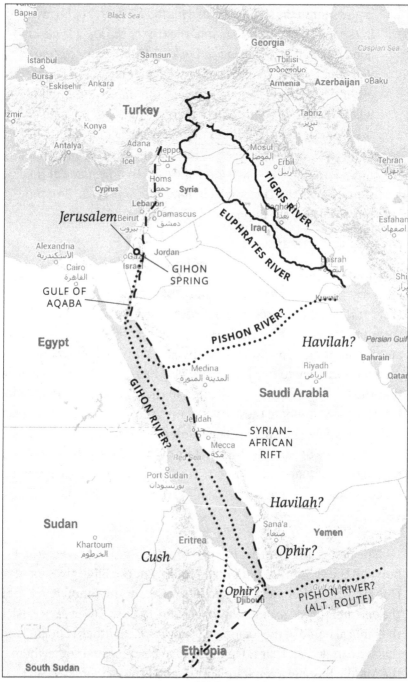

Pishon

The first river, the Pishon, is a little bit more problematic to locate geographically.[2] There are, however, a couple of clues that can help us. It says about the river Pishon, *"It is the one that flowed around the whole land of Havilah, where there is gold. And the gold of that land is good; bdellium and onyx stone are there."* (Gen 2:11–12)

The Bible connects the area of *"Havilah, where there is gold,"* with the center of the Arabian Peninsula where Ophir was situated.[3] This area has, throughout history, always been known for its gold. King Solomon built a fleet of ships that brought gold from Ophir (see 1 Ki 9:28). Also, southwestern Arabia (around today's Yemen) is known for its gold as well as bdellium and onyx stone.

There is today a dry riverbed in this area, traversing the entire Arabian Peninsula from west to east, which some believe could once have been the Pishon River.[4] Whatever the case, the Pishon seems clearly connected with the Arabian Peninsula.

Syrian-African Rift

We now have three landmarks to navigate from, the area between (1) Iraq/Turkey, (2) Ethiopia/Sudan, and (3) the Arabian Peninsula. There is a well-known geological phenomenon called the Syrian-African Rift, which stretches from southern Turkey to Ethiopia, connecting these three key landmarks. Jerusalem is located right along this rift!

---

2   Some say that it is the Nile, others that it was the Ganges River in India.

3   The Scriptures connect Havilah with the sons of Joktan. *"Sheba, Ophir, Havilah, and Jobab; all these were the sons of Joktan."* (Gen 10:28–29) Havilah is also connected with the sons of Ishmael. *"They settled from Havilah to Shur, which is opposite Egypt in the direction of Assyria. He settled over against all his kinsmen."* (Gen 25:18) All this points to the region of the Arabian Peninsula where Ophir also was.

4   Farouk El–Baz, "A River in the Desert," *Discover*, July 1993, cited by http://en.wikipedia.org/wiki/Pishon.

During the Flood of Noah, as well as when the earth was divided in the time of Peleg (Gen 10:25), the earth's geography changed quite dramatically compared to what it looked like in the days of Adam and Eve. Peter wrote, *"... the earth was formed out of water and through water by the word of God, and that by means of these the world that then existed was deluged with water and perished."* (2 Pe 3:5–6)

It is very possible that when the Syrian-African Rift was formed, it caused major shifts. First, the original headwaters of the rivers flowing from the Garden of Eden moved. Secondly, the Pishon River dried up, and thirdly, the Gihon River became the Gulf of Aqaba and the Red Sea, which even today continues on to encircle the land of Cush (i.e. Ethiopia/Sudan).

Gihon Spring

The Gihon Spring is mentioned in the Bible. It is situated in the ancient City of David in Jerusalem, just south of the Temple Mount. The water from the Gihon Spring flowed, in biblical times into the Dead Sea, which is part of the Syrian-African Rift.

This means that Jerusalem could very well be where the Garden of Eden was located, as it is situated right in the center of the area of the four rivers![5] After the fall of man, the Garden of Eden was, according to Jewish tradition, taken up into heaven.

The River of Life

There are, however, other indications in the Scriptures than the four rivers showing that Jerusalem is where the Garden of Eden was. It is written that the river from the Garden of Eden was connected with the tree of life. ***"The tree of life was in the midst of the garden, and***

---

5   The well-known Jewish Bible commentator Rashi believed that the Pishon River is the same as the Nile. Even if Rashi is right, Jerusalem would still be in the middle of the area of the four rivers.

the tree of the knowledge of good and evil. ***A river flowed out of Eden to water the garden.***"(Gen 2:9–10)

This is interesting, because we find the tree of life and the river of life mentioned once again at the end of the Bible in the Book of Revelation. The first promise to those who overcome says, *"To the one who conquers I will grant to eat of the tree of life, which is in the paradise of God."* (Rev 2:7) This verse connects the tree of life with *"the paradise of God,"* which is another name for the Garden of Eden.

The end of the Book of Revelation describes the new Jerusalem that is coming down from heaven.

> *"Then I saw a new heaven and a new earth, for the first heaven and the first earth had passed away, and the sea was no more. And I saw the holy city, new Jerusalem, coming down out of heaven from God, prepared as a bride adorned for her husband."* (Rev 21:1–2)

The final chapter of the Bible tells us that the river of life and the tree of life will be in this city.

> *"Then the angel showed me **the river of the water of life**, bright as crystal, flowing from the throne of God and of the Lamb through the middle of the street of the city; **also, on either side of the river, the tree of life** with its twelve kinds of fruit, yielding its fruit each month. The leaves of the tree were for the healing of the nations."* (Rev 22:1–2)

The river will flow from the throne of God in the new Jerusalem and the tree of life will be on both sides of the river.

Our Destiny Is Linked With Jerusalem

Before we proceed further, it will be helpful to find out what the first generations of followers of Messiah, both Jews and Gentiles, believed regarding new Jerusalem. There is an interesting quote found in a book called *Dialogue with Trypho the Jew*, written in the middle of the second century by one of the earliest church fathers named Justin Martyr.

This book was written after Emperor Hadrian had crushed the second Jewish uprising against Rome, known as the Bar Kochba Revolt in 132–135 CE. The first Jewish revolt sixty years earlier had resulted in the destruction of the Temple by Titus in 70 CE. After the second revolt, Emperor Hadrian was furious with the Jewish people. He decided to once and for all end all Jewish ambitions of ever rebuilding Jerusalem and the Temple. So after Jerusalem had been leveled to the ground he rebuilt it as a Roman, pagan city and renamed it Aelia Capitolina. Aelia was part of his family name and Capitolina referred to the three capitoline gods of Rome: Jupiter, Juno, and Minerva.

Hadrian built a temple to Jupiter on the Temple Mount. He placed Roman armies all around the city and forbade all Jews from setting foot in the city on pain of death. The area where the Davidic kings were buried was desecrated and changed into a quarry where he could get stones to build his pagan temples. A temple to the goddess Venus was built over the place where today the Church of the Holy Sepulcher is located. In order to infuriate the Jewish people as much as possible, he renamed the entire area Palestine, in honor of the greatest enemies to the Jewish people, the long since extinct Philistines.

It is with this background in mind that we need to look at what Justin Martyr wrote in his book *Dialogue with Trypho the Jew.* Trypho was an imaginary Jewish rabbi that Justin invented as a rhetorical device. In the book the Jewish rabbi asks Justin an interesting question. He says, "Do you acknowledge for a truth that this place Jerusalem will be rebuilt, and expect that your people will be gathered together and rejoice with Christ, together with the patriarchs and the prophets, and the saints of our race, or even of them who became proselytes, before your Christ came ... ?"

Justin then answers the question saying,

> "I have acknowledged to you earlier that I and many others
> do hold this opinion, even as you also know well that this is
> to take place. ... I, and all other entirely orthodox Christians,
> know that there will be a resurrection of the flesh, and also
> a thousand years in Jerusalem built up and adorned and en-
> larged, as the prophets Ezekiel and Isaiah, and all the rest,
> acknowledge. ...

> "And, further, a man among us named John, one of the
> apostles of Christ, prophesied in a Revelation made to him
> that they who have believed our Christ will spend a thou-
> sand years in Jerusalem, and that afterwards the universal,
> and, in one word, eternal resurrection of all at once, will
> take place, and also the judgment."[6]

It is very interesting to notice two things in Justin's response. First
of all, according to him, all "entirely orthodox Christians," i. e. all
Christians with the correct doctrine, in the second century had exactly the same hope for the future as the Jewish people had in those
days, and always have had up to this day; that Jerusalem one day will
be restored again, "built up and adorned and enlarged, as the prophets Ezekiel and Isaiah, and all the rest, acknowledge."

Secondly, Justin says that the heavenly, new Jerusalem that the
Apostle John describes in the Book of Revelation is the restored Jerusalem that the Hebrew prophets Isaiah, Ezekiel and the others spoke
of. And this is what all "entirely orthodox Christians" in the second
century believed. They obviously must have been taught this from
the original Jewish apostles.

Sadly, a century later, this biblical hope began to change. We know
from the Christian church historian Eusebius that two centuries later,

---

6   Justin Martyr, *Dialogue with Trypho*, ch. 80–81.

in the time of Constantine, this view was considered heretical. Euse-bius called it "unspiritual," "childish," and "Jewish." "New Jerusalem" became another expression for heaven. This thinking has more or less remained the same in the church up to our time.

But from the beginning it was not so. The early believers all looked forward to a restored, earthly Jerusalem, just as the Hebrew prophets had spoken. The heavenly Jerusalem that will come down out of heav-en one day is the restored Jerusalem that Isaiah, Jeremiah, Ezekiel, Zechariah and the other prophets spoke about. This is very important to bear in mind. That the city is coming down out of heaven from God simply means that it is God who is restoring the city. It is His work.

The Tree of Life

Let us look at the text again about new Jerusalem with the river of life and the tree of life in it.

> *"Then the angel showed me **the river of the water of life**, bright as crystal, flowing from the throne of God and of the Lamb through the middle of the street of the city; also, on either side of the river, **the tree of life** with its twelve kinds of fruit, **yielding its fruit each month. The leaves of the tree were for the healing of the nations.**"* (Rev 22:1–2)

Now, let us compare this prophecy by John with what Ezekiel prophesied about the restoration of Jerusalem.

> *"Then he brought me back to the door of the Temple, and behold, water was issuing from below the threshold of the Temple toward the east (for the Temple faced east). **The wa-ter was flowing down from below the south end of the threshold of the Temple**, south of the altar ...*

"As I went back, I saw on the bank of the river very many trees on the one side and on the other. And he said to me, 'This water flows toward the eastern region and goes down into the Arabah, and enters the sea; when the water flows into the sea, the water will become fresh. And wherever the river goes, every living creature that swarms will live, and there will be very many fish. For this water goes there, that the waters of the sea may become fresh; so everything will live where the river goes. Fishermen will stand beside the sea. From Engedi to Eneglaim it will be a place for the spreading of nets. Its fish will be of very many kinds, like the fish of the Great Sea. But its swamps and marshes will not become fresh; they are to be left for salt. And on the banks, on both sides of the river, there will grow all kinds of trees for food. Their leaves will not wither, nor their fruit fail, but they will bear fresh fruit every month, because the water for them flows from the sanctuary. Their fruit will be for food, and their leaves for healing." (Eze 47:1,7–12)

Whereas John's vision of the river of life in "new Jerusalem" has no other geographical reference points, Ezekiel mentions several. The Apostle John wrote that the river will flow *"from the throne of God and of the Lamb."* (Rev 22:1) Ezekiel says that the river will come from the Temple in Jerusalem. He has, however, already established in Ezekiel 43 that the Temple in Jerusalem is where God's throne will be located forever when the Messiah returns.

"As the glory of the LORD entered the Temple by the gate facing east, the Spirit lifted me up and brought me into the inner court; and behold, the glory of the LORD filled the Temple. While the man was standing beside me, I heard one speaking to me out of the Temple, and he said to me, 'Son of man, this is the place of my throne and the place of the

soles of my feet, where I will dwell in the midst of the people
of Israel forever.'" (Eze 43:4–7)

John's account in the Book of Revelation and Ezekiel's match perfectly. Whereas John mentions that the river of life will come from
God's throne, Ezekiel explains that the new Temple in Jerusalem is
that throne.

Before going further, we need to answer an objection that is sometimes raised against the understanding that Ezekiel and John describe
the same city, as Justin Martyr said. John wrote, *"And I saw no temple*
in the city, for its temple is the Lord God the Almighty and the Lamb."
(Rev 21:22)

The Greek language has, however, two different words that are
used about the Temple. The first one is *hieron,* which is used about
the entire Temple, including the outer courts. The second one is *naos,*
which in its strictest sense can refer to only the inner sanctuary, the
Most Holy Place where God's presence resided.[7] This is the word that
John used when he wrote that he saw no "temple" in the city because
the Lord Almighty and the Lamb is the Most Holy Place. This does not
necessarily mean that there was no *hieron,* no Temple structure, in
the city. It is the *hieron,* the outward Temple structure that Ezekiel
describes in chapters 40–48. There need not be any contradiction between John and Ezekiel.

John mentions the river of life flowing *"through the middle of the*
street of the city;" Ezekiel, however, describes in detail geographically
where the river is flowing. It flows *"from below the south end of the*
threshold of the Temple, south of the altar ... toward the eastern region
and goes down into the Arabah, and enters the sea." (Eze 47:1,8) The
Arabah is the Judean wilderness and "the sea" is the Dead Sea. Ezekiel
mentions the names of Engedi to Eneglaim. Engedi is well known

---

7   *The Revelation of Jesus Christ, LGV,* translation and notes by Tim Warner (©
     answersinrevelation.org, revised January, 2013), p. 39, http://goo.gl/3EnFKc.

from the Scriptures as well as from its present location by the Dead Sea. It is one of the areas where David hid from King Saul.

Furthermore, Ezekiel wrote about the trees surrounding the river, *"And on the banks, on both sides of the river, there will grow all kinds of trees for food. Their leaves will not wither, nor their fruit fail, but* **they will bear fresh fruit every month,** *because the water for them flows from the sanctuary.* **Their fruit will be for food, and their leaves for healing.**" (47:12) There will be fresh fruit from the trees every month and the leaves from the trees will be used for healing.

It is obvious that John refers to the same thing when it says, *"also, on either side of the river, the tree of life with its twelve kinds of fruit,* **yielding its fruit each month. The leaves of the tree were for the healing of the nations.**" (Rev 22:2)

The prophet Zechariah also wrote about the river of life. **"On that day living waters shall flow out from Jerusalem, half of them to the eastern sea and half of them to the western sea. It shall continue in summer as in winter. And the LORD will be king over all the earth.** *On that day the LORD will be one and his name one."* (Zec 14:8–9)

Here, it also says that living waters shall flow out from Jerusalem. Zechariah prophesied that the water will not only flow towards the Dead Sea, but also westward towards the Mediterranean.

The prophet Joel also spoke about the river,

> *"So you shall know that I am the LORD your God, who dwells in Zion, my holy mountain. And Jerusalem shall be holy, and strangers shall never again pass through it. And in that day the mountains shall drip sweet wine, and the hills shall flow with milk, and all the streambeds of Judah shall flow with water;* **and a fountain shall come forth from the house of the LORD and water the Valley of Shittim.**" (Joel 3:17–18)

According to Bible scholars, the Valley of Shittim is most likely an extension of the Kidron Valley going into the Dead Sea.[8] Joel is, in other words, describing the same river as Ezekiel saw.

We can conclude that the new Jerusalem that John saw, is referring to the restored Jerusalem that Ezekiel, Zechariah and Joel described, just like Justin Martyr wrote in his book. The new Jerusalem is not a place that will hover over the earth like a chandelier city, as some believe. It will come down and be located on the earth, in the very place where present Jerusalem is.

Point being, if the river of life and the tree of life will be in a restored Jerusalem coming down from heaven, it makes sense that this is also the place where the original Garden of Eden once was.

A Common Objection

People sometimes object that the city that John describes is much larger than the one described by Ezekiel. It says, *"The city lies four-square; its length the same as its width. And he measured the city with his rod, 12,000 stadia. Its length and width and height are equal."* (Rev 21:16) One Greek "stadia" equaled approximately 200 yards, which, according to many, would make the city about 1,500 miles long and wide, and just as high. Ezekiel definitely does not describe anything remotely that large. Were Justin Martyr and all "entirely orthodox Christians," so mistaken in the second century, just 50 years after the Apostle John wrote the Book of Revelation?

---

8   "Joel seems to have had in mind the acacias of the Kidron Valley; apparently the drought had especially parched them. But in contrast with 'Valley of Jehoshaphat' and 'Valley of Verdict,' the valley of acacias implies a future paradise for Israel." (Garrett, Duane A. *Hosea, Joel.* Vol. 19A. The New American Commentary. Nashville: Broadman & Holman Publishers, 1997. Joel 3:17–18). "the Dead Sea, near which latter Shittim was situated" (Jamieson, Robert, A. R. Fausset, and David Brown. *Commentary Critical and Explanatory on the Whole Bible.* Oak Harbor, WA: Logos Research Systems, Inc., 1997. Joel 3:17–18.)

Not really. Pastor Tim Warner has proposed the following harmonization of Revelation and Ezekiel. He points out that the word "stadia" can literally just mean "a fixed standard of length."[9] Since it is an angel from heaven that is measuring the city, we need not assume that the length means the traditional Greek or Roman standard of length. It says,

> *"And the one who spoke with me had **a measuring rod of gold** to measure the city and its gates and walls. The city lies foursquare; its length the same as its width. And he measured the city **with his** rod, 12,000 stadia. Its length and width and height are equal. He also measured its wall, 144 cubits by human measurement, which is also an angel's measurement."* (Rev 21:15–17)

The rod that the angel had was a heavenly fixed standard of length, as opposed to the "human measurement" cubit mentioned in verse 17 about the wall.

It is not specified if the 12,000 heavenly stadia measure each side of the city or the entire circumference. But if it refers to the circumference, it would make 1,000 stadia between each of the twelve gates, which seems logical.

Ezekiel mentions both the length of each side as well as the circumference. In Ezekiel the circumference is 18,000 measures. *"In the midst of it shall be the city, and these shall be its measurements: the north side 4,500 cubits, the south side 4,500, the east side 4,500, and the west side 4,500 ... The circumference of the city shall be 18,000* [cubits]*."* (Eze 48:15–16,35)

The word "cubit" is not in the original Hebrew text. It only says *"In the midst of it shall be the city, and these shall be its measurements:*

---

9   Tim Warner, "The 'New Jerusalem' is Jerusalem Restored" (© answersinrevelation.org), http://goo.gl/641xzO.

the north side 4,500, the south side 4,500, the east side 4,500, and the west side 4,500... The circumference of the city shall be 18,000."

Just like there is a normal cubit and a "royal," longer cubit, it is possible that the "golden," heavenly measuring rod used by the angel in Revelation to measure the city is 50% longer than the rod mentioned in Ezekiel. If so, the measurements in Ezekiel with 18,000 rods around the city and in Revelation with 12,000 golden, heavenly rods agree perfectly.

Basically all Bible commentators agree that what John describes in Revelation should often not be taken literally, just like the Messiah described in Revelation is not literally a lion or a lamb with seven eyes. The main message is that the city is a cube with the number 12, describing the fullness of God's people. The Temple gives us God's pattern for holiness, where the Most Holy Place, the place of God's throne, was a cube. John describes the new Jerusalem as the holy city, the fullness and perfection of holiness, where God will dwell, just like He used to dwell in the Holy of Holies in the Temple. That is why it is described as a cube, just like the Holy of Holies was.

Jeremiah prophesied:

> *"And when you have multiplied and been fruitful in the land, in those days, declares the LORD, they shall no more say, 'The ark of the covenant of the LORD.' It shall not come to mind or be remembered or missed; it shall not be made again. At that time **Jerusalem shall be called the throne of the LORD**, and all nations shall gather to it, to the presence of the LORD in Jerusalem, and they shall no more stubbornly follow their own evil heart."* (Jer 3:16–17)

The whole city of Jerusalem, not just the Most Holy Place in the Temple, will be called the throne of the LORD. The whole city will be holy. *"Thus says the LORD: I have returned to Zion and will dwell in the midst of Jerusalem, and Jerusalem shall be called **the faithful city, and the mountain of the LORD of hosts, the holy mountain.**"* (Zec 8:3)

God will dwell in the city, not just in the Most Holy Place in the Temple. That is what John also describes.

The new Jerusalem is also called the *"bride."* It says in Revelation 21:2, *"And I saw the holy city, new Jerusalem, coming down out of heaven from God, prepared as a bride adorned for her husband."* And then it continues:

> *"Then came one of the seven angels who had the seven bowls full of the seven last plagues and spoke to me, saying, '**Come, I will show you the Bride, the wife of the Lamb**.' And he carried me away in the Spirit to a great, high mountain, **and showed me the holy city Jerusalem** coming down out of heaven from God, having the glory of God, its radiance like a most rare jewel, like a jasper, clear as crystal."* (Rev 21:9–11)

The classic song "Jerusalem of Gold," written by Naomi Shemer in 1967 when Jerusalem was reunited, is inspired by this prophetic vision of Jerusalem as the holy city. At sunset, Jerusalem almost glows as if it were made of gold. But one day Jerusalem will really glow, *"having the glory of God, its radiance like a most rare jewel, like a jasper, clear as crystal."* (21:11)

Paul wrote, *"But, as it is written, 'What no eye has seen, nor ear heard, nor the heart of man imagined, what God has prepared for those who love him.'"* (1 Co 2:9)

Eden in the East

It says in Genesis, *"...then the LORD God formed the man of dust from the ground and breathed into his nostrils the breath of life, and the man became a living creature. And the LORD God planted a garden in **Eden, in the east**, and there he put the man whom he had formed."* (Gen 2:7–8)

If God created Adam on the foundation stone of the Temple Mount, and it says that God planted a garden in Eden, **in the east**, then the Garden of Eden was just east of the Temple Mount towards the Jordan Valley and the Dead Sea. We read in Genesis 13:10 about this area,

> *"Lot lifted up his eyes and saw all the valley of the Jordan, that it was well watered everywhere—this was before the Lord destroyed Sodom and Gomorrah—**like the garden of the Lord**."* (NASB)

Before God destroyed Sodom and Gomorrah, the area east of Jerusalem was *"like the garden of the Lord."* The area still carried a resemblance to the Garden of Eden. According to Ezekiel, the river of life will one day flow exactly through this region. It is very possible that it did this once before and this is why the area just east of the Temple Mount was like the Garden of Eden.

It was in *"the garden of the Lord"* that Adam walked and fellowshipped with God before the fall. *"Then they heard the sound of the LORD God as he was walking in the garden in the cool of the day."* (Gen 3:8) This is how it will become once again. *"To the one who conquers I will grant to eat of the tree of life, which is in the paradise of God."* (Rev 2:7) The new Jerusalem coming down from heaven will be the restored Garden of Eden—the paradise of God.

> *"And I heard a loud voice from the throne saying, 'Behold, the dwelling place of God is with man. He will dwell with them, and they will be his people, and God himself will be with them as their God. **He will wipe away every tear from their eyes, and death shall be no more**, neither shall there be mourning nor crying nor pain anymore, for the former things have passed away.'"* (Rev 21:3–4)

This verse is a quote from Isaiah where he prophesies about Jerusalem, God's holy mountain,

> *"And he will swallow up on this mountain the covering that is cast over all peoples, the veil that is spread over all nations. He will swallow up death forever; and the Lord GOD will wipe away tears from all faces, and the reproach of his people he will take away from all the earth, for the LORD has spoken."* (Isa 25:7–8)

Obviously, this is talking about the same thing. Notice, however, that Isaiah contains one small phrase not quoted in Revelation. John wrote, *"He will wipe away every tear from their eyes, and death shall be no more."* Isaiah wrote, *"He will swallow up death forever; and the Lord GOD will wipe away tears from all faces, and the reproach of his people he will take away **from all the earth**."* Isaiah says that when God wipes away tears from all faces, He will also remove His people's disgrace from all **the earth**. This will happen on earth, in the restored Jerusalem, the city that will come down from heaven.

John also wrote, *"Then I saw a new heaven and a new earth, for the first heaven and the first earth had passed away, the sea was no more."* (Rev 21:1) Personally, I love the ocean. I think that it is one of the most beautiful parts of God's creation. Will there be no sea in the new restored earth?

It is possible that John is again speaking symbolically, but we also need to remember that the Scriptures speak about several seas. Zechariah 14:8, for example, mentions both the eastern sea and the western sea. John did not write, **"the seas were** no more," but *"the sea was no more."* Apparently, it refers to a special sea, and the Greek has the definite article attached to it: "the sea." Which sea is he referring to?

Isaiah also speaks about a sea that will be no more in connection with the final ingathering of God's people. It is written:

*"And **the LORD will utterly destroy the tongue of the Sea of Egypt**, and will wave his hand over the River with his scorching breath, and strike it into seven channels, and he will lead people across in sandals. And there will be a highway from Assyria for the remnant that remains of his people, as there was for Israel when they came up from the land of Egypt."* (Isa 11:15–16)

"And the LORD will utterly destroy the tongue of the Sea of Egypt." This is the sea that the children of Israel crossed when they came out of Egypt. Isaiah says here that it will one day completely cease to exist when God regathers His people. This is also what John wrote, *"the sea was no more."*

Eden and God's Holy Mountain

We will look at one last passage that also connects the Garden of Eden to Jerusalem. Over and over again the Scriptures refer to Jerusalem as God's "holy mountain." It is, in fact, one of the names for Jerusalem (see for example Ps 48:1; Isa 27:13; 56:7; 66:20; Eze 20:40; Joel 2:1; 3:17; Obad 1:16, Zec 8:3).

It is written in Ezekiel about Lucifer before he fell:

*"**You were in Eden, the garden of God**; every precious stone was your covering, sardius, topaz, and diamond, beryl, onyx, and jasper, sapphire, emerald, and carbuncle; and crafted in gold were your settings and your engravings. On the day that you were created they were prepared. You were an anointed guardian cherub. I placed you; **you were on the holy mountain of God**; in the midst of the stones of fire you walked."* (Eze 28:13–14)

Here it says in verse 13 that Lucifer was in the Garden of God, and then it says in verse 14 that he was *"on the holy mountain of God."*

Once again we see how the Garden of Eden is connected with Jerusalem.

It is written about the Garden of Eden:

> *"And the LORD God planted a garden in Eden, in the east, and there he put the man whom he had formed. And out of the ground the LORD God made to spring up every tree that is pleasant to the sight and good for food. The tree of life was in the midst of the garden, and the tree of the knowledge of good and evil."* (Gen 2:8–9)

It says that the garden was located **in** Eden. Three things are mentioned in this passage: (1) Eden, (2) the garden in Eden, and (3) the tree of life in the midst of the garden.

With the Garden of Eden and God's holy mountain in Jerusalem so intimately linked, we can see some amazing parallels. The Tabernacle, and the Temples that stood in Jerusalem, reflect the pattern of the Garden of Eden, with Eden corresponding to the outer court, the Garden to the Holy Place, and the tree of life *"in the midst of the Garden"* to the Most Holy Place, where the ark of the covenant was.

Jerusalem and *"the mountain of the house of the LORD"* (Isa 2:2), is the place from which righteousness and peace will one day flow to all nations like a river of life. Just like the Dead Sea will come to life, the restoration of Israel will be life from the dead for the whole world. No wonder that God calls Jerusalem *"the joy of all the earth."*

> *"Great is the LORD and greatly to be praised in the city of our God! His holy mountain, beautiful in elevation, is the joy of all the earth, Mount Zion, in the far north, the city of the great King ... As we have heard, so have we seen in the city of the LORD of hosts, in the city of our God, which God will establish forever. Selah."* (Ps 48:1–2,8)

2

THE CITY WITH FOUNDATIONS

"...he was looking forward to the city that has foundations, whose designer and builder is God." —Hebrews 11:10

T he first time that Jerusalem is mentioned in the Scriptures by name, is in connection with Abraham, the father of all who believe (see Ro 4:11–12). The Book of Hebrews tells us that Abraham had a specific goal in his life. It says that he was looking for a particular city.

> *"By faith Abraham obeyed when he was called to go out to a place that he was to receive as an inheritance. And he went out, not knowing where he was going.* **By faith he went to live in the land of promise, as in a foreign land,** *living in tents with Isaac and Jacob, heirs with him of the same promise.* **For he was looking forward to the city that has foundations, whose designer and builder is God.***"* (Heb 11:8–10)

It is written here that Abraham left Ur of the Chaldeans to go to *"the land of promise"* (11:9) and that he obeyed when he was called *"to go out to a place that he was to receive as an inheritance."* (11:8) But when he came to the land, it says that he lived there *"as in a foreign land."* (11:9) Moreover, it says that Isaac and Jacob also were heirs of the same promise and that they also lived in tents as strangers in the same Promised Land.

So what was the goal Abraham had? What was this city that he was looking forward to? Let us read on in the text.

> *"These* [the Patriarchs] *all died in faith, not having received the things promised, but having seen them and greeted them from afar, and having acknowledged that they were strangers and exiles on the earth. For people who speak thus make it clear that they are seeking a homeland. If they had been thinking of that land from which they had gone out, they would have had opportunity to return. But as it is, they desire a better country, that is, a heavenly one. **Therefore God is not ashamed to be called their God, for he has prepared for them a city.**"* (Heb 11:13–16)

Here we see that Abraham, Isaac and Jacob, were strangers and exiles on the earth and were looking for a heavenly country. Most Christians draw the conclusion from these words that what Abraham, Isaac and Jacob really were looking forward to, was to go to heaven. But this seems illogical for two reasons.

First of all, if Abraham really was looking for heaven, why would he leave Chaldea and go to another geographical place here on the earth? Secondly, it says that Abraham was called to go to a place that he was to receive as an inheritance, and that he continued to live by faith in this place even though he was a stranger in it during his whole life. How can we solve this mystery?

It seems like basically all Bible translators also have misunderstood the text, because they have chosen to translate one and the same Greek word in two different ways in this passage. It is the word *ge*, which can mean both "land" and "earth." Hebrews 11:9 reads,

"By faith he went to live in the land [Greek *ge*] *of promise, as in a foreign land* [literally "as an alien or stranger"], *living in tents with Isaac and Jacob, heirs with him of the same promise."*

The Greek word *ge* is translated as "land" in this verse, because it seems perfectly logical to do so. But then in Hebrews 11:13, the same Greek word is translated "earth" instead of "land."

"These all died in faith, not having received the things promised, but having seen them and greeted them from afar, and having acknowledged that they were strangers and exiles on the earth [Greek *ge*]."

Why do the translators change the translation of the same Greek word *ge* in this verse, from "land" to "earth"? Hebrews 11:9 has already stated that Abraham, Isaac and Jacob lived as strangers in the land, i. e. the Promised Land. But here it all of a sudden says that the patriarchs acknowledged, *"that they were strangers and exiles **on the earth**."* That is very different.

Let us look at the passages in the Book of Genesis where it is written that Abraham, Isaac and Jacob acknowledged that they were strangers in the Land of Promise. We find the first instance in chapter 23, when Abraham is about to buy a burial place for his wife Sarah.

*"And Abraham rose up from before his dead and said to the Hittites, **I am a sojourner and foreigner among you**; give me property among you for a burying place, that I may bury my dead out of my sight."* (Gen 23:3–4)

Abraham did not tell the Hittites that he was eager to buy a burial place for his wife because he was a sojourner and foreigner **on the earth**. That would not have made any sense. If he was a stranger on earth, what difference did it make where he buried his wife? He could have buried her anywhere. No, Abraham was a man of faith and he wanted a burial place for his wife in the Promised Land, as a statement of faith that he would one day inherit it, in the resurrection. He confessed that **in this life** he was a sojourner and stranger in the land among the Hittites.

The Scripture says that Abraham had to pay *"four hundred shekels of silver, **according to the weights current among the merchants"*** (Gen 23:16) for the cave and the field. These specific silver coins, *"current among the merchants,"* were called "centenaria." According to the most famous Jewish Bible commentator Rashi, they were worth 2500 regular silver coins.[1] If Rashi is right, it means that Abraham bought the field for 1 million silver coins. Today, it would be an amount equivalent to millions of U.S. dollars that Abraham paid for burying Sarah in Hebron.

Abraham did not object to the amount. He was willing to pay the price that Ephron asked, in order to give the matriarch and queen of the chosen people of God a worthy burial place in the Promised Land. Scripture emphasizes that the burial place was in the Land. *"After this, Abraham buried Sarah his wife in the cave of the field of Machpelah east of Mamre (that is, Hebron) **in the land of Canaan**. The field and the cave that is in it were made over to Abraham as property for a burying place by the Hittites."* (Gen 23:19–20)

Later on God spoke to Isaac and said,

> *"Sojourn in this land, and I will be with you and will bless you, for to you and to your offspring I will give all these lands, and I will establish the oath that I swore to Abraham your father. I will multiply your offspring as the stars of heaven and will give to your offspring all these lands."* (Gen 26:3–4)

---

1   Nosson Scherman, *Artscroll Series: Chumash Stone Edition Travel Size (Ashkenaz)* (Brooklyn, NY: Mesorah Publications Ltd., 1998), p. 109.

God told Isaac to sojourn in the Land that he would give him as an inheritance. He did not say, "Sojourn in this land because one day I will take you to heaven." He said, *"for to you and to your offspring I will give **all these lands**."* (26:3) Isaac was a stranger and alien in the Promised Land.

Psalm 105 recounts God's promise to the Patriarchs and their experience in the Promised Land.

> *"He remembers his covenant forever, the word that he commanded, for a thousand generations, the covenant that he made with Abraham, his sworn promise to Isaac, which he confirmed to Jacob as a statute, to Israel as an everlasting covenant, saying, 'To you I will give the land of Canaan as your portion for an inheritance.' **When they were few in number, of little account, and sojourners in it**, wandering from nation to nation, from one kingdom to another people, he allowed no one to oppress them; he rebuked kings on their account."* (Ps 105:8–14)

Verse 12 says, *"When they were few in number, of little account, and sojourners in it..."* The context makes it very clear that "it" is referring to the land of Canaan. The patriarchs were sojourners and strangers in Canaan. They lived by faith in the Promised Land, looking for the fulfillment of the promise that they would one day inherit the entire land.

Verses 14–16 in Hebrews 11 give us a clue why almost all the translators change the translation of the Greek *ge* to "earth" instead of "land."

> *"For people who speak thus make it clear that they are seeking a homeland. If they had been thinking of that land from which they had gone out, they would have had opportunity to return. But as it is, they desire **a better country, that is, a***

*heavenly one. Therefore God is not ashamed to be called
their God, for he has prepared for them a city."*

Here, the author of the Book of Hebrews begins to talk about a
heavenly country. That is why the translators seem to think that
Abraham, Isaac and Jacob said that they were strangers on earth and
were longing to go to heaven. But if that were true, it does not make
sense that they would go to another land on earth, in the first place. It
also contradicts the fact that they lived by faith in the promise of receiving the land of Canaan. But it fits perfectly with the theology that
began to develop in the church, particularly from the time of Constantine, which we mentioned in the previous chapter, where the
Promised Land becomes synonymous with heaven.

We have to understand that **there is a difference between heav-
en and a country that is called** *"a heavenly one."* As we have already
discovered, new Jerusalem is not the same as heaven. But it is a heavenly city, where God will dwell among His people. It is *"the city that
has foundations"* that will one day come down from heaven. That is
why it is called "heavenly," and this is the city that Abraham was looking for when he went to the Promised Land. The fact that Abraham
journeyed to the the land of Israel proves to us that the heavenly new
Jerusalem is going to be located here on earth, in the Promised Land.
That is why Abraham was so eager to also bury his wife there.

This new Jerusalem here on earth is the city where we will one day
recline with Abraham, Isaac and Jacob at the feast in the kingdom of
heaven! Isaiah describes this feast,

> *"On this mountain the LORD of hosts will make for all peo-
> ples a feast of rich food, a feast of well–aged wine, of rich
> food full of marrow, of aged wine well refined. And he will
> swallow up on this mountain the covering that is cast over
> all peoples, the veil that is spread over all nations. He will
> swallow up death forever; and the Lord GOD will wipe away
> tears from all faces, and the reproach of his people he will*

take away from all the earth, for the LORD has spoken." (Isa 25:6–8)

Notice that the LORD will remove the disgrace of his people *"from all **the earth**."* The new Jerusalem where death is swallowed up forever will be on the earth, not in heaven. Jesus said in Matthew 8:11, *"I tell you, many will come from east and west and recline at table with Abraham, Isaac, and Jacob in the kingdom of heaven."* It does not say "many will come from the earth," but *"many will come from the east and the west."* The parallel text in Luke says, *"And people will come from east and west, and from north and south, and recline at table in the kingdom of God."* (Lk 13:29) God will fulfill his promise to Abraham and he will inherit the Land of promise where he sojourned all of his life. And we will also be there with him!

Hebrews 11:39–40 explains about all the heroes of faith, *"And all these, though commended through their faith, did not receive what was promised, since God had provided something better for us, that **apart from us they should not be made perfect**."*

What a glorious promise! "... ***apart from us they should not be made perfect***." God planned that the Patriarchs and all the heroes throughout history that have gone before us will not inherit the promise ahead of us. At the resurrection of the righteous we will all be gathered from the four corners of the earth to meet the Lord in the air, and then sit down with Abraham, Isaac, and Jacob in the kingdom of Heaven in the renewed and restored Jerusalem.

> *"For behold, **I create new heavens and a new earth**, and the former things shall not be remembered or come into mind. But be glad and rejoice forever in that which I create; **for behold, I create Jerusalem to be a joy**, and her people to be a gladness. I will rejoice in Jerusalem and be glad in my people; no more shall be heard in it the sound of weeping and the cry of distress."* (Isa 65:17–19)

Some ask, "In that case, will we never get to heaven?" Yes—and no. When we die, our spirits are in the presence of God in heavenly Jerusalem (see Heb 12:22–23 and 2 Co 5:6–8). This is, however, likened in the Scriptures to us being "asleep" (see 1 Th 4:14). The Scriptural testimony is that we will fully "get to heaven" at the resurrection of those who sleep, when heaven comes to earth!

> *"Then I saw a new heaven and a new earth, for the first heaven and the first earth had passed away, and the sea was no more. And I saw the holy city, new Jerusalem, **coming down out of heaven from God**, prepared as a bride adorned for her husband. And I heard a loud voice from the throne saying, 'Behold, **the dwelling place of God is with man. He will dwell with them**, and they will be his people, and God himself will be with them as their God.'"* (Rev 21:1–3)

Abraham and Melchizedek

As already stated, the first time that Jerusalem is mentioned by name in the Scriptures is in connection with Abraham. It is, of course, not a coincidence that Abraham, who was looking for the "city that has foundations," is so connected to Jerusalem.

We find the story of Abraham's first recorded encounter with Jerusalem in Genesis 14. The background is Abraham's victory over the four kings who had conquered Sodom and taken his nephew Lot captive. The city was at this time not called "Jerusalem," but "Salem." We know, however, from Psalm 76 that it is a reference to Jerusalem. It states there, *"His abode has been established in Salem, his dwelling place in Zion."* (Ps 76:2) This shows us that "Salem" refers to Jerusalem and Zion, the place where both of the Temples stood.

> *"After his return from the defeat of Chedorlaomer and the kings who were with him, the king of Sodom went out to*

meet him at the Valley of Shaveh (that is, the King's Valley). **And Melchizedek king of Salem brought out bread and wine. (He was priest of God Most High.)** *And he blessed him and said, 'Blessed be Abram by God Most High, Possessor of heaven and earth; and blessed be God Most High, who has delivered your enemies into your hand!' And Abram gave him a tenth of everything."* (Gen 14:17–20)

This chapter begins by telling us that these things happened in *"the days of Amraphel king of Shinar"* (14:1). Shinar is the same as Babylon. According to the Jewish sages, Amraphel is the same as Nimrod, who we know is a picture of the anti-messiah.[2] Lot was living in Sodom, which is a picture of the society that will exist when the Messiah comes. *"Likewise, just as it was in the days of Lot ... so will it be on the day when the Son of Man is revealed."* (Lk 17:28,30) In other words, the text is dealing with a prophetic picture of the end times.

Let us look at the same incident as it is described in the Book of Hebrews,

"This Melchizedek was king of Salem and priest of God Most High. He met Abraham returning from the defeat of the kings and blessed him, and Abraham gave him a tenth of everything. First, his name means 'king of righteousness'; then also, 'king of Salem' means 'king of peace.' Without father or mother, without genealogy, without beginning of days or end of life, like the Son of God he remains a priest forever." (Heb 7:1–3 NIV)

Melchizedek was king of Salem. Salem, or *shalem* in Hebrew, means wholeness, or completeness, and it is also where we get the Hebrew word *shalom* from, meaning "peace." Melchizedek was "king of peace." Also, Melchizedek's name means "king of righteousness."

---

2   Scherman, *Artscroll Series: Chumash Stone Edition*, p. 61.

This king of righteousness and peace is one of the clearest prophetic foreshadows in the Scriptures of the Messiah, the Righteous One, who is also our High Priest. He laid down his life to restore mankind back to God, symbolized by the bread and wine that Melchizedek gave to Abraham. Melchizedek is a picture of the Messiah ruling and reigning from Jerusalem.

Messiah is a High Priest in the order of Melchizedek and destined to rule all the nations in righteousness and peace from Jerusalem. *"We have this as a sure and steadfast anchor of the soul, a hope that enters into the inner place behind the curtain, where Jesus has gone as a forerunner on our behalf, having become a high priest forever after the order of Melchizedek."* (Heb 6:19–20) Psalm 110:4 declares about the Messiah, *"The LORD has sworn and will not change his mind: 'You are a priest forever, in the order of Melchizedek.'"*

Jesus will one day inherit the throne of David (see Lk 1:32–33). Both Melchizedek and David ruled as kings from Jerusalem. So will Jesus, the Son of God, our true and eternal High Priest. At His return, in the resurrection and "the Messianic rebirth of the world," He will establish His throne in Jerusalem as the eternal King/Priest. Zechariah also bore witness about the Messiah, whom he calls "the Branch," that He will be both king and priest.

> *"Thus says the LORD of hosts, 'Behold, the man whose name is the Branch: for he shall branch out from his place, and he shall build the Temple of the LORD. It is he who shall build the Temple of the LORD and shall bear royal honor, and shall sit and rule on his throne.* ***And there shall be a priest on his throne, and the counsel of peace shall be between them both.****'"* (Zec 6:12–13)

> *"Jesus said to them, Truly I say to you,* ***in the new age [the Messianic rebirth of the world], when the Son of Man shall sit down on the throne of His glory,*** *you who have [become My disciples, sided with My party and] followed Me will also*

sit on twelve thrones and judge the twelve tribes of Israel."
(Mt 19:28 Amplified Translation)

Abraham is the father of all who believe. Just as Abraham encountered Melchizedek in Salem after defeating Chedorlaomer and the kings allied with him, we shall be gathered to be with the Messiah in Jerusalem after the anti-messiah and the kings allied with him have been defeated.

Moses did not record anything about the genealogy of Melchizedek. This is a prophecy of the eternal character of Jesus' priesthood as the Son of God. *"Without father or mother, without genealogy, without beginning of days or end of life, like the Son of God he remains a priest forever."* (Heb 7:3 NIV)

God's ways are eternal. (Hab 3:6) Everything recorded in the Scriptures is a prophecy pointing to the culmination of all things in the Messiah and a restored Jerusalem. Jerusalem is the eternal city of worship and learning about God and His ways. It is the city of truth, where the Messiah will rule forever as King of righteousness and peace, over the whole earth.

> *"For out of Zion shall go the law, and the word of the LORD from Jerusalem. He shall judge between the nations, and shall decide disputes for many peoples; and they shall beat their swords into plowshares, and their spears into pruning hooks; nation shall not lift up sword against nation, neither shall they learn war anymore."* (Isa 2:3–4)

The Binding of Isaac

The next time that Jerusalem appears in the Scriptures is also in connection with Abraham—to be specific, in the story of the binding of Isaac. We read about this in Genesis 22, which begins:

"After these things God tested Abraham and said to him, 'Abraham!' And he said, 'Here am I.' He said, 'Take your son, your only son Isaac, whom you love, and go to the land of Moriah, and offer him there as a burnt offering on one of the mountains of which I shall tell you.'" (Gen 22:1–2)

This is a powerful prophecy about Jerusalem and the Messiah. The name Abraham means, "father of multitudes." God came to Abraham and said to him, "Father of Multitudes! Go and sacrifice the one and only son you have." What a test! He had waited all of his life for a son, and now God was telling Abraham to sacrifice him.

The story of the binding of Isaac is the only place in the Torah that the word *yachid*, meaning "one and only one," occurs. The connection with the well-known words in John 3:16 is very obvious: *"For God so loved the world, that he gave his only Son, that whoever believes in him should not perish but have eternal life."* Many Jews read Genesis 22 at the beginning of their morning prayers every day. Abraham's binding of Isaac is viewed as the very foundation of Israel's relationship with God. It is in this story that the word "worship" occurs for the first time in the Bible. Jerusalem is the place of worship. *"Let us go to his dwelling place; let us worship at his footstool!"* (Ps 132:7)

God is very specific in His dealings with mankind. He is a God of order, and His ways never change. Jerusalem is His chosen place. Ezekiel 38:12 literally calls Jerusalem *"the navel of the earth."* It is the literal connecting point between heaven and earth. Abraham was not supposed to sacrifice Isaac in any other place, but in *"the land of Moriah,"* exactly *"on one of the mountains of which I shall tell you."* (Gen 22:2) "Moriah" refers to Jerusalem since the Bible informs us that King Solomon later on built the Temple on Mount Moriah (see 2 Ch 3:1).

What did God tell Abraham about this place? We continue to read in the story,

"So Abraham rose early in the morning, saddled his donkey, and took two of his young men with him, and his son Isaac.

And he cut the wood for the burnt offering and arose and
went to the place of which God had told him. On the third
day Abraham lifted up his eyes and saw the place from
afar. *Then Abraham said to his young men, 'Stay here with*
the donkey; I and the boy will go over there and worship and
come again to you.'" (22:3–5)

What did Abraham see when he lifted up his eyes? It says that he
saw "the place." "The place" in Hebrew is *ha-makom*. It is mentioned
three times in this chapter, in verses 3, 4 and 9. *Ha-makom* is an important concept in the Scriptures, used about the place where God
dwells and reveals Himself—particularly the Temple.

Abraham saw *"the place"* from afar *"on the third day."* Throughout
the Scriptures "the third day" always points to the resurrection. Jesus
explained this to His disciples after His resurrection. *"Then he opened*
their minds to understand the Scriptures, and said to them, 'Thus it is
written, that the Messiah should suffer and on the third day rise from
the dead." (Lk 24:45–46) According to Jesus, this is the summary of all
the Scriptures.

The Book of Hebrews confirms to us what Abraham saw,

"By faith Abraham, when he was tested, offered up Isaac,
and he who had received the promises was in the act of of-
fering up his only son, of whom it was said, 'Through Isaac
shall your offspring be named.' **He considered that God**
was able even to raise him from the dead, from which, fig-
uratively speaking, he did receive him back." (Heb 11:17–
19)

When Abraham lifted his eyes *"on the third day,"* he saw *"from*
afar," in the distant future, Golgotha and the death and resurrection
of Messiah 2,000 years later! Jesus said, *"Your father Abraham re-*
joiced that he would see my day. He saw it and was glad." (Jn 8:56)
Further on in the story, Abraham told Isaac, *"God will provide for*

himself the lamb for a burnt offering, my son." (Gen 22:8) Jesus is the Lamb of God, just as John the Baptist explained. *"The next day he saw Jesus coming toward him, and said, 'Behold, the Lamb of God, who takes away the sin of the world!'"* (Jn 1:29)

The story continues, *"And Abraham took the wood of the burnt offering and laid it on Isaac his son. And he took in his hand the fire and the knife.* **So they went both of them together**." (Gen 22:6) It is important to note in the text, not only Abraham's obedience, but also Isaac's complete obedience and surrender to his father. This is repeated again in verse 8, *"So they went both of them together."* From the surrounding chapters, we know that Isaac was at this time somewhere between 30 and 37 years old. He was probably just as old as the Messiah was when He surrendered to His Father's will and prayed in the garden, *"My Father, if it be possible, let this cup pass from me; nevertheless, not as I will, but as you will."* (Mt 26:39)

The Hebrew root word for "the wood" that Abraham placed on Isaac is the same corresponding word used about the cross that Jesus carried on his back (see for example 1 Pe 2:24, Ac 5:30). One of the oldest Jewish commentaries on Genesis 22:6 says Isaac carried the wood for the burnt offering "like one who carries his cross on his shoulder" on the way to be crucified.[3] It is written in the Gospel of John, *"...and he went out,* **bearing his own cross**, *to the place called the place of a skull, which in Aramaic is called Golgotha."* (Jn 19:17)

"When they came to the place of which God had told him, Abraham built the altar there and laid the wood in order **and bound Isaac his son and laid him on the altar, on top of the wood**." (Gen 22:9) Among the Jewish people, this whole passage is called "the binding of Isaac" or just "the binding." The Hebrew word for this binding is *akedah*. It is the only time that this form of the word occurs in the Scriptures. According to the Jewish commentator Rashi, the word means

---

3   *Bereishis Rabba* 22:6. This *midrash* uses the word *tzlav*, the Hebrew word for the cross, or execution stake, reflecting a time when the Jews suffered under Roman rule.

that the hands and feet of Isaac were tied behind his back, and they were tied so hard that they left marks on Isaac's hands and feet![4] Jesus told Thomas after His resurrection, *"Put your finger here, and see my hands; and put out your hand, and place it in my side. Do not disbelieve, but believe."* (Jn 20:27)

It is obvious that Abraham could never have bound his son like this without Isaac's consent. The binding of Isaac was a unique event, pointing forward to the most unique, as well as crucial event in human history: the sacrifice of Messiah at Golgotha!

One *midrash*, a Jewish commentary on the Scriptures, says that Isaac asked his father to bind him in this way so that he would not be able to resist the knife and become unacceptable as a sacrifice.

> "Isaac said, 'Father, I am a vigorous young man and you are old. I fear that when I see the slaughtering knife in your hand I will instinctively jerk and possibly injure you. I might also injure myself and thus become unfit for the sacrifice. Or an involuntary movement by me might prevent you from performing the ritual slaughter properly. Therefore, bind me well, so that at the final movement I will not be deficient in filial honor and respect, and thereby not fulfill the commandment properly.' Thereupon Abraham immediately bound Isaac, his son" (*Midrash*).[5]

It is written about Messiah, *"He was oppressed, and he was afflicted, yet he opened not his mouth; like a lamb that is led to the slaughter,*

---

4   Rashi on Genesis 22:9, citing *Shabbat* 54a and *Bereishith Rabbathi, The Complete Jewish Bible with Rashi Commentary* (© 1993–2015 Chabad–Lubavitch Media Center), http://goo.gl/1zQwNR.

5   Scherman, *Artscroll Series: Chumash Stone Edition*, p. 103. *Midrash* means "searched out." It is a Jewish exposition of a Scriptural passage with rabbinic sermon illustrations.

and like a sheep that before its shearers is silent, so he opened not his mouth." (Isa 53:7)

Just when the edge of the knife was about to pierce Isaac, the silence was broken. *"[T]he angel of the LORD called to him from heaven and said, 'Abraham, Abraham!' And he said, 'Here am I.'"* (Gen 22:11) Whenever God repeats a name twice like this, it is always an expression of God's special love and affection. Now God did not just say "Abraham," like He did in Genesis 22:1. He said "Abraham, Abraham!" Abraham had passed the final and most crucial test of his life.

> *"And he said, 'Here am I.' He said, 'Do not lay your hand on the boy or do anything to him, for now I know that you fear God, seeing you have not withheld your son, your only son, from me.' And* **Abraham lifted up his eyes and looked, and behold, behind him was a ram, caught in a thicket by his horns.** *And Abraham went and took the ram and offered it up as a burnt offering instead of his son. So Abraham called the name of that place, 'The LORD will provide'; as it is said to this day, 'On the mount of the LORD it shall be provided.'"* (22:11–14)

Abraham had told Isaac that God would provide the lamb for the sacrifice. The ram that was caught in a thicket points to the Lamb of God who takes away the sin of the world—the substitutional sacrifice that God provided to take our place, just like the ram took Isaac's place. The Hebrew word for "thicket" is the same word that is used about the thorns that were around the head of Messiah when his hands and feet were nailed to the tree, as it says, *"and twisting together a crown of thorns, they put it on his head."* (Mt 27:29) Thorns are symbol of the curse, as God told Adam, *"Because you have listened to the voice of your wife and have eaten of the tree of which I commanded you, 'You shall not eat of it,' cursed is the ground because of you; in pain you shall eat of it all the days of your life; thorns and thistles it shall bring forth for you."* (Gen 3:17–18) *"Messiah redeemed*

us from the curse of the law by becoming a curse for us—for it is writ-
ten, 'Cursed is everyone who is hanged on a tree.'" (Gal 3:13)

"*The LORD will provide*" is *YHWH Yireh* in Hebrew. It can also be
translated, "the LORD shall see" or "the LORD shall be seen." It is
from the word *Yireh* that the first part of the name "Jerusalem" is de-
rived. Before the binding of Isaac, the place was only called "Salem,"
which means "wholeness" or "being complete." It is also the root
from which the word peace, *shalom*, comes.

After the binding of Isaac, the place became known as "Jerusalem," meaning: "The LORD will provide wholeness, completeness
and peace." Jerusalem is the place where God has provided all of hu-
manity with salvation, wholeness and peace with God—yes, everything that we need—both now and for eternity. "*He who did not spare
his own Son but gave him up for us all, how will he not also with him
graciously give us all things?*" (Rom 8:32)

> "*Blessed be the God and Father of our Lord Jesus the Messi-
> ah, who has blessed us in Messiah with every spiritual bless-
> ing in the heavenly places, even as he chose us in him before
> the foundation of the world, that we should be holy and
> blameless before him. In love.*" (Eph 1:3–4)

Jerusalem can also be understood as meaning, "The LORD will be
seen or revealed, bringing wholeness, completeness and peace." Finally, the Hebrew word *yireh* can also mean "to come down." The
LORD's wholeness, completeness and peace for mankind will come
down from heaven at the revelation of Messiah. "*Blessed is he who
comes in the name of the Lord.*" (Mt 23:39)

Among the Jewish people, Jerusalem is today called Yerushalayim
instead of Yerushalem, which is the Hebrew word for Jerusalem. The
ending "*–ayim*" is a so–called "dual plural ending" in Hebrew. Jerusalem is the only city in the world that exists in two realms. There is
both a heavenly Jerusalem and an earthly Jerusalem, hence the plural
name Yerushalayim is used by the Jewish people. In Jerusalem, God

will both provide peace between man and Him and peace between man and man.

Eight Provisions in Jerusalem

The Scriptures record at least eight things that God provided (or will provide) in Jerusalem.

1. In the Garden of Eden, God killed the first sacrifice that provided the garments of skin to cover Adam and Eve's nakedness after the fall. *"And the LORD God made for Adam and for his wife garments of skins and clothed them."* (Gen 3:21)

2. It was in Jerusalem that Melchizedek, the King of Righteousness, provided Abraham with bread and wine, a foreshadowing of the body and blood of Messiah. *"And Melchizedek king of Salem brought out bread and wine. (He was priest of God Most High.) And he blessed him."* (Gen 14:18–19)

3. It was in Jerusalem, on Mount Moriah, that God provided the substitutionary sacrifice for Isaac—the ram caught in a thicket. *"And Abraham lifted up his eyes and looked, and behold, behind him was a ram, caught in a thicket by his horns. And Abraham went and took the ram and offered it up as a burnt offering instead of his son. So Abraham called the name of that place, 'The LORD will provide'; as it is said to this day, 'On the mount of the LORD it shall be provided.'"* (Gen 22:13–14)

4. It was in Jerusalem, on the same mountain, that God provided salvation when He heard the prayers of David and the angel of death drew back his sword. *"Then the LORD commanded the angel, and he put his sword back into its sheath. At that time, when David saw that the LORD had answered him at the*

threshing floor of Ornan the Jebusite, he sacrificed there." (1 Ch 21:27–28)

5. It was in Jerusalem, on Mount Moriah, that both Temples were later built, where God provided atonement for the sins of His people every year. *"For on this day shall atonement be made for you to cleanse you. You shall be clean before the LORD from all your sins."* (Lev 16:30)

6. It was in Jerusalem, on Golgotha, that God provided eternal salvation for mankind, through the death of His Son on the cross. *"He who did not spare his own Son but gave him up for us all, how will he not also with him graciously give us all things?"* (Rom 8:32)

7. It was in Jerusalem that God, for the first time, poured out His Holy Spirit on all flesh. *"And while staying with them he ordered them not to depart from Jerusalem, but to wait for the promise of the Father, which, he said, 'you heard from me; for John baptized with water, but you will be baptized with the Holy Spirit not many days from now.'"* (Ac 1:4–5)

8. It is to Jerusalem that Messiah will return to be seen, providing peace and righteousness over all the earth. *"that times of refreshing may come from the presence of the Lord, and that he may send the Messiah appointed for you, Jesus."* (Ac 3:20)

Jerusalem is the place where God has provided and will provide everything for the salvation of mankind through the death, resurrection and return of His Son! Jerusalem is the navel of the earth. Just as the navel of an infant is the place where it receives its nourishment from the mother in the womb, Jerusalem is the place where heaven meets earth. It is the place where the tree of life stood, and will once again stand in the restored Jerusalem, the city with foundations God has built. There is no city like Jerusalem.

Truly on the Mount of the LORD, in Jerusalem, it has been provided—and shall be provided for all of mankind's needs. No wonder it is written about Jerusalem in Psalm 87 that *"All my springs are in you."*

> *"On the holy mount stands the city he founded; the LORD loves the gates of Zion more than all the dwelling places of Jacob. Glorious things of you are spoken, O city of God. Selah Among those who know me I mention Rahab and Babylon; behold, Philistia and Tyre, with Cush—'This one was born there,' they say. And of Zion it shall be said, 'This one and that one were born in her'; for the Most High himself will establish her. The LORD records as he registers the peoples, 'This one was born there.' Selah **Singers and dancers alike say, 'All my springs are in you.'"** (Ps 87)*

3

THE HOUSE OF GOD

"How awesome is this place! This is none other than the house of God, and this is the gate of heaven."
—Genesis 28:17

After the Messiah, Moses is the greatest of all the prophets in the Bible. The Book of Hebrews says, *"Now Moses was faithful in all God's house as a servant, to testify to the things that were to be spoken later, but Messiah is faithful over God's house as a son. And we are his house if indeed we hold fast our confidence and our boasting in our hope."* (Heb 3:5–6) Moses was entrusted by God to see the full blueprint of God's house, and he spoke about what was to come for God's people.

The statement above, that Moses was faithful in all God's house, is a quote from God's conversation with Aaron and Miriam, when they had criticized Moses. He said to them:

> *"Hear my words: If there is a prophet among you, I the LORD make myself known to him in a vision; I speak with him in a dream. Not so with my servant Moses. He is faithful in all my house. With him I speak mouth to mouth, clearly, and not in riddles, and he beholds the form of the LORD. Why then were you not afraid to speak against my servant Moses?'*

And the anger of the LORD was kindled against them, and he departed." (Nu 12:6–9)

Unfortunately, it is all too common for Christians to speak against Moses. Messiah is greater than Moses. But we do not honor Jesus by belittling Moses. On the contrary, we honor Jesus much more when we exalt Moses by recognizing who he is, and then explaining that the Messiah is even greater than Moses. Jesus said, *"If you believed Moses, you would believe me; for he wrote of me. But if you do not believe his writings, how will you believe my words?"* (Jn 5:46–47) We do not believe in Jesus **instead** of Moses. We believe in Jesus **because** of Moses! Jesus confirmed every stroke of a pen in the Torah of Moses. *"For truly, I say to you, until heaven and earth pass away, **not an iota, not a dot**, will pass from the Law until **all** is accomplished."* (Mt 5:18)

We have already looked at what Moses wrote about Jerusalem in the Book of Genesis, in connection with Abraham. Now we will continue to see what else Moses prophesied about the city that God calls His own.

Isaac and Jerusalem

"These are the generations of Isaac, Abraham's son: Abraham fathered Isaac, and Isaac was forty years old when he took Rebekah to be his wife, the daughter of Bethuel the Aramean of Paddan-aram, the sister of Laban the Aramean. And Isaac prayed to the LORD for his wife, because she was barren. And the LORD granted his prayer, and Rebekah his wife conceived." (Gen 25:19–21)

Isaac is a picture of the Son, the Messiah. While Scripture covers the life of Abraham and also the life of Jacob in many chapters, relatively few things are mentioned about Isaac.

One of the few things that is said about Isaac is that he was a man of prayer. In the verses above from Genesis 25, it says that Isaac prayed that his wife Rebekah would become pregnant. The root of the Hebrew word translated as "prayer" denotes "abundance."[1] The idea is that Isaac prayed abundantly for Rebekah to become pregnant. In the same way, we see in the Gospels that Jesus prayed all the time.[2]

God had told Isaac,

> *"Sojourn in this land, and I will be with you and will bless you, for to you and to your offspring I will give all these lands, and I will establish the oath that I swore to Abraham your father.* **I will multiply your offspring as the stars of heaven and will give to your offspring all these lands.** *And in your offspring all the nations of the earth shall be blessed, because Abraham obeyed my voice and kept my charge, my commandments, my statutes, and my laws."* (Gen 26:3–5)

When Isaac was forty years old, he married Rebekah. By the time Rebekah became pregnant, Isaac was sixty years old (Gen 25:20,26). Even though Isaac and Rebekah had received the promise that *"I will multiply your offspring as the stars of heaven,"* Isaac still had to pray continually for twenty years for Rebekah to conceive. What a test of endurance in prayer!

Jewish tradition says that Isaac often visited Mount Moriah, where the promise was first given, in order to pray for its fulfillment. This is where Isaac first heard the promise from heaven, when he lay on the altar and the angel spoke to his father Abraham, *"I will surely bless you, and I will surely multiply your offspring as the stars of heaven and as the sand that is on the seashore."* (Gen 22:17)

In the same way, we have to come before God in prayer through Jesus' sacrifice on Golgotha, and remind the Father of His promises to

---

1 *va–ye'etar,* from the root *atar* (עתר); Rashi on Genesis 25:21.

2 See Mt 14:23–25; 26:36–44; Mk 1:33–35; Lk 3:21; 6:12–13; 9:28–30; 11.1.

us. *"He who did not spare his own Son but gave him up for us all, how will he not also with him graciously give us all things?"* (Rom 8:32) We need to learn to endure in prayer, like Isaac. It is written, *"And the LORD granted his prayer, and Rebekah his wife conceived."* (Gen 25:21)

Jewish tradition says, "Why were our ancestor childless? Because the Holy One, blessed be He, yearns for the prayers of the righteous!"[3] It took twenty years of enduring prayer for Isaac. This is also a picture of the Messiah praying for twenty centuries at the right hand of God to see the full harvest, the reward of his suffering.

> *"Out of the anguish of his soul he shall see and be satisfied; by his knowledge shall the righteous one, my servant, make many to be accounted righteous, and he shall bear their iniquities."* (Isa 53:11)

Jacob's Dream at Bethel

Both Abraham and Isaac worshipped in Jerusalem. The Jewish people also believe that Jacob actually had his dream about the ladder stretching up to heaven, in Jerusalem on Mount Moriah. There are several reasons for this, as we will see.

Jacob had his dream about the ladder when he fled from his brother Esau. Jacob's flight from his brother to stay in a foreign land for twenty years before he returned again, is a prophecy about the Jewish people's present exile, which is nearing its end, after twenty centuries.

Just before Jacob left the Promised Land he had an unexpected encounter with God.

---

3   *Midrash ha–Gadol* on Genesis, p. 433, cited by *Bar–Ilan University's Parashat Hashavua Study Center* (Parashat Toledot 5768/Nov. 10, 2007), http://goo.gl/GHmSpZ.

*"And he came to a certain place and stayed there that night,
because the sun had set. Taking one of the stones of the
place, he put it under his head and lay down in that place to
sleep. And he dreamed, and behold, there was a ladder set
up on the earth, and the top of it reached to heaven. And
behold, the angels of God were ascending and descending on
it!"* (Gen 28:11–12)

It says that this took place when *"the sun had set."* When Jacob
returned to the Land, the Bible says that the *"sun rose." "The sun rose
upon him as he passed Penuel, limping because of his hip."* (Gen 32:31)
With the exile of the Jewish people, and the destruction of the Temple
2,000 years ago, a spiritual decline (darkness) began in the world. In
the same way, the Jewish people's return marks the beginning of the
final restoration and the Messianic age. *"Arise, shine, for your light
has come, and the glory of the LORD has risen upon you. For behold,
darkness shall cover the earth, and thick darkness the peoples; but the
LORD will arise upon you, and his glory will be seen upon you."* (Isa
60:1–2)

Darkness is also a picture of suffering and tribulation, just as sun-
shine represents peace and healing. *"But for you who fear my name,
the sun of righteousness shall rise with healing in its wings."* (Mal 4:2)

The text in Genesis 28 says that Jacob came *"to a certain place,"*
and stayed there overnight. It was not any place, but a specific place.
In the Hebrew text, it simply says that Jacob came to "the place" and
stayed there at night. The definite article tells us that it was not only a
special place, but also a known place that has been mentioned earlier.

This is one of the reasons why the Jewish scholars believe that it
refers to the same specific place that God showed Abraham when he
went to sacrifice Jacob's father Isaac as a burnt offering, which we
studied in the previous chapter. There it says, *"And he cut the wood
for the burnt offering and arose and went to **the place** of which God
had told him. On the third day Abraham lifted up his eyes and saw **the
place** from afar."* (Gen 22:3–4) As we mentioned in Chapter 2, the He-

brew expression *ha-makom,* which means "the place," refers to the place where God's presence is. It can also refer to God's personal, holy name, YHWH.

Moreover, the Hebrew text in verse 11 literally says, *"And **he encountered the place** and spent the night there."* The Hebrew word *yifga,* which is translated "encountered" here, comes from the root word *paga,* which is also used about prayer.[4] This indicates that Jacob did not primarily encounter a geographical place, but God Himself. Prayer is made to God, not to a place. Jacob had come to *ha-makom,* the place where God dwells.

Because of this, the sages say that the place where Jacob had this dream and encountered God was at Mount Moriah, where Abraham bound Isaac, and where both the Temples later stood. The word *yifga,* "encounter," also implies that Mount Moriah could have been brought to Jacob in the dream or that Jacob was transported in the dream to Mount Moriah. There is definitely a spiritual connection between the experience Jacob had and the Temple Mount, where God has chosen to place His Name forever. *"God said to David and to Solomon his son, 'In this house, and in Jerusalem, which I have chosen out of all the tribes of Israel, I will put my name forever.'"* (2 Ch 33:7)

In the days of the apostles, the Temple was called "the place." The chief priests said about Jesus, *"If we let him go on like this, everyone will believe in him, and **the Romans will come and take away** both **our place** and our nation."* (Jn 11:48) The NIV translation reads, *"If we let him go on like this, everyone will believe in him, and then **the Romans will come and take away** both **our Temple** and our nation."* Here we see that the Temple was called "the place"—in Hebrew *ha-makom.*

Likewise, Stephen was accused by false witnesses, *"This man never ceases to speak words **against this holy place** and the law, for we have heard him say that this **Jesus of Nazareth will destroy this place***

---

4   Nosson Scherman, *Artscroll Series: Chumash Stone Edition Travel Size (Ashkenaz)* (Brooklyn, NY: Mesorah Publications Ltd., 1998), p 145.

and will change the customs that Moses delivered to us." (Ac 6:13–14) What "place" was it that Jesus was falsely accused of destroying? It was the Temple. Mark wrote about the trial of Jesus before the Sanhedrin, *"We heard him say, 'I will destroy this Temple that is made with hands, and in three days I will build another, not made with hands.' Yet even about this their testimony did not agree."* (Mk 14:58–59)

The "place" that the people accused Jesus of destroying was the Temple. The Temple was known by the expression "the place."

Jacob's unexpected encounter with God at Bethel is a prophecy about the divine encounter that the Jewish people had, just before the long exile began, in the person of Jesus, the Messiah. Jesus spoke of Himself as the Temple. He said, *"'Destroy this temple, and in three days I will raise it up.' The Jews then said, 'It has taken forty–six years to build this Temple, and will you raise it up in three days?' But he was speaking about the temple of his body."* (Jn 2:19–21)

Jesus also interpreted the Bethel experience as a reference to Himself. He told Nathanael, *"'Because I said to you, "I saw you under the fig tree," do you believe? You will see greater things than these.' And he said to him, 'Truly, truly, I say to you, you will see heaven opened, and the angels of God ascending and descending on the Son of Man.'"* (Jn 1:50–51) The disciples, who would have known the whole Law of Moses by heart, understood immediately that Jesus was referring to Jacob's dream at Bethel. Jesus was saying the He is the House of God, "the place" where God's presence dwells.

The parallel between Jacob and Nathanael is striking. Nathanael did not expect anything good to come out of Nazareth. (Jn 1:45–46) Likewise, Jacob had not expected to meet God at Bethel. Both were surprised. Both ran into "the place" where the angels of God are ascending and descending, without prior warning.

We once again see how deeply connected the Messiah is to the Temple and Jerusalem. It is important to understand that even though Jesus spoke of His body as "the place," this does not contradict or exclude the importance of the Temple Mount, and a literal Temple in Jerusalem. At the final restoration, when the world is born again, "the place" in Jerusalem will be filled with the presence of God as Messiah takes up His residence there. Ezekiel wrote about this:

> "As **the glory of the LORD entered the Temple** by the gate facing east, ... I heard one speaking to me out of the Temple, and he said to me, 'Son of man, **this is the place of my throne** and the place of the soles of my feet, where I will dwell in the midst of the people of Israel forever.'" (Eze 43:4,6–7)

> "Then Jacob awoke from his sleep and said, 'Surely the LORD is in this place, and **I did not know it.**' And he was afraid and said, 'How awesome is this place! This is none other than the house of God, and this is the gate of heaven.'" (Gen 28:16–17)

Jacob did not know that he had come to the house of God and the gate of heaven. It was a complete surprise to him. In the same way, when Messiah came the first time, this was hidden from most of Jacob's descendants. They did not know it. But one day, they will realize with the same fear and trembling that Jacob had after his encounter, "How awesome is this man! He is none other than the house of God, and He is the gate of heaven."

God's Unshakable Promise to Jacob

> "And behold, the LORD stood above it and said, 'I am the LORD, the God of Abraham your father and the God of Isaac. **The land on which you lie I will give to you and to your offspring.** Your offspring shall be like the dust of the earth, and you shall spread abroad to the west and to the east and to the north and to the south, and in you and your offspring shall all the families of the earth be blessed. Behold, **I am with you and will keep you wherever you go, and**

will bring you back to this land. For I will not leave you until I have done what I have promised you.'" (Gen 28:13–15)

Here, we see God's irrevocable promise to the descendants of Jacob. *"Behold, I am with you and will keep you wherever you go, and will bring you back to this land. For I will not leave you until I have done what I have promised you."* (28:15) For 2,000 years, God has kept His people during their long exile to the ends of the earth; and in our day, He has begun to bring them back again to their Land, just as He promised Jacob. This is a unique, unparalleled phenomenon in the history of mankind. Truly, the Creator of heaven and earth is the shepherd of Israel.

> *"Hear the word of the LORD, O nations, and declare it in the coastlands far away; say, 'He who scattered Israel will gather him, and will keep him as a shepherd keeps his flock.'"* (Jer 31:10)

God's promise to all of Jacob's descendants stands firm. ***"The land on which you lie I will give to you and to your offspring.*** *Your offspring shall be like the dust of the earth, and you shall spread abroad to the west and to the east and to the north and to the south, and **in you and your offspring shall all the families of the earth be blessed."*** (Gen 28:13–14)

In the Book of Acts it is recorded how Peter explained to the Jews who had gathered for afternoon prayer in the Temple, *"**You are the sons of the prophets and of the covenant** that God made with your fathers, saying to Abraham, 'And in your offspring shall all the families of the earth be blessed.'"* (Ac 3:25) The Jewish people are still heirs to the promise given to the patriarchs.

Jacob inherited the promise made to Abraham, *"in you and your offspring shall all the families of the earth be blessed."* (Gen 28:14) Not one dot in the Law shall disappear, as long as heaven and earth exist.

Every part of the promise God gave to Jacob and his descendants will be fulfilled. ***"The land on which you lie I will give to you and to your offspring** ... [I] will bring you back to this land. For I will not leave you until I have done what I have promised you."* (Gen 28:13,15)

The place where Jacob slept and had his dream is located within the area where the politicians of the world want to establish a Palestinian state. There is a spiritual battle today for this small piece of land, and it involves the entire world. The leaders in Jerusalem 2,000 years ago chose to hand Jesus over to be killed, and instead they asked that a murderer would be released. Similarly, the leaders of the nations today want to give freedom to a terrorist state and hand the Jewish state over to be killed. The remaining area of the Promised Land (within the "Auschwitz borders" from 1949) is impossible to defend.

We have to remember that it is the credibility of the Creator of the universe that is at stake here. He is the one who has made the promise. He cannot lie and He cannot go back on His word. His promise will be fulfilled. *"I will not leave you until I have done what I have promised you."* Paul wrote about this election of Jacob, *"though they were not yet born and had done nothing either good or bad—**in order that God's purpose of election might continue, not because of works but because of his call**—she was told, 'The older will serve the younger.' As it is written, 'Jacob I loved, but Esau I hated.'"* (Rom 9:11–13)

As we just mentioned, the exact same promise given to Abraham was repeated again to Jacob, *"in you and your offspring shall all the families of the earth be blessed."* (Gen 28:14) Concerning Abraham, Paul wrote that the "offspring" is a reference to Messiah. Isaac, who was born supernaturally through the power of the promise, is a picture of this. Here at Bethel, God said that through the offspring **of Jacob**, all the families of the world will be blessed. This is a reference to the Jewish people. Jacob's twelve sons were all born in natural ways. Before Jacob left the Promised Land, God promised him that his descendants would become a blessing to all the nations of the world.

In the same way, Paul also wrote, *"For I tell you that Messiah became **a servant to the circumcised** to show God's truthfulness, in or-*

der to confirm the promises given to the patriarchs." (Rom 15:8) Messiah did not come to take away all the promises from the Jewish people, but to confirm them. The promise that the descendants of Jacob would bless all the families of the earth has been fulfilled already, in many different ways, even though the greatest fulfillment is in the future.

The Holy Scriptures have been given to the world through the Jewish people. Messiah came, according to the flesh, from Israel. The gospel has come to the nations from this people, and so on. In our day, the tiny nation of Israel has already begun to fill the world with fruit in fulfillment of Isaiah 27:6, *"In days to come Jacob shall take root, Israel shall blossom and put forth shoots and fill the whole world with fruit."* According to the Jewish Virtual Library, 22% of all Nobel Prices throughout history up to 2013 have been given to Jews even though they make up less than 0.2% of the global population.[5] The State of Israel is a leader in the world today in water technology, medicine, and high tech. The list of contributions from this numerically small nation goes on and on. And just like the Messiah came the first time **through** the Jewish people, He will also return **to** the Jewish people, which will bless the world with life from the dead.

The Messiah is "the desire of all nations" as it is written, *"And I will shake all nations, and the desire of all nations shall come: and I will fill this house with glory, saith the Lord of hosts."* (Hag 2:7 KJV) And to where will the Messiah come? He will come to Zion. *"'And a Redeemer will come to Zion, to those in Jacob who turn from transgression,' declares the LORD."* (Isa 59:20) This is why it says, *"May the LORD bless you from Zion, he who made heaven and earth!"* (Ps 134:3)

---

5   *Jewish Virtual Library*, "Jewish Biographies: Nobel Prize Laureates" (© 2015 American–Israeli Cooperative Enterprise), http://goo.gl/sAmWU2.

Jacob's Promise

> *"So early in the morning Jacob took the stone that he had*
> *put under his head and set it up for a pillar and poured oil*
> *on the top of it. He called the name of that place Bethel, but*
> *the name of the city was Luz at the first."* (Gen 28:18–19)

The stone that Jacob put under his head and then poured oil on
top of is a messianic prophecy. Messiah means "Anointed One" and
the stone that Jacob rested on is the first object in the Scriptures to be
anointed. It says in Isaiah about Messiah, *"Behold, I am the one who*
has laid as a foundation in Zion, a stone, a tested stone, a precious
cornerstone, of a sure foundation: 'Whoever believes will not be in
haste.'" (Isa 28:16) Messiah came to confirm all the promises made to
the patriarchs. He is the guarantee that all of them will be fulfilled—
the sure foundation that the Jewish people can rest upon. *"For all the*
promises of God find their Yes in him." (2 Co 1:20)

> *"Then Jacob made a vow, saying, 'If God will be with me and*
> *will keep me in this way that I go, and will give me bread to*
> *eat and clothing to wear, so that I come again to my father's*
> *house in peace,* **then the LORD shall be my God, and this**
> **stone, which I have set up for a pillar, shall be God's house**.
> *And of all that you give me I will give a full tenth to you.'"*
> (Gen 28:20–22)

Jacob's promise that the LORD would be his God is understood in
different ways among the Jewish sages. But prophetically, the fulfillment of Jacob's promise refers to the new covenant that Israel will enter into in the end times, through Messiah, as it is written in Jeremiah
31:33, *"But this is the covenant that I will make with the house of Israel*
after those days, declares the LORD: I will put my law within them,
and I will write it on their hearts. **And I will be their God, and they**

shall be my people." It is only through the power of the new covenant that it is possible for the LORD to truly be our God, the supreme King of our lives.

The angels that Jacob saw ascended and descended on the ladder from heaven. *"And he dreamed, and behold, there was a ladder set up on the earth, and the top of it reached to heaven. And behold, the angels of God were ascending and descending on it!"* (Gen 28:12) When Jacob returned again to the Promised Land, it is written that he once again encountered God's angels. *"Jacob went on his way, and the angels of God met him. And when Jacob saw them he said, 'This is God's camp!' So he called the name of that place Mahanaim."* (Gen 32:1–2) *Mahanaim* means "two camps." Here, we see a reversal of what happened at Bethel when Jacob left the Land.

The late international Bible teacher Derek Prince used to tell a story about a pastor in New Zealand, who in a dream saw a host of angels in heaven, ready to be released onto the earth. In a second dream, he saw the angels released to the earth. He told his colleagues and friends about his dreams, saying that he believed that there would soon be a great revival in the area. Months went by without anything extraordinary taking place. Then he got the idea to check if something had happened somewhere else in the world at the time he had his second dream, when the angels were released on earth. He soon made the discovery that it was the first day of the Six Day War, when Israel recaptured all of Judea and Samaria, including Jerusalem.

When Jacob returned again to the Promised Land, the peace did not last long. He settled with all of his sons in Shechem, where he bought some land from Hamor's sons. One of them, called Shechem, however, raped Jacob's daughter Dinah. Her brothers were very upset over this immoral and disgraceful act, and made a plan to take their sister back. In the end, Shimon and Levi took matters into their own hands and murdered all the men of Shechem.

Jacob became very troubled and told Shimon and Levi, *"You have brought trouble on me by making me stink to the inhabitants of the land, the Canaanites and the Perizzites. My numbers are few, and if they gather themselves against me and attack me, I shall be destroyed, both I and my household."* (Gen 34:30)

It was in this difficult situation that God told Jacob to go back again to Bethel and fulfill the promise he had made.

> *"God said to Jacob, 'Arise, go up to Bethel and dwell there. Make an altar there to the God who appeared to you when you fled from your brother Esau.' So Jacob said to his household and to all who were with him, 'Put away the foreign gods that are among you and purify yourselves and change your garments. Then let us arise and go up to Bethel, so that I may make there an altar to the God who answers me in the day of my distress and has been with me wherever I have gone.' So they gave to Jacob all the foreign gods that they had, and the rings that were in their ears. Jacob hid them under the terebinth tree that was near Shechem."* (Gen 35:1–4)

The Jewish rabbis say that Jacob's neglecting of the vow he had made to God at Bethel when he had left the Promised Land, led to the tragic incident with Dinah. Jacob had vowed that he would make the stone at Bethel into a house of God.[6] Jacob had returned safely to the Land from Paddan-aram. But he had not yet fulfilled his promise.

Just as Dinah was raped and the inhabitants of Shechem were destroyed, so also has the return of the Jewish people back to Israel in our day led to wars and atrocities, because the Jewish people have not yet crowned their Messiah as king. It was at Bethel that Jacob's name-change was finally complete. Jacob's return to Bethel is therefore like a sequel to the incident at Peniel. As it says in Hosea, *"He strove with the angel and prevailed; he wept and sought his favor* [Peniel]. *He met God at Bethel, and there God spoke with us."* (Hos 12:4)

---

6   Rashi and Radak on Genesis 35:1–7, Scherman, *Artscroll Series: Chumash Stone Edition*, p. 186.

The circumstances of Jacob's return to Bethel mirrored those at Peniel, when Esau came against him with an army of 400 men. They similarly included a fear of being destroyed, just as he had been afraid that Esau was going to kill him. He said, *"My numbers are few, and if they gather themselves against me and attack me, I shall be destroyed, both I and my household."* (Gen 34:30)

The way out of such danger is always radical repentance and a commitment to serve God. *"So Jacob said to his household and to all who were with him, 'Put away the foreign gods that are among you and purify yourselves and change your garments. Then let us arise and go up to Bethel, so that I may make there an altar to the God who answers me in the day of my distress and has been with me wherever I have gone.'"* (Gen 35:2–3)

This is the only ultimate solution to the danger that Israel is facing today. The Bible tells us what the result was when Jacob's household repented, *"And as they journeyed, a terror from God fell upon the cities that were around them, so that they did not pursue the sons of Jacob."* (35:5) Likewise, it is written in Psalm 105:12–15,

> *"When they were few in number, of little account, and so-journers in it* [the Promised Land], *wandering from nation to nation, from one kingdom to another people, he allowed no one to oppress them; he rebuked kings on their account, saying, 'Touch not my anointed ones, do my prophets no harm!'"*

It was during his second visit to Bethel that Jacob fulfilled his promise to take the stone that he had leaned against when he was in trouble, and that the angels had ascended and descended upon, and make it into God's house. *"... and this stone, which I have set up for a pillar, shall be God's house."* (Gen 28:22) Jacob anointed that stone.

> *"God appeared to Jacob again, when he came from Paddan-aram, and blessed him. And God said to him, 'Your name is*

Jacob; no longer shall your name be called Jacob, but Israel shall be your name.' So he called his name Israel. And God said to him, 'I am God Almighty: be fruitful and multiply. A nation and a company of nations shall come from you, and kings shall come from your own body. The land that I gave to Abraham and Isaac I will give to you, and I will give the land to your offspring after you.' Then God went up from him in the place where he had spoken with him." (Gen 35:9– 13)

Jacob's first encounter with God at Bethel was a complete surprise to him. As we already mentioned, it was a prophecy about Messiah's first coming to His people, which led to their dispersion. Jacob's second encounter with God at Bethel, which led to his name being changed to Israel, was a result of His willful obedience. It is a prophecy about Messiah's return, when all Israel shall be saved.

Jacob's second encounter with God at Bethel was not a dream. It was not a prophetic revelation. This time, it was God Himself who visited Jacob. The incident is prophetic of the restored and reborn Messianic Israel that will rule with Messiah from Zion.

"And Jacob set up a pillar in the place where he had spoken with him, a pillar of stone. He poured out a drink offering on it and poured oil on it. So Jacob called the name of the place where God had spoken with him Bethel." (Gen 35:14–15)

As we mentioned earlier, the stone that Jacob anointed with oil is the first object in Scripture to be anointed. Messiah means the "Anointed One." This time, Jacob did not just anoint the stone. He also poured out a drink offering on it. This is a prophecy about the day when Messiah has been welcomed by Jacob's descendants, and God's House is restored.

The Temple without Messiah cannot endure. Before the leaders in Jerusalem handed Jesus over to the Romans to be crucified, He told them,

> *"O Jerusalem, Jerusalem, the city that kills the prophets and stones those who are sent to it! How often would I have gathered your children together as a hen gathers her brood under her wings, and you would not! See, your house is left to you desolate. For I tell you, you will not see me again, until you say, 'Blessed is he who comes in the name of the Lord.'"* (Mt 23:37–39)

Jacob's second anointing of the stone at Bethel is a picture of Israel's spiritual rebirth when they embrace their Messiah, the anointed King. We know that this will take place in Jerusalem. The Jewish sages are adamant that Jacob's encounters with God at Bethel took place on Mount Moriah. There is at least absolutely no doubt that this is prophetically what the story is all about.

The place where Jacob had his dream is holy ground. It is the gate to heaven—the place where heaven and earth meet. It was the place that God showed Abraham and provided the substitute sacrifice. The city of the great King!

> *"Then Jacob awoke from his sleep and said, 'Surely the LORD is in this place, and I did not know it.' And he was afraid and said, **How awesome is this place**! This is none other than the house of God, and this is the gate of heaven.'"* (Gen 28:16–17)

It is on the Temple Mount that Messiah, the pillar of stone that Jacob rested on, will be anointed by Israel in the latter days, to become the House of God, and God's glory will be revealed to the whole world.

*"And I saw no temple in the city, for its temple is the Lord
God the Almighty and the Lamb."* (Rev 21:22)

It is noteworthy that in Isaiah's famous prediction about the nations coming to Jerusalem in the Messianic Era, the Temple is called
"the house of the God of Jacob." (Isa 2:3)

*"A glorious throne set on high from the beginning is the
place of our sanctuary."* (Jer 17:12)

4

THE CHOSEN PLACE

"You will bring them in and plant them on your own mountain, the place, O LORD, which you have made for your abode, the sanctuary, O Lord, which your hands have established. The LORD will reign forever and ever."
—Exodus 15:17-18

The next time that we find a reference to Jerusalem in the Scriptures is in Exodus 15, in connection with the "Song at the Sea," the wonderful song of triumph and victory after the crossing of the Red Sea.

The exodus from Egypt is the primary picture we have in the Scriptures of our salvation through Jesus. The freedom from slavery in Egypt came when the children of Israel slaughtered a lamb for each household and put its blood on the doorposts of their homes. When the angel of death that struck Egypt saw the blood, he passed over the house.

It was at the special time of sacrifice, at three in the afternoon during the Feast of Passover, right when the priests in the Jerusalem Temple were slaughtering thousands of Passover lambs, that Jesus died on the cross as the Lamb of God to take away the sins of the world. Just as the blood of the Passover lambs in Egypt brought freedom from slavery and Pharaoh's power, the blood of Jesus broke the power of sin and Satan over our lives.

The passing through the Red Sea—or, as it is more correctly called, the Sea of Reeds—is a picture of our resurrection from death together with Messiah, to a walk in newness of life, free from Satan and the power of sin. A whole new life in freedom from slavery began for the children of Israel after they had passed through the Red Sea. But this was not the goal or the end. The triumphant Song at the Sea ends with these words:

> *"You have led in your steadfast love the people whom you have redeemed; you have guided them by your strength to your holy abode. The peoples have heard; they tremble; pangs have seized the inhabitants of Philistia. Now are the chiefs of Edom dismayed; trembling seizes the leaders of Moab; all the inhabitants of Canaan have melted away. Terror and dread fall upon them; because of the greatness of your arm, they are still as a stone, till your people, O LORD, pass by, till the people pass by whom you have purchased. You will bring them in and plant them on your own mountain, the place, O LORD, which you have made for your abode, the sanctuary, O Lord, which your hands have established. The LORD will reign forever and ever."* (Ex 15:13–18)

This is a prophetic song. It is common for prophecy in the Bible to be written in past tense, to emphasize the surety of the promise. It could as well be written:

> *"You [**will lead**] in your steadfast love the people whom you have redeemed; you [**will guide**] them by your strength to your holy abode. The peoples [**will hear**]; they [**will tremble**]; pangs [**will seize**] the inhabitants of Philistia ..."*

The end of the journey, the goal set before the redeemed community is clearly spelled out here: *"you have guided them by your strength to **your holy abode**."* (15:13) The song ends, *"You will bring them in* *and plant them **on your own mountain, the place,** O LORD, which you have made for your abode, **the sanctuary, O Lord, which your hands have established.** The LORD will reign forever and ever."* (15:17–18)

There is no doubt as to what place this is referring to. It is not a place in the desert. The verses in between show the geographic area. They refer to *"the inhabitants of Philistia,"* *"Edom,"* *"Moab,"* and *"all the inhabitants of Canaan."* In short we are talking about the Promised Land.

Moreover, the expressions in the Song at the Sea like *"your holy abode,"* *"your own mountain,"* and *"the sanctuary, O Lord, which your hands have established,"* all refer to *ha-makom,* **"the** place," the Temple Mount in Jerusalem.

We see here, once again, how Jerusalem is described in the plans of God for His people in the Torah of Moses, even before they enter into the Promised Land. God had a plan from the beginning for the place He had chosen from eternity. Right at the exodus from Egypt, the focus is once again on this special place. This is the final destination for God's people. The mighty song of salvation and deliverance by the sea ends, *"The LORD will reign forever and ever."* (15:18) It is from Jerusalem, particularly from the Temple Mount, that God will reign forever and ever, just as Ezekiel prophesied:

> *"I heard one speaking to me out of **the Temple,** and he said to me, Son of man, **this is the place of my** throne and the place of the soles of my feet, where I will dwell in the midst of the people of Israel **forever.**"* (Eze 43:6–7)

Psalm 87:1–3 declares that the Temple Mount is the very foundation for His kingdom. *"He has set his foundation on the holy mountain; the LORD loves the gates of Zion more than all the dwellings of Jacob. Glorious things are said of you, O city of God."* (NIV)

Moses Longed for Jerusalem

Moses was never allowed to enter the Promised Land. God only let him see it from a distance. But Moses longed to see the Land and especially Jerusalem. In the Book of Deuteronomy it is recorded how he told the people of Israel,

> *"And I pleaded with the LORD at that time, saying, 'O Lord GOD, you have only begun to show your servant your greatness and your mighty hand. For what god is there in heaven or on earth who can do such works and mighty acts as yours? **Please let me go over and see the good land beyond the Jordan, that good hill country and Lebanon.**'"* (Dt 3:23–25)

Moses pleaded with God to be allowed to enter the Promised Land and see it with his own eyes. The LORD had previously told him that he would not be allowed to enter. But, Moses still continued to pray for it to happen. Moses is an example for us to never give up praying until God answers us, or expressly tells us not to pray any longer. When God had said that He would consume Israel, Moses had prayed, and God heard his plea and turned from the disaster He had intended to bring upon the people. Perhaps God would relent from what He had prescribed for Moses, as well? Finally, God told him, *"Enough from you; do not speak to me of this matter again."* (Dt 3:26)

Scripture says that Moses "pleaded" with the LORD. The Hebrew word means, "to ask a superior for an undeserved favor." Moses prayed to God and said, *"O Lord GOD ..."* In Scripture, this is a relatively unique way of addressing God. It seldom appears, but when it does, it is always in connection with expressions of great humility and respect before God's greatness and sovereignty. Abraham was the first to call God "Lord"—*Adonai* in Hebrew. *"After these things the word of the LORD came to Abram in a vision: 'Fear not, Abram, I am your shield; your reward shall be very great.' But **Abram said, 'O Lord GOD,*** *what will you give me, for I continue childless, and the heir of my house is Eliezer of Damascus?'"* (Gen 15:1–2)

After the exile in Babylon, "Lord"—in Hebrew, the plural form *Adonai*—became the most common way of addressing God, instead of using His personal name, *YHWH*. This was the custom among the Jewish people in the time of Jesus, and this also became the custom among His followers to this day. Among Jews today, *HaShem*—which means "The Name"—is commonly used when speaking **about** God. During prayer, however, the expression *Adonai* is used, rather than *HaShem*.

Abraham, Moses, Jeremiah, and Ezekiel all addressed the God of Israel, *YHWH*, as "Lord"—especially when they wished to express extra humility, respect, and reverence. Moses pleaded with God by using the expression, "Lord."

"O Lord GOD, you have only begun to show your servant your greatness and your mighty hand." (Dt 3:24) Through Moses, God **began** to reveal His greatness and might to the world. Moses' successor, Joshua, is a picture of Messiah. Through the coming of Messiah in power and great glory, God will be revealed as King and show **all** of His greatness and might. What a day that will be!

Moses called the land of Israel *"the good land"* and *"that good hill country."* (Dt 3:25) The land of Israel is truly a good and beautiful land. Ezekiel describes the land of Israel as *"the most glorious of all lands"* (Eze 20:6). Three times, Daniel calls Israel *"the glorious land"* (Dan 8:9; 11:16,41). It is written about the land of Israel that it is a land *"that the LORD your God cares for. The eyes of the LORD your God are always upon it, from the beginning of the year to the end of the year."* (Dt 11:12) He is ever mindful of His Land. God will one day judge all the nations of the world because they have divided His own Land. (Joel 3:6)

Literally, it says in the Hebrew in Deuteronomy 3:25, *"Please let me go over and see the good land beyond the Jordan,* **that beautiful mountain, and Lebanon.***"* In the literal sense, this speaks of the mountains of Israel and Lebanon. But prophetically, *"that beautiful* *mountain, and Lebanon"* is referring to Mt. Zion and the Temple. It is written, *"Out of Zion, the perfection of beauty, God shines forth."* (Ps 50:2) Jerusalem is the beautiful, good mountain, the mountain of the LORD. This is what Moses longed to see. Just like Abraham, Moses was looking for the city with foundations, whose builder and maker is God. He is an example for us as watchmen on the walls of Jerusalem, watching and praying, *"waiting for the redemption of Jerusalem."* (Lk 2:38)

"Lebanon," which comes from the word "white" in Hebrew, is a descriptive word used for the Temple, where Israel's sins, though red as blood, became white as snow on the Day of Atonement. Also, the Temple was completely covered on the inside with cedar wood from Lebanon. *"The cedar within the house was carved in the form of gourds and open flowers. All was cedar; no stone was seen."* (1 Ki 6:18) This made Lebanon into a code word for the Temple. Zechariah prophesied, *"Open your doors, O Lebanon, that the fire may devour your cedars!"* (Zec 11:1) This was understood as a prophecy about the coming destruction of the Temple.

Moses desired to see Jerusalem and the Temple. In the Spirit, he saw it. The LORD said to him, *"Go up to the top of Pisgah and lift up your eyes westward and northward and southward and eastward, and look at it with your eyes, for you shall not go over this Jordan."* (Dt 3:27) The expressions *"... lift up your eyes ... and look at it with your eyes"* refer to more than Moses seeing with only his physical eyes. The LORD showed him the land and the city where His glory will rest when Messiah comes. *"In that day the root of Jesse, who shall stand as a signal for the peoples—of him shall the nations inquire, and his resting place shall be glorious."* (Is 11:10)

The Torah commands, *"And you shall eat and be full, and you shall bless the LORD your God for the good land He has given you."* (Dt 8:10) Since Moses, in his prayer, connected *"the good land"* with Jerusalem, calling it *"that beautiful mountain and Lebanon,"* Jewish people always pray for both the restoration of Israel, Jerusalem and the Temple after each meal. This is a biblical habit and command that is a blessing for all of us to follow, as it also says, "*If I forget you, O Jerusalem, let my right hand forget its skill! Let my tongue stick to the roof of my mouth, if I do not remember you, if I do not set Jerusalem above my highest joy!*" (Ps 137:5–6) The third prayer in the traditional Jewish prayer after meals goes:

> "Have mercy, O LORD our God, on Israel Your people, on Jerusalem Your city, on Zion the dwelling place of Your glory, and on the kingdom of the house of David, Your Anointed One. Rebuild Jerusalem, Your holy city, swiftly in our days. Blessed are You, LORD, who in His mercy rebuilds Jerusalem. Amen!"

It is a blessing to make this prayer part of our prayer habits after every meal, in fulfillment of the commandment, *"And you shall eat and be full, and you shall bless the LORD your God for the good land He has given you."* (Dt 8:10)

High Places and Pagan Worship

In the Book of Deuteronomy, Moses gives instructions regarding the special place that God will choose to make His habitation.

> *"These are the statutes and rules that you shall be careful to do in the land that the LORD, the God of your fathers, has given you to possess, all the days that you live on the earth. You shall surely destroy all the places where the nations whom you shall dispossess served their gods, on the high mountains and on the hills and under every green tree. You shall tear down their altars and dash in pieces their pillars and burn their Asherim with fire. You shall chop down the carved images of their gods and destroy their name out of that place. You shall not worship the LORD your God in that way. But **you shall seek the place that the LORD your God***

will choose out of all your tribes to put his name and make his habitation there. There you shall go." (Dt 12:1–5)

It says here, *"You shall surely destroy all the places where the nations whom you shall dispossess served their gods, **on the high mountains and on the hills** ...you shall **seek the place that the LORD your God will choose.**"* (12:2,5)

The first place that God chose in the Promised Land for the Tabernacle was Shiloh, where it stood for almost 400 years. After that, He chose Jerusalem, to place His Name there forever. The pagans worship their gods *"on the high mountains and on the hills."* That is why it is said of Jerusalem, *"As the mountains **surround** Jerusalem, so the LORD surrounds his people."* (Ps 125:2)

Neither the hill in Shiloh where the Tabernacle stood, nor the Temple Mount in Jerusalem is the highest place in its respective area. On the contrary, higher mountains surround both Shiloh and Jerusalem. It is written about Solomon when he fell away from the LORD,

> *"Then Solomon built **a high place** for Chemosh the abomination of Moab, and for Molech the abomination of the Ammonites, on the mountain east of Jerusalem."* (1 Ki 11:7)

This is a reference to the Mount of Olives, which is the highest mountain in the area of Jerusalem.

The One Chosen Place

> *"But you shall seek **the place** that the LORD your God will choose out of all your tribes to put his name and make his habitation there. There you shall go."* (Dt 12:5)

The expression "the place"—in Hebrew, *ha-makom*, is found no fewer than six times in Deuteronomy 12! Together with other phrases and words like "there," "that place," etc., *ha-makom* is referred to 14 times in this chapter. Verses 9–11 explain which place it is:

> *"... for you have not as yet come to the rest and to the inheritance that the LORD your God is giving you. But when you go over the Jordan and live in the land that the LORD your God is giving you to inherit, and **when he gives you rest from all your enemies around, so that you live in safety, then to the place that the LORD your God will choose**, to make his name dwell there, there you shall bring all that I command you."*

This shows us that the Torah is referring here to Jerusalem. It was David who gave Israel rest from all their enemies. It is written about David:

> *"Now when the king lived in his house and the LORD had given him rest from all his surrounding enemies, the king said to Nathan the prophet, 'See now, I dwell in a house of cedar, but the ark of God dwells in a tent.' And Nathan said to the king, 'Go, do all that is in your heart, for the LORD is with you.'"* (2 Sa 7:1–3)

God spoke to David that his son Solomon would build the Temple. At the dedication, King Solomon prayed,

> *"Blessed be the LORD, the God of Israel, who with his hand has fulfilled what he promised with his mouth to David my father, saying, 'Since the day that I brought my people out of the land of Egypt, I chose no city out of all the tribes of Israel in which to build a house, that my name might be there, and I chose no man as prince over my people Israel; **but I have chosen Jerusalem that my name may be there, and I have chosen David** to be over my people Israel.'"* (2 Ch 6:4–6)

The Temple in Jerusalem was the specific place that God chose for His Name. It is interesting that Jerusalem is situated between three valleys, which together form the Hebrew letter *shin* (ש). The Hinnom Valley forms the southern and western boundary. This corresponds to the bottom and left stroke of *shin* (ש). The Kidron Valley is the eastern boundary and corresponds to the right stroke of *shin* (ש). Then there is a third valley in between these two valleys called the Tyropoeon Valley or Central Valley. This valley corresponds to the middle stroke of the letter *shin* (ש).

Shin (ש) is the first letter in one of the Hebrew names for God, *Shaddai*, which means "the Almighty," or "All Sufficient." *Shin* is therefore used as a symbol for God's name, and it is found on the *mezuzah* box on the doorframe of every Jewish home.

God showed the exact place on Mount Moriah to Abraham, and later on also to David. *"Then Solomon began to build the house of the LORD in Jerusalem on Mount Moriah, where the LORD had appeared to David his father, **at the place that David had appointed**, on the threshing floor of Ornan the Jebusite."* (2 Ch 3:1)

When Abraham was about to sacrifice Isaac, it says, *"**On the third day Abraham** lifted up his eyes and **saw the place from afar**."* (Gen 22:4) Abraham saw the resurrection of Messiah on the third day. On a deeper, prophetic level, "the place" —ha-makom—therefore refers, not only to Jerusalem, but also to Messiah, whose body is a Temple. It is only based on this foundation that we can worship God! Jesus is "the place"! We must not worship in any other "place," i.e., on any other foundation than the one that He established through His death and resurrection. All other "places of worship," competing spiritual foundations, must be completely destroyed.

> *"You shall surely destroy all the places where the nations whom you shall dispossess served their gods, on the high mountains and on the hills and under every green tree. You shall tear down their altars and dash in pieces their pillars and burn their Asherim with fire. You shall chop down the*

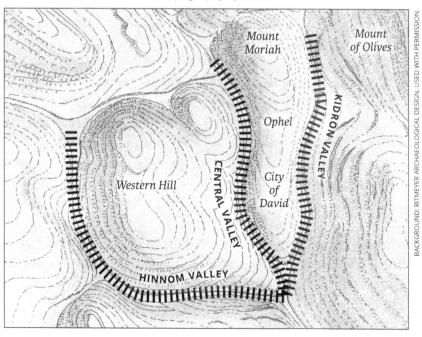

Top: Mezuzah scroll on the doorpost of a Jewish home.
Bottom: Topography of Jerusalem.

*carved images of their gods and destroy their name out of that place. You shall not worship the LORD your God in that way. But **you shall seek the place that the LORD your God will choose.*** " (Dt 12:2–5)

"Take care that you do not offer your burnt offerings at any place that you see, but at the place that the LORD will choose in one of your tribes, there you shall offer your burnt offerings, and there you shall do all that I am commanding you." (Dt 12:13–14)

The Hebrew word for sacrifice is *korban,* which comes from the root word "to come near" or "to be drawn near." It is written, *"But now in Messiah Jesus you who once were far off have been brought near by the blood of Messiah."* (Eph 2:13) Glory to God for Messiah's sacrifice that has brought us near to Him!

Jesus and the Temple in Jerusalem are intimately linked to one another as we discovered in the previous chapter. That is why Jesus had to give His life as the ultimate sacrifice in Jerusalem. Luke wrote about Jesus' final journey to Jerusalem.

"At that very hour some Pharisees came and said to him, 'Get away from here, for Herod wants to kill you.' And he said to them, 'Go and tell that fox, 'Behold, I cast out demons and perform cures today and tomorrow, and the third day I finish my course. Nevertheless, I must go on my way today and tomorrow and the day following, for it cannot be that a prophet should perish away from Jerusalem.'" (Lk 13:31–33)

Jesus knew that He was not to die just anywhere, or in any way, or at any time. He was to die exactly in fulfillment of the Scriptures. He had to give His life in Jerusalem, in a specific place. It is written in the Book of Hebrews about this special place:

*"We have an altar from which those who serve the tent have no right to eat. For the bodies of those animals whose blood is brought into the holy places by the high priest as a sacrifice for sin are burned **outside the camp**. So Jesus also suffered outside the gate in order to sanctify the people through his own blood."* (Heb 13:10–12)

The place where the sin sacrifices were burnt and where Jesus died for our sins, were both places outside of the camp. But it was "a clean place" used for the Tabernacle or Temple worship. The place was a special area, connected to the Temple. It is written in the Torah about the sin sacrifice:

*"But the skin of the bull and all its flesh, with its head, its legs, its entrails, and its dung—all the rest of the bull—he shall carry **outside the camp to a clean place, to the ash heap**, and shall burn it up on a fire of wood. On the ash heap it shall be burned up."* (Lev 4:11–12)

The "ash heap," was a clean place outside of the camp that belonged to the Temple ceremonies. The Book of Hebrews compares this place to the place Jesus died to fulfill all that was written. In this way we see how "the place" refers both to the Temple, and to Messiah, His sacrifice and His resurrection.

Between Benjamin's Shoulders

When Moses blessed the twelve tribes of Israel just before he died, he gave a very interesting prophecy about Benjamin.

"Of Benjamin he said, 'The beloved of the LORD dwells in safety. The High God surrounds him all day long, and dwells between his shoulders.'" (Dt 33:12)

Most English translations of this verse are more in line with the likely meaning of the Hebrew text than is the ESV. The NIV translation, for instance, reads, *"About Benjamin he said: 'Let the beloved of the Lord rest secure in him, for he shields him all day long, and the one the Lord loves rests between his shoulders.'"*

"...the beloved of the Lord" refers to the Messiah. When Jesus was baptized, a voice from heaven spoke and said, *'This is my beloved Son, with whom I am well pleased."* (Mt 3:17) Likewise, on the Mount of Transfiguration when *"the power and coming"* (2 Pe 1:16) of the Messiah was revealed to His closest disciples, a voice spoke from heaven, *"This is my beloved Son, with whom I am well pleased; listen to him."* (Mt 17:5)

Ezekiel explains that the Temple will be the throne of the Lord, *"While the man was standing beside me, I heard one speaking to me* **out of the Temple**, *and he said to me, 'Son of man,* **this is the place of my throne and the place of the soles of my feet**, *where I will dwell in the midst of the people of Israel forever.'"* (Eze 43:6–7)

Moses' prophecy about Benjamin shows us that Messiah's throne, His place of rest, will be in Benjamin. Moreover, God chose Benjamin to surround and protect the throne and the resting place of the King of Israel. It says, *"the one the Lord loves rests between his shoulders."* (Dt 33:12 NIV)

The border between Benjamin and Judah is described in the Book of Joshua:

> *"And the southern side begins at the outskirts of Kiriath–jearim. And the boundary goes from there to Ephron, to the spring of the waters of Nephtoah. Then the boundary goes down to the border of the mountain that overlooks the Valley of the Son of Hinnom, which is at the north end of the Valley of Rephaim. And it then goes down the Valley of Hinnom, south of the shoulder of the Jebusites, and downward to En-rogel. Then it bends in a northerly direction going on*

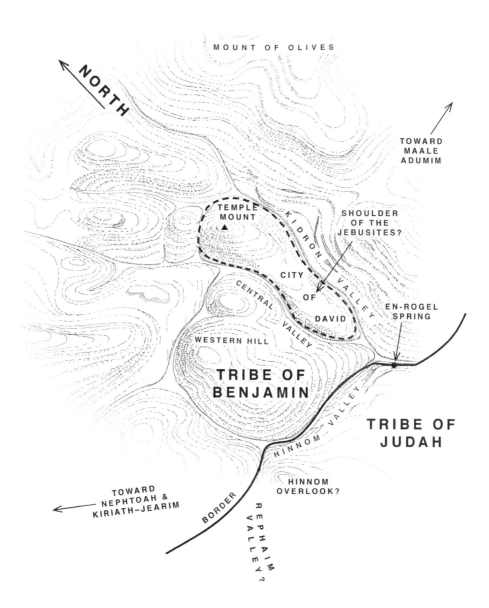

to En–shemesh, and from there goes to Geliloth, which is op-
posite the ascent of Adummim." (Jos 18:15–17)

This shows that Jerusalem was originally located in Benjamin. The
border went *"south of the shoulder of the Jebusites."* The border began
to turn north after En-rogel. This is the name of a well in the Kidron
valley at the southern end of the Mount of Olives. The border turned
north on the east side of the Mount of Olives towards Adummim, the
area where the city Maale Adumim is located today.

The tribe of Benjamin could never conquer Jerusalem. It was David from the tribe of Judah who conquered it after he became king of
Israel, calling it the City of David (see 2 Sa 5:6–9). David also bought
the threshing floor of Ornan the Jebusite, north of the city, where the
Temples later stood. Jerusalem is therefore unique, reminiscent of the
special district of the American capital Washington DC. You can
rightly call the capital of Israel, Jerusalem DC—Jerusalem David's
City. It is the city of the great King.

The Temple Mount is a hill—in a valley—located between the
Mount of Olives to the east, and the so called "Western Hill" (aka the
"Upper City") to the west. Both of these surrounding hills, which are
described as "shoulders," are located in Benjamin. These two "shoulders"—the Mount of Olives to the east and the Western Hill to the
west—surround the Temple Mount. *"... the one the Lord loves rests between his [Benjamin's] shoulders." (Dt 33:12 NIV) This is how exact
Moses prophesied the location of Jerusalem, His holy hill, and the
throne of the Son of David!

According to Jewish tradition, David and Samuel discovered this
place in the Torah of Moses, when the spirit of prophecy rested on
them. We read about this in First Samuel 19:

"Now David fled and escaped, and he came to Samuel at Ra-
mah and told him all that Saul had done to him. And he and
Samuel went and lived at Naioth. And it was told Saul, 'Be-
hold, David is at Naioth in Ramah.' Then Saul sent messen-

gers to take David, and when they saw the company of the prophets prophesying, and Samuel standing as head over them, the Spirit of God came upon the messengers of Saul, and they also prophesied. When it was told Saul, he sent other messengers, and they also prophesied. And Saul sent messengers again the third time, and they also prophesied. Then he himself went to Ramah and came to the great well that is in Secu. And he asked, 'Where are Samuel and David?' And one said, 'Behold, they are at Naioth in Ramah.' And he went there to Naioth in Ramah. And the Spirit of God came upon him also, and as he went he prophesied until he came to Naioth in Ramah. And he too stripped off his clothes, and he too prophesied before Samuel and lay naked all that day and all that night. Thus it is said, 'Is Saul also among the prophets?'" (1 Sa 19:18–24)

As we see in the text, there was a very strong prophetic anointing upon Samuel and David in Rama. The Jewish sages say that this caused them to see the place Moses had described, where *"The beloved of the LORD dwells in safety."* (Dt 33:12)

There are, however, indications that David knew about this place already, before this incident. We will discuss more about this in Chapter 5.

The City of our Appointed Feasts

"Three times a year all your males shall appear before the LORD your God at the place that he will choose: at the Feast of Unleavened Bread, at the Feast of Weeks, and at the Feast of Booths. They shall not appear before the LORD empty-handed." (Dt 16:16)

Jesus said, *"If you believed Moses, you would believe me; for he wrote of me."* (Jn 5:46) Moses wrote about Jesus. All of the Feasts of the LORD point to Messiah. He is the one who fulfills them.

It is also written in Isaiah:

> *"Behold Zion, the city of our appointed feasts! Your eyes will see Jerusalem, an untroubled habitation, an immovable tent, whose stakes will never be plucked up, nor will any of its cords be broken."* (Isa 33:20)

All the Feasts that God gave to His people through Moses point not only to Messiah, but also to Jerusalem. Isaiah calls Jerusalem *"the city of our appointed feasts!"*

All of the LORD's appointed feasts will have their prophetic fulfillment in Jerusalem, through the Messiah. It was in Jerusalem that Jesus died at three in the afternoon during the Feast of Passover, while the Passover lambs were being slaughtered in the Temple. It was at the Temple in Jerusalem at nine in the morning during the morning prayers at the Feast of Weeks, or Pentecost, that the Holy Spirit was poured out to seal the new covenant by writing the Torah on the hearts of the disciples. As the grain offering of new grain from the first harvest was presented before the LORD, the first harvest of 3,000 souls was brought into the kingdom.

It is also in Jerusalem that the Feast of Booths will be fulfilled at the coming of Messiah. *"Then everyone who survives of all the nations that have come against Jerusalem shall go up year after year to worship the King, the LORD of hosts, and to keep the Feast of Booths."* (Zec 14:16) No wonder that Peter said when he saw the power and coming of Messiah on the Mount of Transfiguration, *"Lord, it is good that we are here. If you wish, I will make three tents here, one for you and one for Moses and one for Elijah."* (Mt 17:4)

The Feast of Booths points to the great banquet feast in the kingdom of God, that will be celebrated there.

"On this mountain the LORD of hosts will make for all peoples a feast of rich food, a feast of well-aged wine, of rich food full of marrow, of aged wine well refined. And he will swallow up on this mountain the covering that is cast over all peoples, the veil that is spread over all nations. He will swallow up death forever; and the Lord GOD will wipe away tears from all faces, and the reproach of his people he will take away from all the earth, for the LORD has spoken. It will be said on that day, 'Behold, this is our God; we have waited for him, that he might save us. This is the LORD; we have waited for him; let us be glad and rejoice in his salvation.'" (Isa 25:6–9)

"I tell you, many will come from east and west and recline at table with Abraham, Isaac, and Jacob in the kingdom of heaven." (Mt 8:11)

5

THE CITY OF
THE GREAT KING

"...beautiful in elevation, is the joy of all the earth,
Mount Zion, in the far north, the city of the great King."
—Psalm 48:2

The main person associated with Jerusalem in the Torah is Abraham—particularly through the binding and near sacrifice of his son Isaac on Mount Moriah. It was this incident that changed the name of the city from Salem to Jerusalem, from "the city of peace" to "the city where the LORD shall provide peace," or where "the LORD shall come down and be seen bringing peace." Abraham saw the day of Messiah. The name of the city Jerusalem is prophetic of the coming of Messiah.

In the books of Joshua and Judges, Jerusalem is only mentioned in passing as a Jebusite city. Under Joshua, Israel defeated the king of Jerusalem even though the city itself was not captured. The Book of Joshua tells the story.

> *"As soon as Adoni–zedek, king of Jerusalem, heard how Joshua had captured Ai and had devoted it to destruction, doing to Ai and its king as he had done to Jericho and its king, and how the inhabitants of Gibeon had made peace with Israel*

and were among them, he feared greatly, because Gibeon was a great city, like one of the royal cities, and because it was greater than Ai, and all its men were warriors. So Adoni–zedek king of Jerusalem sent to Hoham king of He-bron, to Piram king of Jarmuth, to Japhia king of Lachish, and to Debir king of Eglon, saying, 'Come up to me and help me, and let us strike Gibeon. For it has made peace with Joshua and with the people of Israel.'" (Jos 10:1–4)

The men of Gibeon asked for help from Joshua, who came and defeated the army led by the king of Jerusalem. It was in connection with this battle for Jerusalem that the sun stood still in Gibeon.

"At that time Joshua spoke to the LORD in the day when the LORD gave the Amorites over to the sons of Israel, and he said in the sight of Israel, 'Sun, stand still at Gibeon, and moon, in the Valley of Aijalon.' And the sun stood still, and the moon stopped, until the nation took vengeance on their enemies. Is this not written in the Book of Jashar? The sun stopped in the midst of heaven and did not hurry to set for about a whole day. There has been no day like it before or since, when the LORD heeded the voice of a man, for the LORD fought for Israel." (Jos 10:12–14)

The tribe of Judah later on defeated the people of Jerusalem and captured the city. *"And the men of Judah fought against Jerusalem and captured it and struck it with the edge of the sword and set the city on fire."* (Jdg 1:8) But the people of Judah could not hold on to the city, so the Jebusites moved back in again. *"But the Jebusites, the inhabitants of Jerusalem, the people of Judah could not drive out, so the Jebusites dwell with the people of Judah at Jerusalem to this day."* (Jos 15:63)

As we mentioned in Chapter 4, Jerusalem is located right on the border between Judah and Benjamin. The Scriptures tell us that nei-ther the tribe of Judah nor the tribe of Benjamin could drive out the

Jebusites from Jerusalem. *"But the people of Benjamin did not drive out the Jebusites who lived in Jerusalem, so the Jebusites have lived with the people of Benjamin in Jerusalem to this day."* (Jdg 1:21) Jerusalem became known as Jebus, a Jebusite city, as we see in the tragic story about the Levite who lost his concubine.

> *"He rose up and departed and arrived opposite Jebus (that is, Jerusalem). He had with him a couple of saddled donkeys, and his concubine was with him. When they were near Jebus, the day was nearly over, and the servant said to his master, 'Come now, let us turn aside to this city of the Jebusites and spend the night in it.' And his master said to him, '**We will not turn aside into the city of foreigners, who do not belong to the people of Israel**, but we will pass on to Gibeah.'"* (Jdg 19:10–12)

We see here that Jerusalem was at this time still occupied by the Jebusites. The city did not belong to the people of Israel. Jerusalem remained as a foreign, Jebusite city, until the time of King David. With him the next major phase in the history of Jerusalem begins.

The Man After God's Own Heart

When Israel had crossed the Red Sea they sang:

> *"You will bring them in and plant them on the mountain of your inheritance—the place, O LORD, you made for your dwelling, the sanctuary, O Lord, your hands established."* (Ex 15:17 NIV)

Later on, Moses prophesied about the special place God would choose for His people. It would happen *"**when he gives you rest from all your enemies around, so that you live in safety.**"* (De 12:10) It was during King David's time that the LORD gave His people this rest.

*"Now when the king lived in his house and **the LORD had given him rest** from all his surrounding enemies, the king said to Nathan the prophet, 'See now, I dwell in a house of cedar, but the ark of God dwells in a tent.' And Nathan said to the king, 'Go, do all that is in your heart, for the LORD is with you.'"* (2 Sa 7:1–3)

When Solomon prayed at the inauguration of the Temple, he made a special reference to Moses' promise that God would choose a place for His name,

*"Praise be to the LORD, the God of Israel, who with his hand has fulfilled what he promised with his mouth to David my father, saying, 'Since the day I brought my people out of Egypt, I have not chosen a city in any tribe of Israel to have a Temple built for my Name to be there, nor have I chosen anyone to be the leader over my people Israel. **But now I have chosen Jerusalem for my Name to be there, and I have chosen David to rule my people Israel.**'"* (2 Ch 6:4–6 NIV)

To summarize, Moses referred to a place in the Song at the Sea. He then prophesied that God would choose this place when he gave Israel rest from all their enemies around, and they lived in safety. David was the warrior who accomplished this for Israel, as he was *"fighting the battles of the LORD."* (1 Sa 25:28)

It was David who received the final revelation about the exact location of the place that Moses had prophesied about, and he established Jerusalem as the capital and center of Israel. With David—the man after God's own heart—the history of Jerusalem really begins. At that time, Jerusalem became known as the "City of David."

Right after David had been anointed as king over all of Israel in Hebron, he immediately mobilized his army to conquer Jerusalem.

"And the king and his men went to Jerusalem against the Je-busites, the inhabitants of the land, who said to David, 'You will not come in here, but the blind and the lame will ward you off'—thinking, 'David cannot come in here.' **Neverthe-less, David took the stronghold of Zion, that is, the city of David.** *And David said on that day, 'Whoever would strike the Jebusites, let him get up the water shaft to attack 'the lame and the blind,' who are hated by David's soul.' There-fore it is said, 'The blind and the lame shall not come into the house.'* **And David lived in the stronghold and called it the city of David.** *And David built the city all around from the Millo inward. And David became greater and greater, for the LORD, the God of hosts, was with him."* (2 Sa 5:6–10)

This is also the first time in the Scriptures that another name con-nected with Jerusalem, namely Zion, appears. Scholars are not really sure what exactly the word Zion means or where it comes from. If it has Hebrew origins, it is most likely connected to a word that means "castle" or "fortress."[1] The original phrase *"the stronghold of Zion"* (5:7) where David settled, supports this. *"And David lived in the strong-hold and called it the city of David."* (5:9)

---

1   "'Zion' may derive from the Hebrew root *ṣiyyôn* ('castle'), from Arabic *sana* ('protect' or 'citadel')" (T. Longman, P. Enns, ed. *Dictionary of the Old Testa-ment: wisdom, poetry & writings, Vol. 3,* InterVarsity Press, 2008, p. 936). Zion "is possibly related to Arabic *ṣâna* from root *ṣ–w–n,* meaning protect, defend; hence *ṣîyôn* may have meant place of defence, fortress" (H. Laird, G. Archer Jr., and B. Waltke, eds. *Theological Wordbook of the Old Testament,* Chicago: Moody Press, 1999, TWOT No. 1910). There are some who say that Zion comes from the Hebrew word *tziun,* which means "signal," or "marker." (L. Ritmeyer, "A Response to Dr. Ernest L. Martin," Prophecy Watchers, Oct. 8, 2014, http://goo.gl/DvsnJk; see also J. Swanson, *Dictionary of Biblical Languages with Se-mantic Domains: Hebrew [Old Testament],* Oak Harbor: Logos Research Sys-tems, Inc., 1997, No. 7483).

The name "Zion" in the Scriptures is strongly connected to King David, the King of Israel. "Zion" is also used specifically about the Temple Mount, the throne of the Lord. This is the real Mount Zion in the Bible.[2] Finally, Zion, just like Jerusalem in the Book of Revelation, is also a metaphor for the people of God, the Bride of Messiah.

Both Christians and Jews today often refer to the hill outside of Jerusalem's Zion Gate, south of the Armenian Quarter in the Old City, as Mount Zion. This clear misidentification dates back to the Crusaders in the Middle Ages, when Christian pilgrims, influenced by pagan and Christian traditions, mistook the highest point in ancient Jerusalem for the original site of the Jewish Temple. But the Torah forbids worshipping the God of Israel on high places, which is why the Temple Mount is not the highest place in the area.

Today the Dormition Church is located upon the hill erroneously called Mount Zion. But this hill is west of the original city of Jerusalem and was not even part of the city that David made into his capital. The hill has nothing whatsoever to do with the original Mount Zion in the Scriptures. Psalm 48 begins:

> "*Great is the LORD and greatly to be praised in the city of our God! His holy mountain, beautiful in elevation, is the joy of all the earth, **Mount Zion, in the far north**, the city of the great King.*" (Ps 48:1–2)

Here we see that Mount Zion is located in the far north of Jerusalem. The Temple Mount was the most northern part of original Jerusalem, in the Bible. This is the biblical Mount Zion. Psalm 48 tells us that the Temple Mount is also the city of the great King. It is God's throne and therefore referred to as "*his holy hill*" (Ps 3:4) and "*my holy hill*" (Ps 2:6).

---

2   Whereas "the stronghold of Zion" refers to the City of David, this expression is never used about the Temple Mount.

Stephen mentioned David in his speech before the Sanhedrin in Jerusalem.

> *"Our fathers had the tent of witness in the wilderness, just as he who spoke to Moses directed him to make it, according to the pattern that he had seen. Our fathers in turn brought it in with Joshua when they dispossessed the nations that God drove out before our fathers. So it was until the days of* **David, who found favor in the sight of God and asked to find a dwelling place for the God of Jacob.***"* (Ac 7:44–46)

Here we see that a whole new chapter in the history of Israel began with David. Stephen said that David found favor in the sight of God and asked that he would find a dwelling place for the God of Jacob. David must have known about the command and the promise God made to Moses, *"But you shall seek the place that the LORD your God will choose out of all your tribes to put his name and make his habitation there. There you shall go."* (Dt 12:5) It was David's desire to establish that dwelling place for God.

In Paul's sermon in the synagogue in Pisidian Antioch he said that David was a man after God's own heart and would do all His will. *"And when he had removed him* [King Saul], *he raised up David to be their king, of whom he testified and said, 'I have found in David the son of Jesse* **a man after my heart, who will do all my will.***'"* (Ac 13:22)

Why did David choose Jerusalem? We have already mentioned the tradition in the previous chapter that God revealed this place to David when he fled from King Saul, and he and Samuel were under the influence of the spirit of prophecy and studied the Torah of Moses together. We do not know if this tradition is true or not, but it certainly is possible. At least it could have served as a confirmation to David that Jerusalem was indeed the location of his future capital.

It is very interesting that Jerusalem is mentioned right after David had defeated Goliath. It says, *"And David took the head of the Philistine and brought it to Jerusalem, but he put his armor in his tent."* (1 Sa

17:54) Why did David take the head of Goliath to Jerusalem? Did he know something about the destiny of Jerusalem already at that time, that it would become his capital? David had just conquered the giant of the land. Was this a prophetic act, that the haughty Jebusites in Jerusalem, who said that they would never be conquered, were next on David's agenda, because this is where he would one day establish his throne?

Psalm 132 gives us a special insight into the heart of David, the man after God's own heart, who would do all His will.

> *"Remember, O LORD, in David's favor, all the hardships he endured, how he swore to the LORD and vowed to the Mighty One of Jacob, 'I will not enter my house or get into my bed, I will not give sleep to my eyes or slumber to my eyelids, until I find a place for the LORD, a dwelling place for the Mighty One of Jacob.' Behold, we heard of it in Ephrathah; we found it in the fields of Jaar."* (Ps 132:1–6)

This is what Stephen was referring to when he said that David *"asked to find a dwelling place for the God of Jacob."* (Ac 7:46) We should have the same passion and dedication to the restoration of Jerusalem and the coming of Messiah as David expresses, here in Psalm 132. He was willing to suffer and sacrifice the comforts of life for the sake of securing *"a dwelling place for the Mighty One of Jacob."* In the same way, we need to prepare the way for Messiah to take up His throne in Jerusalem. *"In that day the root of Jesse, who shall stand as a signal for the peoples—of him shall the nations inquire, and his resting place shall be glorious."* (Isa 11:10)

Psalm 132:6 says, *"Behold, we heard of it in Ephrathah."* "Ephrathah" is another name for Bethlehem. This indicates that David had the longing in his heart to secure a dwelling place for the Mighty One of Jacob ever since his youth, when the Spirit of the LORD came upon him as a shepherd boy. He may also have known about the place already, from that time.

> *"Then Samuel said to Jesse, 'Are all your sons here?' And he said, 'There remains yet the youngest, but behold, he is keeping the sheep.' And Samuel said to Jesse, 'Send and get him, for we will not sit down till he comes here.' And he sent and brought him in. Now he was ruddy and had beautiful eyes and was handsome. And the LORD said, 'Arise, anoint him, for this is he.' Then Samuel took the horn of oil and anointed him in the midst of his brothers. **And the Spirit of the LORD rushed upon David from that day forward.**"* (1 Sa 16:11–13)

From this time, David had a passion to find a resting place for the God of Jacob. King David was the one who officially selected the place for the Temple. As we have already seen, others before David had also known about this place—especially Abraham. *"So Abraham called the name of that place, 'The LORD will provide'; as it is said to this day, 'On the mount of the LORD it shall be provided.'"* (Gen 22:14) Targum Onkelos is one of the paraphrase translations of the Hebrew Bible into Aramaic that were used in synagogue readings in the time of Jesus. It translated this verse, *"God will seek out for Himself this place for the dwelling of His Shechinah and for the offering of sacrifices."* (Gen 22:14, Targum Onkelos)

The exact location, however, was still a mystery for King David. It was not until the serious crisis when the angel had come to destroy Jerusalem after David had broken God's command not to count the people, that the place was revealed to him. At that time, God ordered the prophet Gad to tell David to erect an altar at the threshing floor of Ornan, in order to stop the plague.

> *"Now the angel of the LORD had commanded Gad to say to David that David should go up and raise an altar to the LORD on the threshing floor of Ornan the Jebusite. So David went up at Gad's word, which he had spoken in the name of the LORD."* (1 Ch 21:18–19)

The story continues:

> *"So David paid Ornan 600 shekels of gold by weight for the site. And David built there an altar to the LORD and presented burnt offerings and peace offerings and called on the LORD, and the LORD answered him with fire from heaven upon the altar of burnt offering. Then the LORD commanded the angel, and he put his sword back into its sheath. At that time, when David saw that the LORD had answered him at the threshing floor of Ornan the Jebusite, he sacrificed there. For the tabernacle of the LORD, which Moses had made in the wilderness, and the altar of burnt offering were at that time in the high place at Gibeon, but David could not go before it to inquire of God, for he was afraid of the sword of the angel of the LORD.* **Then David said, 'Here shall be the house of the LORD God and here the altar of burnt offering for Israel.'"** (21:25–22:1)

King David bought the threshing floor of Ornan for 600 shekels of silver. The title deed to the Temple Mount is recorded in the Scriptures about which Jesus said, *"Heaven and earth will pass away, but my words will not pass away."* (Mt 24:35) Jerusalem belongs forever to the King of Israel! This is why Jesus also called Jerusalem an occupied city when it is not under Jewish control (see Lk 21:24). Psalm 125:3 promises, *"For the scepter of wickedness shall not rest on the land allotted to the righteous."*

Later on it is written, *"Then Solomon began to build the house of the LORD in Jerusalem on Mount Moriah, where the LORD had appeared to David his father, at the place that David had appointed, on the threshing floor of Ornan the Jebusite."* (2 Ch 3:1)

Mount Moriah is a reference to the place of the binding of Isaac, when Abraham was told, *"Take your son, your only son Isaac, whom you love, and go to the land of Moriah, and offer him there as a burnt offering on one of the mountains of which I shall tell you."* (Gen 22:2)

The name Moriah comes from the Hebrew word *moreh*, which means "teacher." It is the place from which God one day will teach all nations (see Isa 2:3). It was also here that the Gospel was preached in its fullness for the first time, on the Day of Pentecost.

Psalm 132 continues,

> *"'Let us go to his dwelling place; let us worship at his footstool!' Arise, O LORD, and go to your resting place, you and the ark of your might. Let your priests be clothed with righteousness, and let your saints shout for joy. For the sake of your servant David, do not turn away the face of your anointed one."* (Ps 132:7–10)

In the wilderness, when the Pillar of Cloud over the Tabernacle lifted, it was time for the children of Israel to take down the Tabernacle and journey on. It says,

> *"And whenever the ark set out, Moses said, 'Arise, O LORD, and let your enemies be scattered, and let those who hate you flee before you.' And when it rested, he said, 'Return, O LORD, to the ten thousand thousands of Israel.'"* (Nu 10:35–36)

Psalm 132 refers to these prayers of Moses when it says, *"Arise, O LORD, and go to your resting place, you and the ark of your might."* (Ps 132:8)

The Temple Mount became God's permanent dwelling place or resting place, as opposed to the Tabernacle that was transported from place to place. Isaiah prophesied about Zion:

> *"Behold Zion, the city of our appointed feasts! Your eyes will see Jerusalem, an untroubled habitation, **an immovable tent, whose stakes will never be plucked up**, nor will any of its cords be broken."* (Isa 33:20)

Jerusalem is called *"an immovable tent."* It is God's permanent resting place, which David had in his heart to secure.

The Temple Mount and the Messiah

We are now living in a time that Jesus spoke about to the woman at the well in Samaria.

> *"The woman said to him, 'Sir, I perceive that you are a prophet. Our fathers worshiped on this mountain, but you say that in Jerusalem is the place where people ought to worship.' Jesus said to her, 'Woman, believe me, the hour is coming when neither on this mountain nor in Jerusalem will you worship the Father. You worship what you do not know; we worship what we know, for salvation is from the Jews. But the hour is coming, and is now here, when the true worshipers will worship the Father in spirit and truth, for the Father is seeking such people to worship him. God is spirit, and those who worship him must worship in spirit and truth.'"* (Jn 4:19–24)

Right now, we can worship the Father in spirit and truth anywhere on the earth and He hears us. The kingdom of God is manifest inside of us, through the giving of the Holy Spirit. Jesus said, *"The kingdom of God does not come with observation; nor will they say, 'See here!' or 'See there!' For indeed, the kingdom of God is within you."* (Lk 17:20–21 NKJV) And Paul wrote, *"For the kingdom of God is not a matter of eating and drinking but of righteousness and peace and joy in the Holy Spirit."* (Ro 14:17)

But in the world to come, when Jesus returns in power and glory, the kingdom of God will certainly come *"with observation."* Jesus spoke about the signs of His coming, and said,

*"And **then they will see** the Son of Man coming in a cloud with power and great glory. Now when these things begin to take place, straighten up and raise your heads, because your redemption is drawing near.' And he told them a parable: Look at the fig tree, and all the trees. As soon as they come out in leaf, you see for yourselves and know that the summer is already near. So also, **when you see these things taking place, you know that the kingdom of God is near.**"* (Lk 21:27–31)

When the kingdom of God manifests itself physically in a renewed heaven and earth at the coming of Messiah, God's throne will be established physically in Jerusalem on the Temple Mount. This is the same Mountain from which the Messiah will reign on the throne of His father David.

*"The LORD swore to David a sure oath from which he will not turn back: 'One of the sons of your body I will set on your throne. If your sons keep my covenant and my testimonies that I shall teach them, their sons also forever shall sit on your throne.' For the LORD has chosen Zion; he has desired it for his dwelling place: 'This is my resting place forever; here I will dwell, for I have desired it. I will abundantly bless her provisions; I will satisfy her poor with bread. Her priests I will clothe with salvation, and her saints will shout for joy. There I will make a horn to sprout for David; **I have prepared a lamp for my anointed.** His enemies I will clothe with shame, but on him his crown will shine.'"* (Ps 132:11–18)

Messiah means "anointed." Verse 17 can therefore also be translated, *"There* [on Mount Zion] *I will make a horn to sprout for David; I **have prepared a lamp for my Messiah.**"* Mount Zion is reserved for the Messiah, Jesus of Nazareth. This is what the angel Gabriel promised Mary when he said:

*"Do not be afraid, Mary, for you have found favor with God. And behold, you will conceive in your womb and bear a son, and you shall call his name Jesus. He will be great and will be called the Son of the Most High. And **the Lord God will give to him the throne of his father David, and he will reign over the house of Jacob forever, and of his kingdom there will be no end.**"* (Lk 1:30–33)

If the Messiah is to reign forever on the throne of David, He cannot be just an ordinary man. He must be immortal. Peter said in his sermon on the day of Pentecost in Jerusalem:

*"For David says concerning him, 'I saw the Lord always before me, for he is at my right hand that I may not be shaken; therefore my heart was glad, and my tongue rejoiced; my flesh also will dwell in hope. For **you will not abandon my soul to Hades, or let your Holy One see corruption.** You have made known to me the paths of life; you will make me full of gladness with your presence.'*

*"Brothers, I may say to you with confidence about the patriarch David that he both died and was buried, and his tomb is with us to this day. **Being therefore a prophet, and knowing that God had sworn with an oath to him that he would set one of his descendants on his throne, he foresaw and spoke about the resurrection of the Messiah,** that he was not abandoned to Hades, nor did his flesh see corruption. This Jesus God raised up, and of that we all are witnesses."* (Ac 2:25–32)

The resurrection of Jesus is proof that He is the Messiah. Paul explained in the synagogue in Pisidian Antioch:

"And we bring you the good news that what God promised to the fathers, this he has fulfilled to us their children by raising Jesus, as also it is written in the second Psalm, 'You are my Son, today I have begotten you.' And as for the fact that he raised him from the dead, no more to return to corruption, he has spoken in this way, 'I will give you the holy and sure blessings of David.'" (Ac 13:32–34)

Here, Paul says that Jesus had to die and be raised to life, never to die again in order to fulfill the promise and the oath God had given David that the reign of one of his sons would be forever. He had told him:

*"I will raise up your offspring after you, who shall come from your body, and I will establish his kingdom. He shall build a house for my name, and **I will establish the throne of his kingdom forever**."* (2 Sa 7:12–13)

Jesus has been raised to life in order to reign forever on the throne of his father David. David's throne was not in heaven. It was in Jerusalem. More specifically, it was moved by his son Solomon, right next to the place that David secured for the Temple—the Temple Mount.

Zion: A Place of Conflict and Salvation

David wrote extensively in the Book of Psalms about Zion and the coming Messiah. Many of these Psalms speak about Zion as a place of conflict. There will be an end time battle over the throne of God and His Anointed King.

Two of the most quoted Psalms by the apostles in the Apostolic Scriptures are Psalm 2 and Psalm 110. Psalm 2 reads:

"Why do the nations rage and the peoples plot in vain? The kings of the earth set themselves, and the rulers take counsel

together, against the LORD and against his Anointed, say-
ing, 'Let us burst their bonds apart and cast away their
cords from us.' He who sits in the heavens laughs; the Lord
holds them in derision. Then he will speak to them in his
wrath, and terrify them in his fury, saying, 'As for me, I have
set my King on Zion, my holy hill.' I will tell of the decree: The
LORD said to me, 'You are my Son; today I have begotten
you. Ask of me, and I will make the nations your heritage,
and the ends of the earth your possession. You shall break
them with a rod of iron and dash them in pieces like a pot-
ter's vessel.' Now therefore, O kings, be wise; be warned, O
rulers of the earth. Serve the LORD with fear, and rejoice
with trembling. Kiss the Son, lest he be angry, and you perish
in the way, for his wrath is quickly kindled. Blessed are all
who take refuge in him." (Ps 2:1–12)

The beginning of Psalm 2 was initially fulfilled at the crucifixion of Jesus, according to Acts 4:24–28. But it will also be fulfilled in the end times, through the antichrist. Paul warned the Thessalonians about this coming rebellion against the Messiah.

"Let no one deceive you in any way. For that day will not
come, unless the rebellion comes first, and the man of law-
lessness is revealed, the son of destruction, who opposes and
exalts himself against every so–called god or object of wor-
ship, so that he takes his seat in the Temple of God, proclaim-
ing himself to be God." (2 Th 2:3–4)

We see this rebellion against God everywhere today. It will soon culminate in the appearance of the Lawless One. Satan has always tried to take God's place. That is why it says about Lucifer:

"How you are fallen from heaven, O Day Star, son of Dawn!
How you are cut down to the ground, you who laid the na-

tions low! You said in your heart, 'I will ascend to heaven; above the stars of God I will set my throne on high; **I will sit on the mount of assembly in the far reaches of the north**; *I will ascend above the heights of the clouds; I will make myself like the Most High.'"* (Isa 14:12–14)

This is why the antichrist will take his seat in the Temple of God in Jerusalem, proclaiming himself to be God. The Davidic Psalms about Zion are full of the end time conflict over God's throne. Psalm 110 reads:

"The LORD says to my Lord: 'Sit at my right hand, until I make your enemies your footstool.' The LORD sends forth from Zion your mighty scepter. Rule in the midst of your enemies! Your people will offer themselves freely on the day of your power, in holy garments; from the womb of the morning, the dew of your youth will be yours. The LORD has sworn and will not change his mind, 'You are a priest forever after the order of Melchizedek.' The Lord is at your right hand; he will shatter kings on the day of his wrath. He will execute judgment among the nations, filling them with corpses; he will shatter chiefs over the wide earth. He will drink from the brook by the way; therefore he will lift up his head." (Ps 110:1–7)

The apostles used the first verse in Psalm 110 to prove the resurrection and ascension of Messiah. They quote this verse more times than any other verse from the entire Hebrew Bible. The Psalm then continues with the proclamation of the LORD stretching forth Messiah's mighty scepter from Zion. It is from Zion that He will rule the nations with a rod of iron, as it also says in the second Psalm, *"You shall break them with a rod of iron and dash them in pieces like a potter's vessel."* (Ps 2:9)

The prophet Joel proclaimed the same message:

"The LORD will roar from Zion and thunder from Jerusa-
lem; the earth and the sky will tremble. But the LORD will be
a refuge for his people, a stronghold for the people of Israel.
Then you will know that I, the LORD your God, dwell in Zion,
my holy hill." (Joel 3:16–17 NIV)

Because the kings of the earth have rebelled against Messiah, Isaiah prophesied that there will come a day when the LORD will take
vengeance. *"For the LORD has a day of vengeance, a year of recom-*
pense for the cause of Zion." (Isa 34:8)

Psalm 48 deals in more detail with the battle over Zion. After a
statement in verse 2 that Zion is the city of the great King, it continues
to describe what will happen with those nations that attack His city,
rebelling against His throne:

"Within her citadels God has made himself known as a for-
*tress. For behold, **the kings assembled; they came on to-***
***gether**. As soon as they saw it, they were astounded; they*
were in panic; they took to flight. Trembling took hold of
them there, anguish as of a woman in labor. By the east wind
you shattered the ships of Tarshish. As we have heard, so
have we seen in the city of the LORD of hosts, in the city of
our God, which God will establish forever. Selah" (Ps 48:3–8)

This is written about as well, in the Book of Zechariah:

"Then the LORD will go out and fight against those nations
as when he fights on a day of battle. On that day his feet
shall stand on the Mount of Olives that lies before Jerusalem
on the east, and the Mount of Olives shall be split in two
from east to west by a very wide valley, so that one half of
the Mount shall move northward, and the other half south-
ward. And you shall flee to the valley of my mountains, for
the valley of the mountains shall reach to Azal. And you

*shall flee as you fled from the earthquake in the days of Uz-
ziah king of Judah. Then the LORD my God will come, and
all the holy ones with him. On that day there shall be no
light, cold, or frost. And there shall be a unique day, which is
known to the LORD, neither day nor night, but at evening
time there shall be light."* (Zec 14:3–7)

Paul described it in this way: *"And then the lawless one will be revealed, whom the Lord Jesus will overthrow with the breath of his
mouth and destroy by the splendor of his coming."* (2 Th 2:8 NIV)

*"The LORD is righteous; he has cut the cords of the wicked.
May all who hate Zion be put to shame and turned back-
ward! Let them be like the grass on the housetops, which
withers before it grows up."* (Ps 129:4–6)

Walid Shoebat, who wrote the book *God's War on Terror*, has said
that while most Christians believe in the second coming of Christ,
hardly anyone seems to have any idea what He will do when He
comes. He is coming to make war, to rescue Zion and Jerusalem, and
to defeat all her enemies. What a day that will be!

Zion and Jerusalem is not just the place of the ultimate end time
conflict and battle. It is, most of all, the place of salvation. Many of the
Psalms of David include prayers like: *"Oh, that salvation for Israel
would come out of Zion!"* (Ps 14:7) An incredibly powerful statement is
made about Zion in Psalm 50:

*"The Mighty One, God the LORD, speaks and summons the
earth from the rising of the sun to its setting. Out of Zion,
the perfection of beauty, God shines forth. Our God comes;
he does not keep silence; before him is a devouring fire,
around him a mighty tempest. He calls to the heavens above
and to the earth, that he may judge his people."* (Ps 50:1–4)

The Jewish sages see Psalm 50:2 as a prophecy about the rock, the Foundation Stone, upon which the Ark of Covenant was placed in the Holy of Holies in the Temple. *"Out of Zion, the perfection of beauty, God shines forth."* Moreover, they see these verses in Psalm 50 as speaking of God creating the heavens and the earth by the words of His mouth, as it says, *"God the LORD, speaks and summons the earth from the rising of the sun to its setting."*

> *"By the word of the LORD the heavens were made, and by the breath of his mouth all their host."* (Ps 33:6)

The rock in the Holy of Holies, which today is situated right under the golden Dome of the Rock on the Temple Mount, is therefore called the "Foundation Stone," *Even HaShtiya* in Hebrew.

We can also see an indication in this Psalm that it is from this place, from Zion, that God will create the new heavens and the new earth. *"I assure you that when the world is made new and the Son of Man sits upon his glorious throne* [on Mount Zion], *you who have been my followers will also sit on twelve thrones, judging the twelve tribes of Israel."* (Mt 19:28 NLT)

> *"For behold, I create new heavens and a new earth, and the former things shall not be remembered or come into mind. But be glad and rejoice forever in that which I create; for behold, I create Jerusalem to be a joy, and her people to be a gladness. I will rejoice in Jerusalem and be glad in my people; no more shall be heard in it the sound of weeping and the cry of distress."* (Isa 65:17–19)

This causes us to pray even more diligently: *"Oh, that salvation for Israel would come out of Zion! When God restores the fortunes of his people, Let Jacob rejoice, let Israel be glad."* (Ps 53:6)

We can therefore see an interesting paradox in the Scriptures about Zion. Isaiah 59:20 says, *"And a Redeemer will come to Zion, to those in Jacob who turn from transgression," declares the LORD."* Here it is stated that a Redeemer, that is the Messiah, will come **to** Zion when the people repent of their sins. However, when Paul quoted this verse in Romans, he changed the order. He wrote,

> *"And in this way all Israel will be saved, as it is written, 'The Deliverer will come **from** Zion, he will banish ungodliness from Jacob.'"* (Ro 11:26)

Will the Messiah come from Zion or to Zion? Both are true. He will come to Zion and from Zion He will bring salvation for Israel and the whole world.

> *"... therefore thus says the Lord GOD, 'Behold, I am the one who has laid as a foundation in Zion, a stone, a tested stone, a precious cornerstone, of a sure foundation: 'Whoever believes will not be in haste.'"* (Isa 28:16)

6

A PRAISE IN THE EARTH

"...give him no rest until he establishes Jerusalem
and makes it a praise in the earth." —Isaiah 62:7

A Spiritual Decline

After King David had conquered Jerusalem and made it the capital of Israel, his son Solomon built the Temple on the exact site that David had chosen. Just as Moses was not allowed to enter the Promised Land but Joshua led the people into it, David was not allowed to build the Temple. Instead, the one who built it was David's son Solomon, which prophetically points to the Messiah, the great Son of David.

At the dedication of the Temple, God told Solomon, *"I have heard your prayer and your plea, which you have made before me. I have consecrated this house that you have built, by putting my name there forever. My eyes and my heart will be there for all time."* (1 Ki 9:3)

Israel prospered greatly during King Solomon's reign (see 1 Ki 8:65). There was peace with all the surrounding neighbors and Israel had finally settled all the land that Moses had promised the children of Israel during his farewell speech to them (see Nu 34:1–15). It was a foretaste of the coming Messianic kingdom, which will include even more territory, according to God's promise to Abraham (see Gen 15:18–21).

The Book of Kings describes the situation in Israel during the reign of Solomon.

> **"Judah and Israel were as many as the sand by the sea. They ate and drank and were happy.** *Solomon ruled over all the kingdoms from the Euphrates to the land of the Philistines and to the border of Egypt. They brought tribute and served Solomon all the days of his life. Solomon's provision for one day was thirty cors of fine flour and sixty cors of meal, ten fat oxen, and twenty pasture–fed cattle, a hundred sheep, besides deer, gazelles, roebucks, and fattened fowl. For he had dominion over all the region west of the Euphrates from Tiphsah to Gaza, over all the kings west of the Euphrates. And* **he had peace on all sides around him. And Judah and Israel lived in safety, from Dan even to Beersheba, every man under his vine and under his fig tree, all the days of Solomon."** (1 Ki 4:20–25)

First Kings continues with a description of the elaborate throne that Solomon made for himself:

> **"The king also made a great ivory throne and overlaid it with the finest gold.** *The throne had six steps, and at the back of the throne was a calf's head, and on each side of the seat were armrests and two lions standing beside the armrests, while twelve lions stood there, one on each end of a step on the six steps.* **The like of it was never made in any kingdom.** *All King Solomon's drinking vessels were of gold, and all the vessels of the House of the Forest of Lebanon were of pure gold. None were of silver; silver was not considered as anything in the days of Solomon. For the king had a fleet of ships of Tarshish at sea with the fleet of Hiram. Once ev-*

*ery three years the fleet of ships of Tarshish used to come bringing gold, silver, ivory, apes, and peacocks. **Thus King Solomon excelled all the kings of the earth in riches and in wisdom. And the whole earth sought the presence of Solomon to hear his wisdom,** which God had put into his mind."* (1 Ki 10:18–24)

This was a foretaste of the coming Messianic kingdom. Isaiah wrote about His throne, *"In that day the root of Jesse, who shall stand as a signal for the peoples—of him shall the nations inquire, and **his resting place shall be glorious.**"* (Isa 11:10)

Kings and potentates came from the ends of the earth to hear the wisdom of Solomon.

"Now when the queen of Sheba heard of the fame of Solomon concerning the name of the LORD, she came to test him with hard questions. She came to Jerusalem with a very great retinue, with camels bearing spices and very much gold and precious stones. And when she came to Solomon, she told him all that was on her mind. And Solomon answered all her questions; there was nothing hidden from the king that he could not explain to her." (1 Ki 10:1–3)

In the same way, the kings of the earth will come to Jerusalem to hear the word of the LORD from Messiah. *"For out of Zion shall go the law, and the word of the LORD from Jerusalem. He shall judge between the nations, and shall decide disputes for many peoples."* (Isa 2:3–4) *"Many peoples and strong nations shall come to seek the LORD of hosts in Jerusalem and to entreat the favor of the LORD."* (Zec 8:22)

Jesus said, *"The queen of the South will rise up at the judgment with this generation and condemn it, for she came from the ends of the earth to hear the wisdom of Solomon, and behold, something greater than Solomon is here."* (Mt 12:42)

However, at the end of Solomon's life, he began to forsake the God of Israel. When his son Rehoboam took over the throne, the kingdom was divided in two and the people began to worship the gods of the peoples around them. But God did not forget the oath that he had sworn to David. As the spiritual decline continued with succeeding generations of Davidic kings, God raised up prophets who spoke in the midst of the spiritual darkness and confusion about a coming glorious restoration of Jerusalem. They called the people to repentance, but they also painted a beautiful picture of a future full of hope for Jerusalem. These prophets' words are still waiting for their fulfillment.

The Promise of a Future Restoration

The promised restoration contained much more than just a return to the way things were in Jerusalem under King David, or even King Solomon. The prophets spoke about the kingdom of God being established from Jerusalem, over a renewed earth, through the Messiah, "the root and offspring of David." Foremost among these prophets was Isaiah, who prophesied extensively about Jerusalem and the coming, anointed King, Messiah:

> *"They shall not hurt or destroy in all my holy mountain; for the earth shall be full of the knowledge of the LORD as the waters cover the sea. In that day the root of Jesse, who shall stand as a signal for the peoples—of him shall the nations inquire, and his resting place shall be glorious."* (Isa 11:9–10)

"The root of Jesse," the Messiah, will one day stand as a signal or banner for all the nations of the world. They will seek him just as the whole earth sought the wisdom of Solomon. His resting place on Mount Zion in Jerusalem will be glorious, far exceeding even the throne of King Solomon.

Probably the most powerful of all the future declarations about Jerusalem is found in the beginning of Isaiah 2.

> *"The word that Isaiah the son of Amoz saw concerning Judah and Jerusalem. It shall come to pass in the latter days that the mountain of the house of the LORD shall be established as the highest of the mountains, and shall be lifted up above the hills; and all the nations shall flow to it, and many peoples shall come, and say: 'Come, let us go up to the mountain of the LORD, to the house of the God of Jacob, that he may teach us his ways and that we may walk in his paths.' For out of Zion shall go the law, and the word of the LORD from Jerusalem. He shall judge between the nations, and shall decide disputes for many peoples; and they shall beat their swords into plowshares, and their spears into pruning hooks; nation shall not lift up sword against nation, neither shall they learn war anymore."* (Isa 2:1–4)

The end of this prophecy *"nation shall not lift up sword against nation, neither shall they learn war anymore,"* is written on a plaque outside of the UN headquarters in New York. But the realization of this glorious prophecy and hope for mankind will not come from New York. It will come from Jerusalem, through the Messiah, Jesus!

Isaiah likewise describes the huge banquet feast that God has prepared for all peoples, which will also take place in Jerusalem at the fulfillment of the Feast of Tabernacles, as we explained in Chapter 4.

Jesus referred to this feast when he said, *"I tell you, many will come from east and west and recline at table with Abraham, Isaac, and Jacob in the kingdom of heaven."* (Mt 8:11) He did not say that people will come from the earth to a feast in heaven.[1] He said, *"many will come from east and west."* What a feast it will be!

---

1   "Heaven," in this text, is just a common, Jewish euphemism for God, not a reference to going to heaven. Note how the parallel passage in Lk 13:29 renders the

Many of those who listened to Jesus were familiar with the prophecy in Isaiah about the coming feast in Jerusalem, and the gospels are full of references to the coming feast in the kingdom of God. Luke describes a conversation with Jesus during a festive Sabbath meal, *"When one of those who reclined at table with him heard these things, he said to him, 'Blessed is everyone who will eat bread in the kingdom of God!'"* (Lk 14:15) Jesus then told the story of a rich man who invited people to a great banquet.

During His last Passover meal with His disciples, Jesus told them,

> *"'I have eagerly desired to eat this Passover with you before I suffer. For I tell you,* **I will not eat it again until it finds fulfillment in the kingdom of God.'** *After taking the cup, he gave thanks and said, 'Take this and divide it among you. For I tell you* **I will not drink again from the fruit of the vine until the kingdom of God comes.'"** (Lk 22:15–18, NIV)

We will celebrate the Passover again, in its fullness, together with Jesus in the kingdom of God. Jesus said, *"It will be good for those servants whose master finds them watching when he comes. Truly I tell you, he will dress himself to serve, will have them recline at the table and will come and wait on them."* (Lk 12:37 NIV) This is truly an incredible promise that Jesus Himself will serve those who are ready for His return! It will be like it was at the last Passover meal with His disciples when He served them and washed their feet.

Isaiah prophesied that it is in Jerusalem that all of God's people who have loved Jerusalem will be comforted one day.

> *"Rejoice with Jerusalem, and be glad for her, all you who love her; rejoice with her in joy, all you who mourn over her; that you may nurse and be satisfied from her consoling breast; that you may drink deeply with delight from her glo-*

"kingdom of heaven" as "kingdom of God."

rious abundance.' For thus says the LORD: 'Behold, I will extend peace to her like a river, and the glory of the nations like an overflowing stream; and you shall nurse, you shall be carried upon her hip, and bounced upon her knees. As one whom his mother comforts, so I will comfort you; you shall be comforted in Jerusalem. You shall see, and your heart shall rejoice; your bones shall flourish like the grass; and the hand of the LORD shall be known to his servants, and he shall show his indignation against his enemies.'" (Isa 66:10–14)

What glorious promises, shining as bright stars in the dark night of spiritual decline, still waiting for their fulfillment! No wonder that God also declares in Isaiah:

"On your walls, O Jerusalem, I have set watchmen; all the day and all the night they shall never be silent. You who put the LORD in remembrance, take no rest, and give him no rest until he establishes Jerusalem and makes it a praise in the earth." (Isa 62:6–7)

God is calling us, in this generation, to join the intercessors over the past millennia on the walls of Jerusalem, reminding Him of all his promises for Jerusalem, until she becomes a praise in the earth!

Abraham only saw the promise of the land from a distance. Even when Israel entered into the land under Joshua, and when Solomon reigned over greater Israel, they were still not the complete fulfillment, but only a foretaste of the coming, glorious kingdom of Messiah. Nevertheless, the fulfillment still concerns the land of Israel and the city of Jerusalem, *"in the new world, when the Son of Man will sit on his glorious throne."* (Mt 19:28) Peter said, *"heaven must receive* [Messiah] *until the time for restoring all the things about which God spoke by the mouth of his holy prophets long ago."* (Ac 3:21)

The promised restoration of Jerusalem **will come**! God **will fulfill** the oath that He swore to David. But He **will not do it** without intercessors calling out to Him and reminding Him of His promises day and night. We encourage you to make it a habit to pray for the restoration of Jerusalem when you give thanks after every meal, as it says in Deuteronomy 8:10, *"When you have eaten and are full, then you shall bless the LORD your God."* (NIV)

We mentioned already in Chapter 1, that the early Christians believed that the prophets "Ezekiel and Isaiah, and all the rest," wrote about the same city that John described in the Book of Revelation. We saw, for instance, how Ezekiel's prophecy about the river from the Temple corresponds to the river in the new Jerusalem, flowing from the throne of God and the Lamb. Let us also look at some examples from Isaiah.

> *"O afflicted one, storm–tossed and not comforted, behold, I will set your stones in antimony, and lay your foundations with sapphires. I will make your pinnacles of agate, your gates of carbuncles, and all your wall of precious stones."* (Isa 54:11–12)

Isaiah 54 is a prophecy about Jerusalem. It begins, *"'Sing, O barren one, who did not bear; break forth into singing and cry aloud, you who have not been in labor! For the children of the desolate one will be more than the children of her who is married,' says the LORD."* (Isa 54:1) Paul quotes this verse in Galatians, and applies it to the new Jerusalem.

> *"But the Jerusalem above is free, and she is our mother. For it is written, 'Rejoice, O barren one who does not bear; break forth and cry aloud, you who are not in labor! For the children of the desolate one will be more than those of the one who has a husband.'"* (Gal 4:26–27)

Let us compare the prophecy about the new Jerusalem in Isaiah 54:11–12 with John's description of new Jerusalem in the Book of Revelation. The parallel to foundations of precious stones is striking.

> *"The foundations of the wall of the city were adorned with every kind of jewel. The first was jasper, the second sapphire, the third agate, the fourth emerald, the fifth onyx, the sixth carnelian, the seventh chrysolite, the eighth beryl, the ninth topaz, the tenth chrysoprase, the eleventh jacinth, the twelfth amethyst."* (Rev 21:19–20)

We will look at a few more examples from Isaiah without making any comments, because the parallels are self-evident.

> *"And he will swallow up on this mountain the covering that is cast over all peoples, the veil that is spread over all nations.* **He will swallow up death forever; and the Lord GOD will wipe away tears from all faces,** *and the reproach of his people he will take away from all the earth, for the LORD has spoken.* **It will be said on that day, 'Behold, this is our God;** *we have waited for him, that he might save us. This is the LORD; we have waited for him; let us be glad and rejoice in his salvation.'"* (Isa 25:7–9)

Compare this with what John wrote in the Book of Revelation about the new Jerusalem:

> *"And I saw the holy city, new Jerusalem, coming down out of heaven from God, prepared as a bride adorned for her husband. And I heard a loud voice from the throne saying, '****Behold, the dwelling place of God is with man****. He will dwell with them, and they will be his people, and God himself will be with them as their God.* **He will wipe away every tear from their eyes, and death shall be no more,** *neither shall*

*there be mourning nor crying nor pain anymore, for the for-
mer things have passed away.'"* (Rev 21:2–4)

Isaiah further prophesied:

*"For behold, I create new heavens and a new earth, and **the
former things shall not be remembered or come into mind**.
But be glad and rejoice forever in that which I create; **for
behold, I create Jerusalem to be a joy**, and her people to be
a gladness."* (Isa 65:17–18)

Compare this with the Book of Revelation:

*"'...neither shall there be mourning nor crying nor pain any-
more, for **the former things have passed away**.' And he who
was seated on the throne said, '**Behold, I am making all
things new**.' Also he said, 'Write this down, for these words
are trustworthy and true.'"* (Rev 21:4–5)

The Book of Isaiah:

*"The sun shall be no more your light by day, nor for bright-
ness shall the moon give you light; but the LORD will be your
everlasting light, and your God will be your glory. Your sun
shall no more go down, nor your moon withdraw itself; for
the LORD will be your everlasting light, and your days of
mourning shall be ended."* (Isa 60:19–20)

The Book of Revelation:

*"And the city has no need of sun or moon to shine on it, for
the glory of God gives it light, and its lamp is the Lamb."* (Rev
21:23)

The Book of Isaiah:

"And nations shall come to your light, and kings to the brightness of your rising ... Your gates shall be open continually; day and night they shall not be shut, that people may bring to you the wealth of the nations, with their kings led in procession." (Isa 60:3,11)

The new Jerusalem, *"the Bride, the wife of the Lamb,"* in the Book of Revelation,

"By its light will the nations walk, and the kings of the earth will bring their glory into it, and its gates will never be shut by day—and there will be no night there. They will bring into it the glory and the honor of the nations." (Rev 21:24–26)

No wonder that Justin Martyr wrote about the city of Jerusalem, "I, and all other entirely orthodox Christians, know that there will be a resurrection of the flesh, and also a thousand years in Jerusalem built up and adorned and enlarged, as the prophets Ezekiel and Isaiah, and all the rest, acknowledge."[2] Justin Martyr then continued to state that the Apostle John confirmed the Jewish people's eschatological view about Jerusalem in the Book of Revelation.

Jeremiah and Jerusalem

Jeremiah declared that eventually, King Nebuchadnezzar of Babylon would destroy Jerusalem. Because of the sins of the people, he would come and burn it to the ground. We read in 2 Chronicles 36:15–19:

---

2   Justin Martyr, *Dialogue With Trypho*, ch. 80–81.

"The LORD, the God of their fathers, sent persistently to them by his messengers, because he had compassion on his people and on his dwelling place. But they kept mocking the messengers of God, despising his words and scoffing at his prophets, until the wrath of the LORD rose against his people, until there was no remedy. Therefore he brought up against them the king of the Chaldeans, who killed their young men with the sword in the house of their sanctuary and had no compassion on young man or virgin, old man or aged. He gave them all into his hand. And all the vessels of the house of God, great and small, and the treasures of the house of the LORD, and the treasures of the king and of his princes, all these he brought to Babylon. And they burned the house of God and broke down the wall of Jerusalem and burned all its palaces with fire and destroyed all its precious vessels."

But Jeremiah also declared that after 70 years, the desolation of Jerusalem would end.

"This whole land shall become a ruin and a waste, and these nations shall serve the king of Babylon seventy years ... When seventy years are completed for Babylon, I will visit you, and I will fulfill to you my promise and bring you back to this place. For I know the plans I have for you, declares the LORD, plans for wholeness and not for evil, to give you a future and a hope. Then you will call upon me and come and pray to me, and I will hear you. You will seek me and find me. When you seek me with all your heart, I will be found by you, declares the LORD, and I will restore your fortunes and gather you from all the nations and all the places where I have driven you, declares the LORD, and I will bring you back to the place from which I sent you into exile." (Jer 25:11; 29:10–14)

Jeremiah prophesied about the future of Jerusalem and its inhabitants, after the exile to Babylon.

> *"Behold, I will bring to it health and healing, and I will heal them and reveal to them abundance of prosperity and security. I will restore the fortunes of Judah and the fortunes of Israel, and rebuild them as they were at first."* (Jer 33:6–7)

Jeremiah then continued to prophesy about the future of Jerusalem in the Messianic kingdom:

> *"I will cleanse them from all the guilt of their sin against me, and I will forgive all the guilt of their sin and rebellion against me. And **this city shall be to me a name of joy, a praise and a glory** before all the nations of the earth who shall hear of all the good that I do for them. **They shall fear and tremble because of all the good and all the prosperity I provide for it.**"* (33:8–9)

These predictions have obviously never been fulfilled yet. But they will come to pass one day.

> *"Behold, the days are coming, declares the LORD, when I will fulfill the promise I made to the house of Israel and the house of Judah. **In those days and at that time I will cause a righteous Branch to spring up for David, and he shall execute justice and righteousness in the land.** In those days Judah will be saved and **Jerusalem will dwell securely. And this is the name by which it will be called: 'The LORD is our righteousness.'** For thus says the LORD: David shall never lack a man to sit on the throne of the house of Israel, and the Levitical priests shall never lack a man in my presence to offer burnt offerings, to burn grain offerings, and to make sacrifices forever."* (33:14–18)

These messianic prophecies await their final fulfillment as well. Just like Isaiah, Jeremiah also prophesied about a glorious future for Jerusalem, far beyond what existed before the exile to Babylon, a future where Jerusalem will be transformed into a heavenly city. This is the glorious city that Abraham looked forward to (see Heb 11:10)!

> *"And when you have multiplied and been fruitful in the land, in those days, declares the LORD, they shall no more say, 'The ark of the covenant of the LORD.' It shall not come to mind or be remembered or missed; it shall not be made again.* ***At that time Jerusalem shall be called the throne of the LORD****, and all nations shall gather to it, to the presence of the LORD in Jerusalem, and they shall no more stubbornly follow their own evil heart."* (Jer 3:16–17)

Jeremiah repeats the grand, future vision for Jerusalem that Isaiah also described. Jerusalem will be called *"the throne of the LORD."* All nations will gather in Jerusalem to seek God and learn to walk in His ways. The ark of the covenant will not be missed, because the Messiah will be there.

Ezekiel and Jerusalem

The final chapters of the Book of Ezekiel describe the glorious future of Jerusalem and the Temple as God's throne. Ezekiel 40 begins with a vision of the new Jerusalem,

> *"In the twenty–fifth year of our exile, at the beginning of the year, on the tenth day of the month, in the fourteenth year after the city was struck down, on that very day, the hand of the LORD was upon me, and he brought me to the city. In visions of God he brought me to the land of Israel, and set me down on a very high mountain, on which was a structure like a city to the south. When he brought me there, behold,*

there was a man whose appearance was like bronze, with a linen cord and a measuring reed in his hand. And he was standing in the gateway. And the man said to me, 'Son of man, look with your eyes, and hear with your ears, and set your heart upon all that I shall show you, for you were brought here in order that I might show it to you. Declare all that you see to the house of Israel.' And behold, there was a wall all around the outside of the Temple area ..." (Eze 40:1–5)

Ezekiel makes a very important observation, *"In visions of God he brought me to the land of Israel, and set me down on a very high mountain."* (40:2) Then a being *"whose appearance was like bronze"* began to show Ezekiel the heavenly city, beginning with the wall around the Temple area. Notice the similarity with John's description of the new Jerusalem in the Book of Revelation:

"Then came one of the seven angels who had the seven bowls full of the seven last plagues and spoke to me, saying, 'Come, I will show you the Bride, the wife of the Lamb.' And he carried me away in the Spirit to a great, high mountain, and showed me the holy city Jerusalem coming down out of heaven from God, having the glory of God, its radiance like a most rare jewel, like a jasper, clear as crystal. It had a great, high wall ..." (Rev 21:9–12)

Just like Ezekiel, John is likewise brought by the Spirit to *"a great, high mountain"* in order to see the city. The angel begins by showing him the wall around the new Jerusalem. The parallel is striking. No wonder that Christians in the second century believed that Ezekiel and Isaiah and the other prophets described the same restored Jerusalem that John wrote about in the Book of Revelation.

We have mentioned that the common view that Ezekiel and John saw different cities comes from the misunderstanding that their measurements differ greatly. We have already seen that this need not be the case at all.

The very last sentence in Ezekiel says about Jerusalem, *"And the name of the city from that time on shall be, The LORD is there."* (Eze 48:35) God will dwell in Jerusalem forever. No other city on earth has this glorious future. This is Paradise! It is the Garden of Eden, restored again! John wrote in the Book of Revelation:

> *"He who has an ear, let him hear what the Spirit says to the churches. To the one who conquers I will grant to eat of the tree of life, which is in the paradise of God."* (Rev 2:7)

Joel and Jerusalem

The prophet Joel foretells a time when God will judge all nations for dividing His land. He says this will happen when God restores the fortunes of Judah and Jerusalem. We are now living in those days.

> *"For behold, in those days and at that time, when I restore the fortunes of Judah and Jerusalem, I will gather all the nations and bring them down to the Valley of Jehoshaphat. And I will enter into judgment with them there, on behalf of my people and my heritage Israel, **because they have scattered them among the nations and have divided up my land**, and have cast lots for my people, and have traded a boy for a prostitute, and have sold a girl for wine and have drunk it."* (Joel 3:1–3)

The confrontation will lead to a major battle over the fate of Jerusalem, where God will defend His chosen nation. The final battle in history will be fought over Jerusalem, God's own city, the city of the great King.

"Let the nations stir themselves up and come up to the Valley of Jehoshaphat; for there I will sit to judge all the surrounding nations. Put in the sickle, for the harvest is ripe. Go in, tread, for the winepress is full. The vats overflow, for their evil is great. Multitudes, multitudes, in the valley of decision! For the day of the LORD is near in the valley of decision." (3:12–14)

It is this final battle that will lead to the coming of Messiah with the darkening of the heavenly luminaries.

"The sun and the moon are darkened, and the stars withdraw their shining. The LORD roars from Zion, and utters his voice from Jerusalem, and the heavens and the earth quake. But the LORD is a refuge to his people, a stronghold to the people of Israel." (3:15–16)

God will show the whole world that Jerusalem is His city, when He defends His own people Israel.

"So you shall know that I am the LORD your God, who dwells in Zion, my holy mountain. And Jerusalem shall be holy, and strangers shall never again pass through it." (3:17)

Once again, God says that water will flow from the Temple in Jerusalem. It will lead to supernaturally blessed agriculture in the Holy Land, while the surrounding nations will suffer shame because of their violent animosity towards Israel.

*"And in that day the mountains shall drip sweet wine, and the hills shall flow with milk, and all the streambeds of Judah shall flow with water; and **a fountain shall come forth from the house of the LORD** and water the Valley of Shittim* [the Kidron Valley]. *Egypt shall become a desolation and*

*Edom a desolate wilderness, for the violence done to the peo-
ple of Judah, because they have shed innocent blood in their
land. But Judah shall be inhabited forever, and Jerusalem to
all generations. I will avenge their blood, blood I have not
avenged, for the LORD dwells in Zion." (3:18–21)*

These prophecies are not just spiritual promises for the church.
They have never been literally fulfilled in history yet, but they will be
fulfilled in the coming Messianic kingdom. We long for that moment.
May it come soon, in our day!

Zechariah and Jerusalem

Zechariah is one of the last prophets in the Hebrew Scriptures. He
prophesied after the return of the Jewish remnant from Babylon. The
whole book is basically centered on Jerusalem. Already, in Zechariah
1, it says,

> *"So the angel who talked with me said to me, 'Cry out, Thus
> says the LORD of hosts:* **I am exceedingly jealous for Jerusa-
> lem and for Zion.** *And I am exceedingly angry with the na-
> tions that are at ease; for while I was angry but a little, they
> furthered the disaster. Therefore, thus says the LORD,* **I have
> returned to Jerusalem with mercy;** *my house shall be built
> in it, declares the LORD of hosts, and the measuring line
> shall be stretched out over Jerusalem. Cry out again, Thus
> says the LORD of hosts: My cities shall again overflow with
> prosperity, and the* **LORD will again comfort Zion and
> again choose Jerusalem.'"** *(Zec 1:14–17)*

We see here the deep passion and longing God has in His heart for
Jerusalem. He says, *"**I am exceedingly jealous for Jerusalem and for
Zion.**"*

The prophecy about Jerusalem continues in Zechariah 2. Here, it becomes evident that the prophet is speaking about things that have never been fulfilled yet, in history. It is a Messianic prophecy, similar to the ones in Isaiah and Jeremiah, where many nations will believe in the God of Israel and learn to walk in His ways, as God restores Jerusalem.

> *"Sing and rejoice, O daughter of Zion, for behold, I come and I will dwell in your midst, declares the LORD. And **many nations shall join themselves to the LORD in that day, and shall be my people**. And I will dwell in your midst, and you shall know that the LORD of hosts has sent me to you. And the LORD will inherit Judah as his portion in the holy land, and will again choose Jerusalem."* (Zec 2:10–12)

This is a great promise that has never been fully fulfilled. In the end times, when Jerusalem is restored, many nations will be included among God's people. That is why it says, *"Rejoice, O Gentiles, with his people."* (Ro 15:10)

In Zechariah 8, the prophet continues to prophesy about the LORD's strong jealousy for Jerusalem's restoration:

> *"And the word of the LORD of hosts came, saying, 'Thus says the LORD of hosts: **I am jealous for Zion with great jealousy, and I am jealous for her with great wrath**. Thus says the LORD: I have returned to Zion and will dwell in the midst of Jerusalem, and **Jerusalem shall be called the faithful city, and the mountain of the LORD of hosts, the holy mountain**. Thus says the LORD of hosts: Old men and old women shall again sit in the streets of Jerusalem, each with staff in hand because of great age. And the streets of the city shall be full of boys and girls playing in its streets. Thus says the LORD of hosts: If it is marvelous in the sight of the remnant of this people in those days, should it also be marvelous in*

*my sight, declares the LORD of hosts? Thus says the LORD of hosts: behold, I will save my people from the east country and from the west country, and **I will bring them to dwell in the midst of Jerusalem. And they shall be my people, and I will be their God, in faithfulness and in righteousness.'** ...*

*"For thus says the LORD of hosts: 'As I purposed to bring disaster to you when your fathers provoked me to wrath, and I did not relent, says the LORD of hosts, **so again have I purposed in these days to bring good to Jerusalem and to the house of Judah; fear not.'"** (Zec 8:1–8, 14–15)*

These are powerful words about the LORD's strong determination to restore Jerusalem again in the end times. He says, *"I am jealous for Zion with great jealousy, and I am jealous for her with great wrath."* (8:2) May the same jealous love that God has for Israel also grip our hearts! Just as God purposed to bring disaster to Israel when they sinned, so God has purposed in His heart to bring good to Jerusalem in the end (8:14–15). This was true in the days of Zechariah, but from the context we can see that it also refers to the ultimate restoration of Jerusalem, to become *"the faithful city."* (8:3) This has not happened yet.

The disaster that Zechariah is referring to in this prophecy is primarily the destruction of Jerusalem under Nebuchadnezzar, which was still vivid in the people's mind at this time. Starving mothers had even eaten their own children (see Lamentations). Just as surely as God brought judgment upon His people, He will also zealously restore Jerusalem again in the end times.

Zechariah then continues to emphasize the same prophecies that we find in Isaiah, Jeremiah and Micah, that the nations will stream to Jerusalem to worship the God of Israel.

"Thus says the LORD of hosts: Peoples shall yet come, even the inhabitants of many cities. The inhabitants of one city

shall go to another, saying, 'Let us go at once to entreat the favor of the LORD and to seek the LORD of hosts; I myself am going.' **Many peoples and strong nations shall come to seek the LORD of hosts in Jerusalem** *and to entreat the favor of the LORD.* **Thus says the LORD of hosts: In those days ten men from the nations of every tongue shall take hold of the robe of a Jew, saying, 'Let us go with you, for we have heard that God is with you.'"** (8:20–23)

Once again, we see that the restoration of the Jewish people back to Jerusalem will cause the nations to seek the God of Israel. Jerusalem will become a blessing, not only for the Jewish people, but for the whole world.

Zechariah also prophesied in great detail about the first coming of Messiah to Jerusalem in several places. One of the most well known passages is found in Zechariah 9:

"Rejoice greatly, O daughter of Zion! Shout aloud, O daughter of Jerusalem! behold, your king is coming to you; righteous and having salvation is he, humble and mounted on a donkey, on a colt, the foal of a donkey." (Zec 9:9)

The Jewish sages say that if Israel is not ready, Messiah will come on a donkey. But if Israel is ready, He will come with the clouds of heaven (Dan. 7:13).[3] Today, we know that Messiah will come twice. When He came the first time, the leaders of Israel were not ready to receive Him, therefore He came on a donkey. The Book of Revelation tells us that when He returns, He will come with the clouds of heaven, riding on a white horse.

---

3   b.*Sanhedrin* 98a.

"Behold, he is coming with the clouds, and every eye will see him, even those who pierced him, and all tribes of the earth will wail on account of him. Even so. Amen. ...

Then I saw heaven opened, and behold, a white horse! The one sitting on it is called Faithful and True, and in righteousness he judges and makes war. His eyes are like a flame of fire, and on his head are many diadems, and he has a name written that no one knows but himself. He is clothed in a robe dipped in blood, and the name by which he is called is The Word of God. And the armies of heaven, arrayed in fine linen, white and pure, were following him on white horses. From his mouth comes a sharp sword with which to strike down the nations, and he will rule them with a rod of iron. He will tread the winepress of the fury of the wrath of God the Almighty. On his robe and on his thigh he has a name written, King of kings and Lord of lords." (Rev 1:7; 19:11–16)

What a day! Here, we see clearly what Messiah will do when He comes. He will make war against His enemies—all those who have opposed His throne on Mount Zion!

Jerusalem In the End Times

The final chapters in Zechariah are devoted to the end time scenario in Jerusalem, leading up to the establishment of the Messianic kingdom from God's city. Zechariah 12 begins:

"The oracle of the word of the LORD concerning Israel: Thus declares the LORD, who stretched out the heavens and founded the earth and formed the spirit of man within him: 'Behold, I am about to make Jerusalem a cup of staggering to all the surrounding peoples. The siege of Jerusalem will also be against Judah. On that day I will make Jerusalem a

heavy stone for all the peoples. All who lift it will surely hurt themselves. And all the nations of the earth will gather against it." (Zec 12:1–3)

Before Jerusalem becomes a praise in the earth, it will become a heavy stone for all nations to deal with. Even though all the nations of the earth will gather against Jerusalem, they will not succeed in lifting it. They will instead get hurt. Isaiah also prophesied about this:

"And the multitude of all the nations that fight against Ariel [Jerusalem], all that fight against her and her stronghold and distress her, shall be like a dream, a vision of the night. As when a hungry man dreams he is eating and awakes with his hunger not satisfied, or as when a thirsty man dreams he is drinking and awakes faint, with his thirst not quenched, so shall the multitude of all the nations be that fight against Mount Zion." (Isa 29:7–8)

The Holy One of Israel will not allow the nations to succeed in their plans.

"On that day, declares the LORD, I will strike every horse with panic, and its rider with madness. But for the sake of the house of Judah I will keep my eyes open, when I strike every horse of the peoples with blindness. Then the clans of Judah shall say to themselves, 'The inhabitants of Jerusalem have strength through the LORD of hosts, their God.'" (Zec 12:4–5)

When the nations turn against Israel and Jerusalem, the people of Israel will have no choice but to turn to God. He will be their strength. He will pour out a spirit of grace and supplication on His people, and in their distress, their eyes will be opened to recognize their Messiah.

> *"And on that day I will seek to destroy all the nations that*
> *come against Jerusalem. And I will pour out on the house of*
> *David and the inhabitants of Jerusalem a spirit of grace and*
> *pleas for mercy, so that, when they look on me, on him whom*
> *they have pierced, they shall mourn for him, as one mourns*
> *for an only child, and weep bitterly over him, as one weeps*
> *over a firstborn. On that day the mourning in Jerusalem will*
> *be as great as the mourning for Hadad–rimmon in the plain*
> *of Megiddo. The land shall mourn, each family by itself: the*
> *family of the house of David by itself, and their wives by*
> *themselves; the family of the house of Nathan by itself, and*
> *their wives by themselves."* (Zec 12:9–12)

There will be strong mourning in Jerusalem *"as one mourns for an only child, ... as one weeps over a firstborn."* (12:10) Jesus, is *"the only Son from the Father full of grace and truth ... his only son"* (Jn 1:14; 3:16), *"the firstborn."* (Ro 8:29).

The people will not mourn very long. The mourning will turn into dancing, in Jerusalem. God has waited a long time for this moment, and He will quickly answer His people. Isaiah prophesied, *"Therefore the LORD waits to be gracious to you, and therefore he exalts himself to show mercy to you. For the LORD is a God of justice; blessed are all those who wait for him. For a people shall dwell in Zion, in Jerusalem; you shall weep no more. He will surely be gracious to you at the sound of your cry. As soon as he hears it, he answers you."* (Isa 30:18–19)

Zechariah continues, *"On that day there shall be a fountain opened for the house of David and the inhabitants of Jerusalem, to cleanse them from sin and uncleanness."* (Zec 13:1) It will be a fulfillment of Yom Kippur, the Day of Atonement, when *"You shall be clean before the LORD from all your sins."* (Lev 16:30)

Zechariah 13

A word needs to be said here about Zechariah 13. The Bible is not always written in chronological order, and the prophets spoke about both Messiah's first and second comings—sometimes even in the same verse. An example of this is found in Isaiah 61. The first verses say,

> *"The Spirit of the Lord GOD is upon me, because the LORD has anointed me to bring good news to the poor; he has sent me to bind up the brokenhearted, to proclaim liberty to the captives, and the opening of the prison to those who are bound; to proclaim the year of the LORD's favor, and the day of vengeance of our God; to comfort all who mourn."* (Isa 61:1–2)

Jesus read those words in the synagogue in Nazareth when He began His ministry, and He said, *"Today this Scripture has been fulfilled in your hearing."* (Lk 4:21) But when we look a little closer, we find that Jesus stopped in the middle of the second verse in Isaiah. He read only, *"to proclaim the year of the Lord's favor"* (Lk 4:19) and then He stopped. The rest of the sentence in Isaiah 61:2 is still waiting for its fulfillment at His return: *"...and the day of vengeance of our God; to comfort all who mourn."*

It is the same with Zechariah 13. It has, unfortunately, become a very popular teaching in many Christian circles, that two thirds of the Jewish people in Israel will die in the end times, because Zechariah 13:8 says, *"In the whole land, declares the LORD, two thirds shall be cut off and perish, and one third shall be left alive."* In the Holocaust, one third of the Jews in Europe died, but it is thought that in Israel, two thirds will die. Something worse than the Holocaust is, according to some, seemingly waiting for the Jewish people in Israel. In popular prophecy circles, it is often called "the time of Jacob's trouble" (an expression found in Jeremiah 30:7). During this difficult time, so the thinking goes, the church will be raptured to heaven and feast with Jesus in the marriage supper of the Lamb, while the Jewish people will go through tremendous sufferings.

This is truly a diabolical teaching. Would Jesus be able to feast while two thirds of His people are being slaughtered? Paul said, *"Rejoice, O Gentiles, with his people."* (Ro 15:10) Should we rejoice in heaven while two thirds of God's people are going through something worse than the Holocaust?

If this teaching were correct, then a well-known evangelist in Norway was right when he said that helping, or encouraging, the Jewish people to move back to Israel is the worst thing we can do for them, because two thirds of them are going to die there.

But no, this evangelist was not right! God has not brought His people back to their own Land again in order to kill them. Jacob did not lose one family member when he went through his trouble; he did not even lose one single sheep. Jeremiah 30:7 says, *"Alas! That day is so great there is none like it; it is a time of distress for Jacob; **yet he shall be saved out of it**."* The time of Jacob's trouble in Jeremiah 30, which is a prophetic picture of what the Jewish people will go through in the end times, is talking about salvation—not destruction! There will be terror and fear, just like it was for Jacob when he met his brother Esau, who came against him with 400 armed men, but there will be salvation and deliverance, just as happened for Jacob. The whole chapter in Jeremiah is filled with glorious promises. The next verses continue:

> *"And it shall come to pass in that day, declares the LORD of hosts, that I will break his yoke from off your neck, and I will burst your bonds, and foreigners shall no more make a servant of him. But they shall serve the LORD their God and David their king, whom I will raise up for them. 'Then fear not, O Jacob my servant, declares the LORD, nor be dismayed, O Israel; for behold, I will save you from far away, and your offspring from the land of their captivity. Jacob shall return and have quiet and ease, and none shall make*

him afraid. For I am with you to save you, declares the LORD." (Jer 30:8–11)

And Jeremiah later continues:

"Therefore all who devour you shall be devoured, and all your foes, every one of them, shall go into captivity; those who plunder you shall be plundered, and all who prey on you I will make a prey. For I will restore health to you, and your wounds I will heal, declares the LORD, because they have called you an outcast: 'It is Zion, for whom no one cares!' Thus says the LORD: Behold, I will restore the fortunes of the tents of Jacob and have compassion on his dwellings; the city shall be rebuilt on its mound, and the palace shall stand where it used to be. Out of them shall come songs of thanksgiving, and the voices of those who celebrate. I will multiply them, and they shall not be few; I will make them honored, and they shall not be small." (30:16–19)

This is Jeremiah's description of what will happen in Israel as the Jewish people go through the time of Jacob's trouble, when all the nations of the earth turn against them.

Let us read the verse in Zechariah 13:8 in context, beginning with the previous verse:

"'Awake, O sword, against my shepherd, against the man who stands next to me,' declares the LORD of hosts. 'Strike the shepherd, and the sheep will be scattered; I will turn my hand against the little ones. In the whole land, declares the LORD, two thirds shall be cut off and perish, and one third shall be left alive. And I will put this third into the fire, and refine them as one refines silver, and test them as gold is tested. They will call upon my name, and I will answer them.

I will say, 'They are my people'; and they will say, 'The LORD
is my God.'" (Zec 13:7–9)

Now we see clearly that the context is referring to Messiah's first
coming. Jesus quoted verse seven when He was in the garden of Geth-
semane with His disciples, *"You will all fall away because of me this*
night. For it is written, 'I will strike the shepherd, and the sheep of the
flock will be scattered.'" (Mt 26:31) He had also just explained to them
what would happen to the Jewish people; that they would be scattered to the ends of the earth:

> *"But when you see Jerusalem surrounded by armies, then*
> *know that its desolation has come near. Then let those who*
> *are in Judea flee to the mountains, and let those who are in-*
> *side the city depart, and let not those who are out in the*
> *country enter it, for these are days of vengeance, to fulfill all*
> *that is written ... They will fall by the edge of the sword and*
> *be led captive among all nations, and Jerusalem will be*
> *trampled underfoot by the Gentiles, until the times of the*
> *Gentiles are fulfilled."* (Lk 21:20–22,24)

The "days of vengeance" for rejecting the Messiah have already
been fulfilled more than once for the Jewish people, during their long
exile for the past 2,000 years, just like Isaiah prophesied,

> *"Comfort, comfort my people, says your God. Speak tenderly*
> *to Jerusalem, and cry to her that her warfare is ended, that*
> *her iniquity is pardoned, that **she has received from the***
> ***LORD's hand double for all her sins."*** (Isa 40:1–2)

This is a time of restoration for Jerusalem, not a time of vengeance.
That has already been fulfilled. More than two–thirds of the Jewish
people have died in these judgments. God says in Zechariah, *"I am*
exceedingly angry with the nations that are at ease; for while I was

angry but a little, they furthered the disaster." (Zec 1:15) The remaining third have truly gone through the fire for the past 2,000 years. That fire is not completely over yet. It will not be over until all Israel is saved, as it says, *"They will call upon my name, and I will answer them. I will say, 'They are my people'; and they will say, 'The LORD is my God.'"* (Zec 13:9) But the "two–thirds" part being killed has certainly already been fulfilled.

Zechariah 14

The last chapter in Zechariah pictures the end time scenario in Jerusalem with the coming of Messiah. It begins:

> *"Behold, a day is coming for the LORD, when the spoil taken from you will be divided in your midst. For I will gather all the nations against Jerusalem to battle, and the city shall be taken and the houses plundered and the women raped. Half of the city shall go out into exile, but the rest of the people shall not be cut off from the city.* **Then the LORD will go out and fight against those nations as when he fights on a day of battle**.

> **"On that day his feet shall stand on the Mount of Olives that lies before Jerusalem on the east**, *and the Mount of Olives shall be split in two from east to west by a very wide valley, so that one half of the Mount shall move northward, and the other half southward. And* **you shall flee to the valley of my mountains**, *for the valley of the mountains shall reach to Azal. And* **you shall flee as you fled from the earthquake in the days of Uzziah** *king of Judah. Then the LORD my God will come, and all the holy ones with him."* (Zec 14:1–5)

In Zechariah 12, the nations that are gathered against Jerusalem will be defeated. We saw one fulfillment of this prophecy in 1967, during the miraculous Six Day War. The threats and attacks against Jerusalem will cause a spiritual awakening among the Jewish people.

Here in Zechariah 14, however, in connection with the physical return of Messiah to the Mount of Olives, the enemies of Israel, led by the antichrist, will succeed in temporarily conquering at least part of the city. The Jewish commentator Rashi asks why God would permit the Gentile nations to exile half the city and plunder the homes, etc. His answer is that then they will have no excuse—like trying to claim that they have come to Jerusalem to worship—when God brings his vengeance upon them.[4] This scenario in Zechariah 14 confirms the warnings of Jesus about the very end, when He asks His followers to flee from the area around Jerusalem.

> *"So when you see the abomination of desolation spoken of by the prophet Daniel, standing in the holy place (let the reader understand),* **then let those who are in Judea flee to the mountains.** *Let the one who is on the housetop not go down to take what is in his house, and let the one who is in the field not turn back to take his cloak. And alas for women who are pregnant and for those who are nursing infants in those days!* **Pray that your flight may not be in winter or on a Sabbath.** *For then there will be great tribulation, such as has not been from the beginning of the world until now, no, and never will be."* (Mt 24:15–21)

Jesus goes on to say that this tribulation will be cut short. He will come to save His people. Zechariah goes on to describe this day:

4   Rashi on Zec 14:2, *The Complete Jewish Bible with Rashi Commentary* (© 1993–2015 Chabad–Lubavitch Media Center), http://goo.gl/d2BNLX.

"Then the LORD my God will come, and all the holy ones with him. On that day there shall be no light, cold, or frost. And there shall be a unique day, which is known to the LORD, neither day nor night, but at evening time there shall be light." (Zec 14:5–7)

This will be a unique day. Bible commentators liken the scenario in these verses to the beginning of the creation of the world, before the sun and moon existed. The first day of creation, when God created light, is not called "the first day" in Genesis. In the original Hebrew it is only called "one day." *"God called the light Day, and the darkness he called Night. And **there was evening and there was morning, one day**."* (Gen 1:5, revised) It says here in Zechariah, *"And there shall be a unique day, which is known to the LORD, neither day nor night, but at evening time there shall be light."* (Zec 14:7)

This is the time of the renewal of all things, which Jesus describes in Matthew 19:28, *"in the new age [the Messianic rebirth of the world], when the Son of Man shall sit down on the throne of His glory."* (Amplified translation) Isaiah wrote,

"The wolf shall dwell with the lamb, and the leopard shall lie down with the young goat, and the calf and the lion and the fattened calf together; and a little child shall lead them. The cow and the bear shall graze; their young shall lie down together; and the lion shall eat straw like the ox. The nursing child shall play over the hole of the cobra, and the weaned child shall put his hand on the adder's den. They shall not hurt or destroy in all my holy mountain; for the earth shall be full of the knowledge of the LORD as the waters cover the sea. In that day the root of Jesse, who shall stand as a signal for the peoples—of him shall the nations inquire, and his resting place shall be glorious." (Isa 11:6–10)

The end of verse 5 in Zechariah 14 says, *"Then the LORD my God will come, and all the holy ones with him."* (Zec 14:5) Paul wrote in Romans about *"the revealing of the sons of God,"* that will bring about the liberation of all of creation:

> *"For I consider that the sufferings of this present time are not worth comparing with the glory that is to be revealed to us. For the creation waits with eager longing for the revealing of the sons of God. For the creation was subjected to futility, not willingly, but because of him who subjected it, in hope that the creation itself will be set free from its bondage to decay and obtain the freedom of the glory of the children of God."* (Ro 8:18–21)

Zechariah goes on to describe the water that will flow again from Jerusalem, just like it did in the Garden of Eden. *"On that day living waters shall flow out from Jerusalem, half of them to the eastern sea* [the Dead Sea] *and half of them to the western sea* [the Mediterranean]. *It shall continue in summer as in winter."* (Zec 14:8)

The Messiah will rule from Jerusalem, which will be "built up and adorned and enlarged" as Justin Martyr expressed it in his *Dialogue with Trypho.*

> *"And the LORD will be king over all the earth. On that day the LORD will be one and his name one. The whole land shall be turned into a plain from Geba to Rimmon south of Jerusalem. But Jerusalem shall remain aloft on its site from the Gate of Benjamin to the place of the former gate, to the Corner Gate, and from the Tower of Hananel to the king's winepresses. And it shall be inhabited, for there shall never again be a decree of utter destruction. Jerusalem shall dwell in security."* (Zec 14:9–11)

This is the glorious end of God's program of salvation for the world. All the nations of the earth will celebrate the final feast of the LORD, the Feast of Tabernacles, in Jerusalem every year.

> *"Then everyone who survives of all the nations that have come against Jerusalem shall go up year after year to worship the King, the LORD of hosts, and to keep the Feast of Booths. And if any of the families of the earth do not go up to Jerusalem to worship the King, the LORD of hosts, there will be no rain on them. And if the family of Egypt does not go up and present themselves, then on them there shall be no rain; there shall be the plague with which the LORD afflicts the nations that do not go up to keep the Feast of Booths. This shall be the punishment to Egypt and the punishment to all the nations that do not go up to keep the Feast of Booths."* (14:16–19)

All of Jerusalem will be holy, even down to the pots and pans:

> *"And on that day there shall be inscribed on the bells of the horses, 'Holy to the LORD.' And the pots in the house of the LORD shall be as the bowls before the altar. And every pot in Jerusalem and Judah shall be holy to the LORD of hosts, so that all who sacrifice may come and take of them and boil the meat of the sacrifice in them. And there shall no longer be a trader in the house of the LORD of hosts on that day."* (14:20–21)

"And there shall no longer be a trader in the house of the LORD." (14:21) No wonder that Jesus drove out those who were buying and selling in the Temple.

> *"In the Temple he found those who were selling oxen and sheep and pigeons, and the money–changers sitting there.*

And making a whip of cords, he drove them all out of the
Temple, with the sheep and oxen. And he poured out the
coins of the money–changers and overturned their tables.
And he told those who sold the pigeons, 'Take these things
away; do not make my Father's house a house of trade.' His
disciples remembered that it was written, 'Zeal for your
house will consume me.'" (Jn 2:14–17)

Jesus did this as a prophetic act of what He knew will come one
day, when Jerusalem is restored. *"No longer will there be anything ac-*
cursed, but the throne of God and of the Lamb will be in it, and his
servants will worship him. They will see his face, and his name will be
on their foreheads." (Rev 22:3–4)

"On the holy mount stands the city he founded; the LORD
loves the gates of Zion more than all the dwelling places of
Jacob. Glorious things of you are spoken, O city of God. Selah
Among those who know me I mention Rahab and Babylon;
behold, Philistia and Tyre, with Cush—'This one was born
there,' they say. And of Zion it shall be said, 'This one and
that one were born in her'; for the Most High himself will
establish her. The LORD records as he registers the peoples,
'This one was born there.' Selah. Singers and dancers alike
say, 'All my springs are in you.'" (Ps 87)

"Blessed are those who wash their robes, so that they may
have the right to the tree of life and that they may enter the
city by the gates. Outside are the dogs and sorcerers and the
sexually immoral and murderers and idolaters, and every-
one who loves and practices falsehood. 'I, Jesus, have sent my
angel to testify to you about these things for the churches. I
am the root and the descendant of David, the bright morn-
ing star.' The Spirit and the Bride say, 'Come.' And let the
one who hears say, 'Come.' And let the one who is thirsty

come; let the one who desires take the water of life without price. ...He who testifies to these things says, 'Surely I am coming soon.' Amen. Come, Lord Jesus!'" (Rev 22:14–17,20)

7

BEHOLD YOUR KING!

"Fear not, daughter of Zion; behold, your king is coming, sitting on a donkey's colt!" —John 12:15

As we have seen, specifically from the previous chapter, most of the glorious prophecies about Jerusalem have never been fulfilled in history—yet. But they certainly will be! There is a glorious future for Jerusalem in the Messianic kingdom. Messiah is the key to the complete fulfillment of these prophecies.

The Gospel of John relates how Jesus entered Jerusalem the final time riding on a donkey:

> *"The next day the large crowd that had come to the feast heard that Jesus was coming to Jerusalem. So they took branches of palm trees and went out to meet him, crying out, 'Hosanna! Blessed is he who comes in the name of the Lord, even the King of Israel!' And Jesus found a young donkey and sat on it, just as it is written, 'Fear not, daughter of Zion; behold, your king is coming, sitting on a donkey's colt!' His disciples did not understand these things at first, but when Jesus was glorified, then they remembered that these things had been written about him and had been done to him."* (Jn 12:12–16)

As the Jewish saying goes, "If the people of Israel are ready, the Messiah will come with the clouds of heaven. If they are not ready, he will come on a donkey."[1] The first time Messiah came, the people were not ready. The Gospels tell us that He rode into the city meekly and humbly, on a donkey. His disciples greeted Him with shouts of "*Hoshiana!*" (Hosanna) but the leaders, the elders of the people, did not receive Him. The Scriptures had to be fulfilled that the Messiah must first be rejected by His people, just as Joseph was first rejected by his brothers and sold to the Gentiles, and just as Moses was first rejected when he approached his brothers in Egypt and then had to flee to Midian.

But Jesus also spoke of another day, when Jerusalem will welcome Him. He ended His harsh speech of rebuke to the leadership in the Jerusalem of His day, by saying,

> *"O Jerusalem, Jerusalem, the city that kills the prophets and stones those who are sent to it! How often would I have gathered your children together as a hen gathers her brood under her wings, and you would not! See, your house is left to you desolate. For I tell you, you will not see me again, until you say, 'Blessed is he who comes in the name of the Lord.'"* (Mt 23:37–39)

The word "you," in this passage, is referring to the spiritual leadership in Jerusalem described in the beginning of Matthew 23: *"The scribes and the Pharisees sit on Moses' seat."* (Mt 23:2) There is a day coming when these leaders of the Jewish people who sit on Moses' seat also will welcome Jesus as their Messiah. And just as there were many tears in Egypt when the brothers of Joseph recognized him, the brothers of Jesus will weep in Jerusalem when they recognize Him, as we saw in the previous chapter, when we studied Zechariah 12.

---

1   Adapted from b.*Sanhedrin* 98a.

Just as the prophecies of Messiah's first coming were literally fulfilled, so will all the rest of the prophecies be fulfilled, that speak about His return and the glorious future of Jerusalem that will follow *"in the new world, when the Son of Man will sit on his glorious throne."* (Mt 19:28) After the resurrection of Jesus, the Apostle Peter said to the Jewish people in the Temple:

> *"And now, brothers, I know that you acted in ignorance, as did also your rulers. But what God foretold by the mouth of all the prophets, that his Messiah would suffer, he thus fulfilled. Repent therefore, and turn again, that your sins may be blotted out, that times of refreshing may come from the presence of the Lord, and that he may send the Messiah appointed for you, Jesus, **whom heaven must receive until the time for restoring all the things about which God spoke by the mouth of his holy prophets long ago.**"* (Ac 3:17–21)

We are now living in these times, waiting for the fulfillment of *"all the things about which God spoke by the mouth of his holy prophets long ago."* (Ac 3:21) The Jewish rabbis call the rebirth of the State of Israel in 1948 and the reunification of Jerusalem 1967 "the firstfruits of our redemption." They are signposts, heralding that the Messianic kingdom is near.

Jerusalem and the Gospel

> *"The book of the genealogy of Jesus the Messiah, the son of David, the son of Abraham."* (Mt 1:1)

This is how the New Testament, or the Apostolic Scriptures begin. Gospel means "good news." The expression "gospel" is *besorah* in Hebrew. It is a well-known term in the Hebrew Scriptures, particularly in Isaiah. It is the good news about the kingdom—specifically about its King and His coming to Jerusalem!

> *"Go on up to a high mountain, O Zion,* **herald of good news***; lift up your voice with strength, O Jerusalem,* **herald of good news***; lift it up, fear not; say to the cities of Judah, '***Behold your God!' Behold, the Lord GOD comes with might, and his arm rules for him***; behold, his reward is with him, and his recompense before him. He will tend his flock like a shepherd; he will gather the lambs in his arms; he will carry them in his bosom, and gently lead those that are with young."* (Isa 40:9–11)

> *"How beautiful upon the mountains are the feet of* **him who brings good news***, who publishes peace,* **who brings good news of happiness***, who publishes salvation,* **who says to Zion, 'Your God reigns.'"*** (Isa 52:7)

"The gospel" is literally the good news that the Messiah, the Redeemer, has come to His people. This is why the Gospel of Matthew begins, *"The book of the genealogy of Jesus the Messiah, the son of David, the son of Abraham."* (Mt 1:1)

Abraham and David are the key figures linked to Jerusalem, in the Hebrew Scriptures. It was Abraham who gave the city of Jerusalem its full name, when he came to sacrifice his son. And the city of heavenly peace and fullness is also called the "City of David."

Abraham and David each received a promise of a special son to be his heir. The real fulfillment of these promises refers to more than just Isaac and Solomon. They point to the Messiah. It is through Him that ultimately all the families of the earth will be blessed, and He is also the eternal heir to the throne of David in Jerusalem. That is why Messiah is called both the "son of Abraham" as well as the "son of David." The Messiah is inseparably linked to Jerusalem. He is the King of Jerusalem.

Paul wrote, *"For I am not ashamed of the gospel, for it is the power of God for salvation to everyone who believes, to the Jew first and also to the Greek."* (Ro 1:16) The gospel is, first of all, the good news to the Jewish people that their Messiah has arrived. This good news to the Jewish people is, however, also good news for the whole world, as Paul also wrote, *"'Rejoice, O Gentiles, with his people.' ... And again Isaiah says, 'The root of Jesse will come, even he who arises to rule the Gentiles; in him will the Gentiles hope.'"* (Ro 15:10,12)

After Philip became a disciple of Jesus, he found Nathanael and said to him, *"We have found him of whom Moses in the Law and also the prophets wrote, Jesus of Nazareth, the son of Joseph."* (Jn 1:45) Nathanael did not believe at first that Jesus of Nazareth could be the Messiah of Israel, but when he finally met Jesus and was convinced, he exclaimed in awe, *"Rabbi, you are the Son of God! You are the King of Israel!"* (Jn 1:49) All Christians believe that Jesus is the Son of God. But most Christians have yet to discover that Jesus is also a Jewish rabbi, a Torah teacher, the King of Israel, and the heir to the throne of David.

Matthew goes on to list the genealogy of Jesus, from Abraham and David. He then summarizes the entire genealogy by writing,

> *"So all the generations from Abraham to David were fourteen generations, and from David to the deportation to Babylon fourteen generations, and from the deportation to Babylon to the Messiah fourteen generations."* (Mt 1:17)

What does this mean? What is Matthew's message behind this distinct repetition of the number fourteen? First of all, the numerical value of "David," in Hebrew, is 14. Matthew wrote his Gospel specifically to a Jewish audience. Among the Jewish people, David is synonymous with the Messiah. Matthew is emphasizing that Jesus is the promised Messiah, the Son of David, the King of Israel.

But there is more. The number 14 is also connected with the moon, and in Psalm 89 the moon is called "a faithful witness in the skies," concerning God's promise to David.

> *"I will not violate my covenant or alter the word that went forth from my lips. Once for all I have sworn by my holiness; I will not lie to David. His offspring shall endure forever, his throne as long as the sun before me. **Like the moon it shall be established forever**, a faithful witness in the skies." Selah."* (Ps 89:34–37)

Psalm 89 says that the throne of David shall be established forever, like the moon. *Exodus Rabbah*, a very ancient commentary on Exodus, says, "The moon begins to shine on the first day of the month and goes on shining until the fifteenth day when she is full. After the fifteenth day her light wanes until on the thirtieth day it is not seen at all. With Israel too, there were fifteen generations from Abraham to Solomon. ... [After Solomon] the kings began to wane ... [until] Zedekiah, when the light of the moon vanished completely."[2]

Paul also wrote that the new moon is a shadow of Messiah. "... *a festival or a **new moon** or a Sabbath. **These are a shadow of the things to come**, but the substance belongs to Messiah."* (Col 2:16–17)

When God gave the promise to Abraham, about a son through whom all the families of the earth would be blessed, it was just the beginning. The moon was only a small sliver. Fourteen generations later, King David was born. His son Solomon was the foretaste of the kingdom. The moon was full. Then apostasy set in. The moon began to wane. Zedekiah was the last king to rule on the throne of David in Jerusalem, and the moon became dark.

During the dark time when the moon began to wane, prophets like Isaiah, Jeremiah, Ezekiel and Zechariah prophesied about the coming of Messiah. Matthew points out that fourteen generations af-

---

2   *Exodus Rabbah* 15:26.

ter the exile, the promised seed, Jesus of Nazareth was born. It was "the fullness of time," after fourteen generations. *"But when the fullness of time had come, God sent forth his Son, born of woman, born under the law."* (Gal 4:4) The moon was once again full.

Messiah came at the appointed time, but was rejected by His own. Jesus said, *"... you will not see me again, until you say, 'Blessed is he who comes in the name of the Lord.'"* (Mt 23:39) We are waiting for that day. *"Messiah ... will appear a second time, not to deal with sin but to save those who are eagerly waiting for him."* (Heb 9:28) *"On that day his feet shall stand on the Mount of Olives that lies before Jerusalem on the east, and the Mount of Olives shall be split in two from east to west."* (Zec 14:4)

Psalm 81:3–4 says, *"Blow the trumpet at the new moon, at the full moon, on our feast day. For it is a statute for Israel, a rule of the God of Jacob."*

The Hebrew word for "full," in this verse, is very similar to the Hebrew word for "concealed."[3] Psalm 81:3 can actually be translated, *"Blow the trumpet at the new moon, when the moon is concealed, on our feast day."* There is only one feast that occurs on the new moon. It is the Feast of Trumpets. It is the feast that speaks about the coming of the Messiah. The moon is God's faithful witness in the skies, bearing testimony to the coming of the Son of David!

Born King of the Jews

*"Now after Jesus was born in Bethlehem of Judea in the days of Herod the king, behold, wise men from the east came to Jerusalem, saying, '**Where is he who has been born king of***

---

3   The word in Psalm 81 translated as "full moon" is *keseh* (*kaph, samech, **hei***). However, "full moon" in Hebrew is actually *kese* (*kaph, samech, **aleph***). The word *keseh* (with *hei*), comes from the root *kasah*, which means "hidden."

the Jews? For we saw his star when it rose and have come to worship him.'" (Mt 2:1–2)

Astrology is a perversion of God's design. But the heavens do declare the glory of God, and we know that God used the stars to reveal to these wise men His true gospel story in the stars, the good news that the King of the Jews had arrived.

Jesus was born King of the Jews. What was the star that the wise men of the East had seen? Most likely, it was the combined helical rising on the eastern horizon of the star Regulus and the planet Jupiter, in the constellation of Leo (the Lion).[4] Regulus is *melech* in Hebrew, which means "king." Jupiter is *tzedek* in Hebrew, which means "righteous." Together, Regulus and Jupiter make up the name Melchizedek, the first priest-king of Jerusalem. King David prophesied about the Messiah, *"The LORD has sworn and will not change his mind, 'You are a priest forever after the order of Melchizedek.'"* (Ps 110:4)

We know that such a helical rising of Regulus and Jupiter was seen in the heavens during the Feast of Trumpets in the year 3 BCE. Each year during this feast, the star constellation Virgo (the Virgin) is also "clothed in the sun" and has the moon under her feet, exactly as it is described in the Book of Revelation:

> *"And a great sign appeared in heaven: a woman clothed with the sun, with the moon under her feet, and on her head a crown of twelve stars. She was pregnant and was crying out in birth pains and the agony of giving birth."* (Rev 12:1–2)

Just as the Feast of Trumpets began in the year 3 BCE,[5] both this phenomenon and the rising of the star "Melchizedek," in the constel-

---

4   See research by Frederick A. Larson, bethlehemstar.net.

5   The great majority of ancient scholars like Irenaeus, Clement of Alexandria, Tertullian, Africanus, Hippolytus of Rome, Hippolytus of Thebes, Origen, Eusebius, Epiphanius, Cassiodorus, Orosius, and others, held that Messiah was

lation Leo (the Lion), could be seen in the heavens. More than likely, this was what convinced the wise men of the East that the King of the Jews had been born. The Messiah is "the Lion of the tribe of Judah" (see Gen 49:9–10 and Rev 5:5).

The question by the wise men who had seen the star of the King of the Jews *"in the east at its rising"* (Amplified Bible) made King Herod so nervous that he ended up killing all the baby boys in Bethlehem who were two years or younger. This was the time of the birth that he had learned from the wise men. They had obviously come to Jerusalem to honor the newborn King almost two years after His birth.

> *"Then Herod, when he saw that he had been tricked by the wise men, became furious, and he sent and killed all the male children in Bethlehem and in all that region who were two years old or under, **according to the time that he had ascertained from the wise men**. Then was fulfilled what was spoken by the prophet Jeremiah: 'A voice was heard in Ramah, weeping and loud lamentation, Rachel weeping for her children; she refused to be comforted, because they are no more.'"* (Mt 2:16–18)

Moses wrote about the death of Rachel,

---

born in the year 3 or 2 BCE. For the past century, there has been a consensus among scholars that King Herod died in 4 BCE, which makes the traditional year of birth impossible. There have, however, been several challenges to this consensus over the past four decades. Andrew Steinmann has argued that placing Herod's death in 1 BCE accounts for all of the datable evidence relating to Herod's reign, whereas the current consensus is unable to explain some of the evidence that it dismisses as ancient errors or that it simply ignores (Andrew Steinmann, "When Did Herod the Great Reign?" *Novum Testamentum*, Vol. 51, Number 1, 2009, pp. 1–29).

"So Rachel died, and she was buried on the way to Ephrath (that is, Bethlehem), and Jacob set up a pillar over her tomb. It is the pillar of Rachel's tomb, which is there to this day. Israel journeyed on and pitched his tent beyond the tower of Eder." (Gen 35:19–21)

The Tower of Eder means the "shepherd's tower." Alfred Edersheim wrote in his book *The Life And Times of Jesus The Messiah* that this tower was located close to Bethlehem, on the way to Jerusalem. Edersheim speculates that during the second Temple period, the shepherds who used this tower were guarding the thousands of sheep that were to be sacrificed at the Temple. They were trained to make sure that there were no blemishes on these animals destined for sacrifice.[6]

The Tower of Eder, or *Migdal Eder* in Hebrew, is also mentioned in Micah 4:8, which is a Messianic prophecy, *"And you, O tower of the flock, hill of the daughter of Zion, to you shall it come, the former dominion shall come, kingship for the daughter of Jerusalem."* The Aramaic paraphrased translation from Hebrew, called Targum Jonathan, which was used in the Jewish synagogues around the time of Jesus, therefore translates Genesis 35:21 like this: *"he pitched his tent beyond Migdal Eder, in the place where King Messiah will be revealed in the last days."*

Luke wrote about shepherds in connection with the birth of Messiah.

"And in the same region there were shepherds out in the field, keeping watch over their flock by night. And an angel of the Lord appeared to them, and the glory of the Lord shone around them, and they were filled with fear. And the angel said to them, 'Fear not, for behold, I bring you good

---

6   Alfred Edersheim, *The Life and Times of Jesus the Messiah*, Vol. 1 (Bellingham, WA: Logos Bible Software, 1896), p. 187.

news of a great joy that will be for all the people. For unto you is born this day in the city of David a Savior, who is Messiah the Lord. And this will be a sign for you: you will find a baby wrapped in swaddling cloths and lying in a manger.'" (Lk 2:8–12)

These were not just any shepherds. These could have been the shepherds of *Migdal Eder,* who were trained to inspect all the sacrificial lambs. They were probably familiar with the prophecy in Micah 4:8 and Genesis 35:21 about King Messiah. What thoughts must have filled their hearts as they hurried away to see and inspect the child who had been born in Bethlehem! They found that everything was exactly as they had been told concerning the child, and they were satisfied. *"And the shepherds returned, glorifying and praising God **for all they had heard and seen, as it had been told them.**"* (Lk 2:20)

Before Jesus was born, the angel Gabriel visited a young Jewish woman in Nazareth named Miriam, better known today as Mary. He told her:

*"Do not be afraid, Mary, for you have found favor with God. And behold, you will conceive in your womb and bear a son, and you shall call his name Jesus. He will be great and will be called the Son of the Most High. **And the Lord God will give to him the throne of his father David, and he will reign over the house of Jacob forever,** and of his kingdom there will be no end."* (Lk 1:30–33)

David's throne was not in heaven. It was in Jerusalem. The throne of David in Jerusalem is the final destiny of Jesus of Nazareth. He has been waiting now in heaven for close to 2,000 years, to take up that throne. Heaven must receive Him *"until the time for restoring all the things about which God spoke by the mouth of his holy prophets long ago."* (Ac 3:21) Jesus is eagerly waiting for His return to Jerusalem. He said before the Sanhedrin, when they sentenced Him to death, *"I say to you, hereafter you will see the Son of Man sitting at the right hand of the Power, and coming on the clouds of heaven."* (Mt 26:64 NKJV)

Coming to His Temple

Malachi, the last of the Hebrew prophets, prophesied about the Messiah that He would come suddenly to the Temple in Jerusalem. *"And the Lord whom you seek will suddenly come to his Temple; and the messenger of the covenant in whom you delight, behold, he is coming, says the LORD of hosts."* (Mal 3:1) The first time Jesus was in the Temple was when his parents brought him there to be presented to the LORD, according to the Law of Moses.

> *"Now there was a man in Jerusalem, whose name was Simeon, and this man was righteous and devout, waiting for the consolation of Israel, and the Holy Spirit was upon him. And it had been revealed to him by the Holy Spirit that he would not see death before he had seen the Lord's Messiah. And he came in the Spirit into the Temple, and when the parents brought in the child Jesus, to do for him according to the custom of the Law, he took him up in his arms and blessed God and said, 'Lord, now you are letting your servant depart in peace, according to your word; for my eyes have seen your salvation that you have prepared in the presence of all peoples, a light for revelation to the Gentiles, and for glory to your people Israel."* (Lk 2:25–32)

Simeon was watching and waiting for *"the consolation of Israel."* He was waiting for the good news about Messiah's coming. The Holy Spirit had revealed to him that he would not die until it happened. This is why he came to the Temple—to look for the Messiah. He knew that this was where the Messiah would appear.

There was also another old saint named Anna, who was always in the Temple looking for the good news, fasting and praying day and night.

> *"And there was a prophetess, Anna, the daughter of Phanu-el, of the tribe of Asher. She was advanced in years, having lived with her husband seven years from when she was a virgin, and then as a widow until she was eighty–four. She did not depart from the Temple, worshiping with fasting and prayer night and day. And coming up at that very hour she began to give thanks to God and to speak of him to all who were waiting for the redemption of Jerusalem."* (Lk 2:36–38)

Anna proclaimed the gospel about the King of Israel to those who were waiting for the redemption of Jerusalem. It was no coincidence that she was waiting for the Messiah in the Temple in Jerusalem. This is also where Jesus will come when He returns, as it is written in Ezekiel. He belongs in His Father's house, the Temple, and Mount Zion is where His throne will be one day.

When Jesus came to the Temple in Jerusalem at the age of 12, He did not want to leave the place. He was in love with the Temple, calling it His Father's house. He knew that this was where He belonged.

> *"Now his parents went to Jerusalem every year at the Feast of the Passover. And when he was twelve years old, they went up according to custom. And when the feast was ended, as they were returning, the boy Jesus stayed behind in Jerusalem. His parents did not know it, but supposing him to be in the group they went a day's journey, but then they began to search for him among their relatives and acquaintances, and when they did not find him, they returned to Jerusalem, searching for him.* **After three days they found him in the Temple, sitting among the teachers, listening to them and asking them questions.** *And all who heard him were amazed*

at his understanding and his answers. And when his parents saw him, they were astonished. And his mother said to him, 'Son, why have you treated us so? Behold, your father and I have been searching for you in great distress.' And he said to them, 'Why were you looking for me? Did you not know that I must be in my Father's house?' And they did not understand the saying that he spoke to them." (Lk 2:41–50)

Jesus' parents found Him in the Temple after three days, sitting among the Torah teachers. This truly is His destiny. On the third day, He will return to the Temple and restore it, in order to reign from Jerusalem, just as Isaiah prophesied:

"It shall come to pass in the latter days that the mountain of the house of the LORD shall be established as the highest of the mountains, and shall be lifted up above the hills; and all the nations shall flow to it, and many peoples shall come, and say: 'Come, let us go up to the mountain of the LORD, to the house of the God of Jacob, that he may teach us his ways and that we may walk in his paths.' For out of Zion shall go the law, and the word of the LORD from Jerusalem." (Isa 2:2–3)

No wonder that Jesus was filled with such zeal for the Temple that it consumed Him.

"In the Temple he found those who were selling oxen and sheep and pigeons, and the money–changers sitting there. And making a whip of cords, he drove them all out of the Temple, with the sheep and oxen. And he poured out the coins of the money–changers and overturned their tables. And he told those who sold the pigeons, 'Take these things away; do not make my Father's house a house of trade.' His

disciples remembered that it was written, 'Zeal for your house will consume me.'" (Jn 2:14–17)

From the Gospel of John, we know that Jesus came regularly to Jerusalem for all the pilgrimage feasts. He loved to be in the Temple. He even traveled in the cold and wet winter, all the way from Galilee, to be in Jerusalem for the Feast of Dedication (Hanukkah). Hanukkah was celebrated in memory of the Temple's cleansing and rededication to the LORD, after it had been desecrated by Antiochus Epiphanes. Luke wrote, *"And every day he was teaching in the Temple, but at night he went out and lodged on the mount called Olivet. And early in the morning all the people came to him in the Temple to hear him."* (Lk 21:37–38)

John tells us that Jesus had a special place on the Mount of Olives, just outside Jerusalem, where He used to stay during the feasts: *"When Jesus had spoken these words, he went out with his disciples across the Kidron Valley, where there was a garden, which he and his disciples entered. Now Judas, who betrayed him, also knew the place, for Jesus often met there with his disciples."* (Jn 18:1–2)

Jesus Wept

But the time for the final redemption of Jerusalem had not yet come. Luke described what happened when Jesus was on His way to Jerusalem for the last time:

> *"As they heard these things, he proceeded to tell a parable, because he was near to Jerusalem, and because they supposed that the kingdom of God was to appear immediately. He said therefore, 'A nobleman went into a far country to receive for himself a kingdom and then return.'"* (Lk 19:11–12)

The crowds around Jesus were expecting Him to take up the throne of His father David in Jerusalem at once, and restore the kingdom to Israel. But Jesus disappointed them by telling a parable about "a nobleman" who went to a country far away in order to be appointed king and then return. The listeners must have been familiar with the scene. In those days, the mighty Rome ruled over the world from far away. Anyone who wanted to rule over Judah or Jerusalem had to first travel to Rome and receive authority from the Emperor before he could begin his rule. Many of the leaders had done just that.

But Jesus was not speaking about Rome. He was speaking about Heaven, the ultimate seat of power. In order to be appointed by Heaven, He first had to be obedient unto death.

> *"But we see him who for a little while was made lower than the angels, namely Jesus, crowned with glory and honor because of the suffering of death, so that by the grace of God he might taste death for everyone. For it was fitting that he, for whom and by whom all things exist, in bringing many sons to glory, should make the founder of their salvation perfect through suffering."* (Heb 2:9–10)

> *"And being found in human form, he humbled himself by becoming obedient to the point of death, even death on a cross. Therefore God has highly exalted him and bestowed on him the name that is above every name, so that at the name of Jesus every knee should bow, in heaven and on earth and under the earth, and every tongue confess that Jesus the Messiah is Lord, to the glory of God the Father."* (Php 2:8–11)

But let's not miss the point of Jesus' parable. He will return! He will come back to Jerusalem to take up the throne of His father David and rule forever over the house of Jacob from Jerusalem, and specifically from Mount Zion. The promise will be fulfilled! A gospel without that ultimate fulfillment is no gospel at all!

During the Feast of Passover, the Jewish people expect that the prophet Elijah will come to the Passover meal, in order to introduce the Messiah, the son of David. Orthodox Jews, in fact, pray after every meal all year, "The Compassionate One, may He send us Elijah the Prophet, remembered for good, and may he bring good news to us, the news of goodness, salvations and consolations!"

But when Jesus came to Jerusalem the last time, He knew what was waiting for Him and for the city, and He began to weep.

> *"And when he drew near and saw the city, he wept over it, saying, 'Would that you, even you, had known on this day the things that make for peace! But now they are hidden from your eyes. For the days will come upon you, when your enemies will set up a barricade around you and surround you and hem you in on every side and tear you down to the ground, you and your children within you. And they will not leave one stone upon another in you, because you did not know the time of your visitation.'"* (Lk 19:41–44)

Jesus wept because Jerusalem did not know at that time *"the things that make for peace."* They were hidden from their eyes.

When Jesus asked His disciples who the people said that He was, the answer was that some of them said that He was Jeremiah (see Mt 16:13–14). Jeremiah was called the weeping prophet, because He prophesied about the coming destruction of Jerusalem and the Temple, and wept over it. It was the same with Jesus. He also prophesied about a second destruction of Jerusalem and the Temple. But this was by no means good news to Him. Jeremiah said, *"Oh that my head were waters, and my eyes a fountain of tears, that I might weep day and night for the slain of the daughter of my people!"* (Jer 9:1) Jesus also wept over Jerusalem.

Some Christians seem to think that the destruction of Jerusalem and the Temple was good news to Jesus, that this was His goal, in order to bring in something different and much better. He did come to establish something much better and eternal, but not in contradiction to what already existed. Heaven is not Jesus' ultimate destiny. Jerusalem and the throne of David, are! And He wanted to bring that about already then, but the people were not willing. He lamented, *"O Jerusalem, Jerusalem, the city that kills the prophets and stones those who are sent to it! How often would I have gathered your children together as a hen gathers her brood under her wings, and you would not! See, your house is left to you desolate."* (Mt 23:37–38) And He wept.

Jesus Will Return to Jerusalem as King

The Scriptures had to be fulfilled, just like Simeon prophesied. Jesus would first be a light unto the Gentiles. This has been fulfilled during the last 2,000 years; *"through their trespass salvation has come to the Gentiles."* (Ro 11:11) But ultimately, Jesus will also be for glory to His people Israel! He will restore the kingdom unto Israel from Jerusalem. If He doesn't, He is not the Messiah, and the gospel is no good news at all. Jesus made clear what the end would be, when He stood before the High Priest and was condemned to death.

> *"And the high priest said to him, 'I adjure you by the living God, tell us if you are the Messiah, the Son of God.' Jesus said to him, 'You have said so. But I tell you, from now on you will see the Son of Man seated at the right hand of Power and coming on the clouds of heaven.'"* (Mt 26:63–64)

Jesus will return on the clouds of heaven! Just like His first mission was fulfilled literally, and exactly as the prophets had spoken, so also His second mission will be fulfilled literally, exactly as the prophets have spoken. Jesus is the King of Israel and the promised Ruler over the house of Jacob, forever.

When Jesus returns to Jerusalem, there will be life from the dead, not only for Jerusalem, but for the whole world. *"For if their rejection* [of the Messiah] *means the reconciliation of the world, what will their acceptance* [of the Messiah] *mean but life from the dead?"* (Ro 11:15)

> *"**For behold, I create new heavens and a new earth**, and the former things shall not be remembered or come into mind. But be glad and rejoice forever in that which I create; for behold, **I create Jerusalem to be a joy, and her people to be a gladness**. I will rejoice in Jerusalem and be glad in my people; no more shall be heard in it the sound of weeping and the cry of distress."* (Isa 65:17–19)

Jesus is the Son of David, the King of Israel and Jerusalem is His capital. The gospel truly is good news!

The name Jesus is an English transliteration of a Greek transliteration of His original Hebrew name, Yeshua. In Hebrew, *Yeshua* means "the LORD saves." No one can be a true king without saving his people from their enemies. This is also what Jesus did when He came the first time, and He will do again when He returns. The first time, He defeated Satan and the second time, He will defeat those armies who have come to destroy His people and their city.

When David appeared before Israel the first time, he came to defeat Goliath, the giant of the Philistines and enemy of Israel. At that time, David's brothers also rejected him and hated him.

> *"Now Eliab his eldest brother heard when he spoke to the men. And Eliab's anger was kindled against David, and he said, 'Why have you come down? And with whom have you left those few sheep in the wilderness? I know your presumption and the evil of your heart, for you have come down to see the battle.'"* (1 Sa 17:28)

Just like the people did not know who David was, the people of Israel did not know who Jesus was, when He came the first time.

> *"As soon as Saul saw David go out against the Philistine, he said to Abner, the commander of the army, 'Abner, whose son is this youth?' And Abner said, 'As your soul lives, O king, I do not know.'"* (1 Sa 17:55)

When David had defeated Goliath it says, *"And David took the head of the Philistine and brought it **to Jerusalem**."* (1 Sa 17:54) It was in Jerusalem that Jesus defeated Satan, more precisely at a place called *"the place of a skull, which in Aramaic is called Golgotha."* (Jn 19:17)

After the elders and all of the people of Israel had anointed David king of Israel, he came back again to Jerusalem, to establish his throne there. He defeated the armies of the Philistines and brought Israel peace. It is a picture of what Yeshua, the Savior and King of the Jews, will do when He returns again to Jerusalem.

> *"The LORD has sworn and will not change his mind, 'You are a priest forever after the order of Melchizedek.' The Lord is at your right hand; he will shatter kings on the day of his wrath. He will execute judgment among the nations, filling them with corpses; he will shatter chiefs over the wide earth."* (Ps 110:4–6)

> *"Lift up your heads, O gates! And be lifted up, O ancient doors, that the King of glory may come in. Who is this King of glory? The LORD, strong and mighty, the LORD, mighty in battle! Lift up your heads, O gates! And lift them up, O ancient doors, that the King of glory may come in. Who is this King of glory? The LORD of hosts, he is the King of glory! Selah"* (Ps 24:7–10)

> *"Blessed is he who comes in the name of the LORD! We bless you from the house of the LORD."* (Ps 118:26)

8

DO NOT LEAVE JERUSALEM

"And while staying with them he ordered them
not to depart from Jerusalem." —Acts 1:4

We have established Jesus' strong and deep affinity for Jerusalem and the Temple. However, maybe one of the strongest proofs of this holy bond is what we read about His disciples, after His ascension. Luke ends his gospel by writing:

> *"Then he led them out as far as Bethany, and lifting up his hands he blessed them. While he blessed them, he parted from them and was carried up into heaven. And they worshiped him and returned to Jerusalem with great joy, and were continually in the Temple blessing God."* (Lk 24:50–53)

The disciples returned to Jerusalem, and were continually at the Temple. That is quite a testimony. They did not begin to collect money in order to lay the foundation to the Church of the Holy Sepulcher. That was built hundreds of years later. They stayed continually in the Jewish Temple in Jerusalem, blessing God.

Before His departure into heaven, Jesus had told them,

*"Thus it is written, that the Messiah should suffer and on the third day rise from the dead, and that repentance and forgiveness of sins should be proclaimed in his name to all nations, **beginning from Jerusalem**. You are witnesses of these things. And behold, I am sending the promise of my Father upon you. But **stay in the city** until you are clothed with power from on high."* (Lk 24:46–49)

It was important for the gospel to be preached first in Jerusalem, as it is written. It is, first of all, good news for Jerusalem! Later on, Paul wrote to the Corinthians, *"Was it from you that the word of God first went forth? Or has it come to you only?"* (1 Co 14:36 NASB) There is only one city in the world from which the word of God has originated—and that is Jerusalem, just as it is written, *"For out of Zion shall go the law, and the word of the LORD from Jerusalem."* (Isa 2:3) The roots of our faith are in Jerusalem among the Jewish people, not in Rome, not in Geneva, not in Dallas or any other city. God has laid the foundation in Zion and nowhere else.

It is true that the Book of Acts ends in Rome. Luke wrote, *"'Therefore let it be known to you that this salvation of God has been sent to the Gentiles; they will listen.' He [Paul] lived there [in Rome] two whole years at his own expense, and welcomed all who came to him, proclaiming the kingdom of God and teaching about the Lord Jesus the Messiah with all boldness and without hindrance."* (Ac 28:28–31) But Luke had already established in the first chapter that Jerusalem is the end destination of the gospel. The angels told the disciples who saw their Master ascend into heaven from the Mount of Olives, *"This Jesus, who was taken up from you into heaven, will come in the same way as you saw him go into heaven."* (Ac 1:11) Jesus will return to Jerusalem, not to Rome. The two years that Paul preached in Rome about the kingdom are prophetic of the 2,000 years that Jesus will be "a light for revelation to the Gentiles," until the times of the Gentiles are fulfilled. Then He will restore again the kingdom unto Israel and be for glory to His people.

We read that Jesus repeated the same command to His disciples to stay in Jerusalem also in the Book of Acts. *"And while staying with them **he ordered them not to depart from Jerusalem**, but to wait for the promise of the Father, which, he said, 'you heard from me; for John baptized with water, but you will be baptized with the Holy Spirit not many days from now.'"* (1:4–5)

True, He also gave them the Great Commission to go out into the whole world and preach the gospel. But, the order was important. They must begin in Jerusalem.

> *"'But you will receive power when the Holy Spirit has come upon you, and you will be my witnesses in Jerusalem and in all Judea and Samaria, and to the end of the earth.' And when he had said these things, as they were looking on, he was lifted up, and a cloud took him out of their sight."* (1:8–9)

According to a tradition in the early church, Jesus ordered His apostles specifically to remain in Jerusalem for the first twelve years.[1] It was crucial for the gospel that the apostolic community be established in Jerusalem. This is the geographical foundation and center for belief in Messiah. The Book of Acts tells us about the early disciples,

---

1   Eusebius, *Ecclesiastical History* 5.18.14. "They were to offer the nation of Israel twelve years to repent before they turned their attention to the rest of the world. According to that tradition, the Master said to the twelve, 'If any man of Israel desires to repent and believe on God by my name, his sins shall be forgiven him. After twelve years, go forth into the world, so that no one may say, 'We have not heard' [Clement of Alexandria, *Stromata* 6.5, citing *Preaching of Peter*]. The twelve years comport nicely with the work of Paul and Barnabas who did not begin proclaiming the message to the God-fearing Gentiles of Syria until some twelve years after the Master's resurrection" (D.T. Lancaster, *Torah Club Vol. 6: Chronicles of the Apostles*, Marshfield, MI: First Fruits of Zion, 2011).

"And they devoted themselves to the apostles' teaching and fellowship, to the breaking of bread and the prayers. And awe came upon every soul, and many wonders and signs were being done through the apostles. And all who believed were together and had all things in common. And they were selling their possessions and belongings and distributing the proceeds to all, as any had need. And day by day, attending the Temple together and breaking bread in their homes, they received their food with glad and generous hearts, praising God and having favor with all the people. And the Lord added to their number day by day those who were being saved." (2:42–47)

Here, it once again says that the disciples attended the Temple together every day. It also states that they had favor with all the people, i.e. the Jewish people. In other words, they did not start a new religion. They continued to be Jews, living as Jews and worshipping as Jews. And the Jewish people in Jerusalem looked up to them. Luke repeats this again in Acts 5.

*"Now many signs and wonders were regularly done among the people by the hands of the apostles. And **they were all together in Solomon's Portico**. None of the rest dared join them, **but the people held them in high esteem**. And more than ever believers were added to the Lord, multitudes of both men and women, so that they even carried out the sick into the streets and laid them on cots and mats, that as Peter came by at least his shadow might fall on some of them. The people also gathered from the towns around Jerusalem, bringing the sick and those afflicted with unclean spirits, and they were all healed."* (5:12–16)

What power there was! It even says that **all** were healed.

The believers had a special place in the Temple, where they used to meet. It was called Solomon's Portico, which we also read about in Acts 3, in connection with the healing of the lame man. *"While he clung to Peter and John, all the people, utterly astounded, ran together to them in the portico called Solomon's."* (3:11)

Solomon's Portico was located along the eastern wall of Herod's Temple Mount Plaza. It was called Solomon's Portico because the eastern retaining wall was the only original wall that remained from the Temple of Solomon. King Herod had extended the plaza in all directions except to the east, because of the steep Kidron Valley. This was obviously the meeting place for the first followers of Jesus—in the Temple.

But they did not stay there, just keeping to themselves. Luke wrote that they *"were continually in the Temple **blessing God**."* (Lk 24:53) They participated with the other Jews in the Temple's daily worship services in the mornings and in the afternoons, as we see in Acts 3:1, *"Now Peter and John were going up to the Temple at the hour of prayer, the ninth hour."*

"The hour of prayer, the ninth hour" was the daily worship service that was conducted in the Temple at approximately 3:00 in the afternoon, in connection with the evening sacrifice. This afternoon service correlated to the hour of prayer at about 9:00 a.m., the morning sacrificial service in the Temple.[2] We read about such a prayer service in Luke 1, where it talks about the father of John the Baptist.

> *"In the days of Herod, king of Judea, there was a priest named Zechariah, of the division of Abijah. And he had a wife from the daughters of Aaron, and her name was Elizabeth. And they were both righteous before God, walking blamelessly in all the commandments and statutes of the*

---

2   The biblical hours consisted of dividing daylight into 12 hours, hence the "third hour" (or the "ninth hour") from sunrise would fluctuate somewhat, from winter to summer, depending on the amount of daylight.

*Lord. But they had no child, because Elizabeth was barren, and both were advanced in years. Now while he was serving as priest before God when his division was on duty, according to the custom of the priesthood, he was chosen by lot to enter the Temple of the Lord and burn incense. And **the whole multitude of the people were praying outside at the hour of incense.***" (Lk 1:5–10)

Here, the hour of prayer is called *"the hour of incense."* David likened prayer to the burning of incense. *"Let my prayer be counted as incense before you, and the lifting up of my hands as the evening sacrifice!"* (Ps 141:2) The priests in the Temple burned incense before the LORD twice a day, in connection with the daily sacrifice (see Nu 28:1–8), as well as tended the lamps in the menorah. Meanwhile, the people were outside the building, praying in the Temple courts. King David had written the main script for these worship services, in the Psalms.

In Acts 6:7, it says, *"And the word of God continued to increase, and the number of the disciples multiplied greatly in Jerusalem, and a great many of the priests became obedient to the faith."* There is no reason to believe that these priests stopped serving in the Temple. If they had, the believers could hardly have been held in high esteem among the rest of the Jews in Jerusalem. These priests who believed in the Messiah Jesus continued to slaughter the sacrifices in the Temple.

Paul and the Temple

What about the Apostle Paul? Did he also participate in these Temple services where they sacrificed animals, after he became a disciple? Absolutely! We can, for example, read from his testimony before the crowd in Jerusalem in Acts 22,

"When I had returned to Jerusalem and was praying in the Temple, I fell into a trance and saw him saying to me, 'Make

*haste and get out of Jerusalem quickly, because they will not
accept your testimony about me.'"* (Ac 22:17–18)

Here, we see that when he returned to Jerusalem after His encounter with Jesus on the road to Damascus, he immediately went to
the Temple to pray, just as was his custom before he became a fol-
lower of the Messiah. The Temple was the obvious place to go and
pray for all of the disciples.

When he came to Jerusalem for the last time, Paul was arrested
and he testified before governor Felix about the reason he had come
to Jerusalem in the first place: *"Now after several years I came to bring
alms to my nation and **to present offerings**. While I was doing this,
they found me purified in the Temple, without any crowd or tumult."*
(24:17–18)

Paul said that he had come to Jerusalem in order to bring alms to
his people, and to present offerings. We know what the first part was
all about. Paul had written to the believers in Rome about his journey
to Jerusalem:

> *"At present, however, I am going to Jerusalem bringing aid
> to the saints. For Macedonia and Achaia have been pleased
> to make some contribution for the poor among the saints at
> Jerusalem."* (Ro 15:25–26)

This is very clear. Paul had come to deliver aid to the disciples in
Jerusalem from the believers in Macedonia and Achaia. But Paul also
said to the Roman governor that he had come to Jerusalem to present
offerings, and that those who had arrested him had found him purified in the Temple. What did he mean? Had the Apostle Paul come on
his final journey to Jerusalem in order to offer animal sacrifices in the
Temple? Yes, he had.

We read about this in Acts 21. Luke described what happened
when he came to Jerusalem, together with Paul, on his final visit to
the holy city.

"When we had come to Jerusalem, the brothers received us gladly. On the following day Paul went in with us to James, and all the elders were present. After greeting them, he related one by one the things that God had done among the Gentiles through his ministry. And when they heard it, they glorified God." (Ac 21:17–20)

So far, everything was fine. However, Luke continues,

"And they said to him, 'You see, brother, how many thousands there are among the Jews of those who have believed. They are all zealous for the law, and they have been told about you that you teach all the Jews who are among the Gentiles to forsake Moses, telling them not to circumcise their children or walk according to our customs." (21:20–21)

This was a problem. All the believers in Jerusalem were very zealous for the Law of God. They had learnt this from Jesus, who had taught them:

"Do not think that I have come to abolish the Law or the Prophets; I have not come to abolish them but to fulfill them. For truly, I say to you, until heaven and earth pass away, not an iota, not a dot, will pass from the Law until all is accomplished. Therefore whoever relaxes one of the least of these commandments and teaches others to do the same will be called least in the kingdom of heaven, but whoever does them and teaches them will be called great in the kingdom of heaven." (Mt 5:17–19)

The disciples in Jerusalem were therefore faithful to the Torah of Moses, down to the least of the commandments. But there was a rumor about Paul in Jerusalem that he had forsaken the Torah, or Law, of Moses and was teaching other Jews to do the same, contrary to what Jesus had taught them.

Sadly, this is a rumor that has persisted about Paul through the centuries, up to our time. But Jacob (James, *Ya'akov* in Hebrew) knew that this rumor about Paul was false. How? Because we can read in Galatians how Paul, after several years of ministry, traveled to Jerusalem to specifically talk to the leaders there, including Jacob (James), about the gospel that he preached. Paul wrote,

> *"Then after fourteen years I went up again to Jerusalem with Barnabas, taking Titus along with me. I went up because of a revelation and set before them (though privately before those who seemed influential) the gospel that I proclaim among the Gentiles, in order to make sure I was not running or had not run in vain."* (Gal 2:1–2)

Paul presented to the leaders in Jerusalem the gospel that he preached among the Gentiles. He had been working for many years as an apostle and wanted to be sure that he *"was not running or had not run in vain."* So he checked his message and teachings with the leaders in Jerusalem, who had been apostles before he was. (Gal 1:17) He explained what the result was,

> *"But even Titus, who was with me, was not forced to be circumcised, though he was a Greek ... And from those who seemed to be influential (what they were makes no difference to me; God shows no partiality)—those, I say, who seemed influential added nothing to me. On the contrary, when ... James and Cephas and John, who seemed to be pillars, perceived the grace that was given to me, they gave the right hand of fellowship to Barnabas and me, that we should go to the Gentiles and they to the circumcised. Only, they asked us to remember the poor, the very thing I was eager to do."* (Gal 2:3,6–7,9–10)

Paul was given the task of going to the Gentiles with the gospel and the message that the Gentiles did not have to get circumcised and keep the entire Law of Moses (see Ac 15). Yet a false rumor about Paul had spread to the Jewish believers in Jerusalem, that Paul himself had forsaken the Law and taught other Jews to do the same. Jacob (James), the main apostolic leader in Jerusalem, and Jesus' own brother, said that something had to be done about this rumor. He continued,

> *"'What then is to be done? They will certainly hear that you have come. Do therefore what we tell you. We have four men who are under a vow; take these men and purify yourself along with them and pay their expenses, so that they may shave their heads.* **Thus all will know that there is nothing in what they have been told about you, but that you your-self also live in observance of the law.** *But as for the Gentiles who have believed, we have sent a letter with our judgment that they should abstain from what has been sacrificed to idols, and from blood, and from what has been strangled, and from sexual immorality.' Then Paul took the men, and the next day he purified himself along with them and went into the Temple, giving notice when the days of purification would be fulfilled and the offering presented for each one of them."* (Ac 21:22–26)

Paul had come to Jerusalem in order to present offerings, because he had taken a Nazarite vow. We can read about this in Acts 18:18, *"After this, Paul stayed many days longer and then took leave of the brothers and set sail for Syria, and with him Priscilla and Aquila. At Cenchreae he had cut his hair, for he was under a vow."*

This is referring to a Nazarite vow, when the person was not allowed to cut his hair during the time he was under the vow. For this reason, the vow began and ended with the person cutting his hair. We can read more about this in the Torah,

"And the LORD spoke to Moses, saying, 'Speak to the people of Israel and say to them, When either a man or a woman makes a special vow, the vow of a Nazirite, to separate himself to the LORD, he shall separate himself from wine and strong drink. He shall drink no vinegar made from wine or strong drink and shall not drink any juice of grapes or eat grapes, fresh or dried. All the days of his separation he shall eat nothing that is produced by the grapevine, not even the seeds or the skins. **All the days of his vow of separation, no razor shall touch his head.** *Until the time is completed for which he separates himself to the LORD, he shall be holy.* **He shall let the locks of hair of his head grow long.***" (Nu 6:1–5)

When a person was under a vow, he voluntarily chose to live under the same strict laws as the High Priest. Some, like Samson, Samuel and John the Baptist, lived as Nazarites their whole lives. It is interesting that it is immediately after the presentation of the Nazarite vow that we find the Aaronic blessing in the Torah. Could this have anything to do with Paul's statement to the Romans about his travel plans after he had been in Jerusalem and completed his vow: *"I know that when I come to you I will come in the fullness of the blessing of Messiah."* (Ro 15:29)

In order to end the vow, sacrifices had to be presented before the LORD. This could only be done at the Temple in Jerusalem. The Torah states,

"And this is the law for the Nazirite, when the time of his separation has been completed: he shall be brought to the entrance of the tent of meeting, and he shall bring his gift to the LORD, one male lamb a year old without blemish for a burnt offering, and one ewe lamb a year old without blemish as a sin offering, and one ram without blemish as a peace offering, and a basket of unleavened bread, loaves of fine flour mixed with oil, and unleavened wafers smeared with

*oil, and their grain offering and their drink offerings. And
the priest shall bring them before the LORD and offer his sin
offering and his burnt offering, and he shall offer the ram
as a sacrifice of peace offering to the LORD, with the basket
of unleavened bread. The priest shall offer also its grain offering and its drink offering. And the Nazirite shall shave
his consecrated head at the entrance of the tent of meeting
and shall take the hair from his consecrated head and put it
on the fire that is under the sacrifice of the peace offering.
And the priest shall take the shoulder of the ram, when it is
boiled, and one unleavened loaf out of the basket and one
unleavened wafer, and shall put them on the hands of the
Nazirite, after he has shaved the hair of his consecration,
and the priest shall wave them for a wave offering before
the LORD. They are a holy portion for the priest, together
with the breast that is waved and the thigh that is contrib-
uted. And after that the Nazirite may drink wine. This is the
law of the Nazirite. But if he vows an offering to the LORD
above his Nazirite vow, as he can afford, in exact accordance
with the vow that he takes, then he shall do in addition to
the law of the Nazirite."* (Nu 6:13–21)

We see here that there were a lot of sacrifices that had to be presented before the LORD, in order to end such a vow. Scripture lists no
less than eight specific offerings, altogether worth well over a thousand dollars in today's currency, especially as the animals in the Temple were extra expensive:

1. One male lamb a year old without blemish for a burnt
    offering;
2. One ewe lamb a year old without blemish as a sin offering;
3. One ram without blemish as a peace offering;
4. A basket of unleavened bread;
5. Loaves of fine flour mixed with oil;

6. Unleavened wafers smeared with oil;
7. Grain offering and drink offerings;
8. An offering to the LORD above his Nazirite vow, as he can afford.

For this reason, it was a common problem in Paul's time that people made Nazarite vows, but did not have the means the pay for all the sacrifices, in order to end the vow. Remember that Joseph and Mary could not afford to bring even a one year-old lamb when Mary's days of purification were completed, but presented two turtledoves or two pigeons instead (see Lev 12:8 and Lk 2:24). That is why the Apostle Jacob (James) explained to Paul,

> *"We have four men who are under a vow; take these men and purify yourself along with them **and pay their expenses, so that they may shave their heads. Thus all will know that there is nothing in what they have been told about you, but that you yourself also live in observance of the law."** (Ac 21:23–24)*

Actions always speak louder than words, especially if money is involved. Jacob asked Paul to pay for all the expenses for the four men to end their vows together with him. "Thus," Jacob said, *"all will know that there is nothing in what they have been told about you, but that you yourself also live in observance of the law."* (21:24)

Luke then continues to tell what happened,

> *"Then Paul took the men, and the next day he purified himself along with them and went into the Temple, giving notice when the days of purification would be fulfilled and the offering presented for each one of them. When the seven days were almost completed, the Jews from Asia, seeing him in the Temple, stirred up the whole crowd and laid hands on him, crying out, 'Men of Israel, help! This is the man who is teach-*

*ing everyone everywhere against the people and the law and
this place. Moreover, he even brought Greeks into the Temple
and has defiled this holy place.' For they had previously seen
Trophimus the Ephesian with him in the city, and they supposed that Paul had brought him into the Temple."* (21:26–
29)

They came with false charges. Paul had not brought Gentiles with
him into the Temple and desecrated it, and he was not teaching
against the Law of Moses or the Temple. Luke devotes major portions
of the remaining chapters in the Book of Acts to cover Paul's defenses
against these accusations, in no less than five trials. Paul told Felix,
*"they did not find me disputing with anyone or stirring up a crowd,
either in the Temple or in the synagogues or in the city. Neither can
they prove to you what they now bring up against me."* (24:12–13) And
he summarized his position before the Jewish leaders in Rome,
*"Brothers, though I had done nothing against our people or the cus-
toms of our fathers, yet I was delivered as a prisoner from Jerusalem
into the hands of the Romans."* (28:17)

In summary, we find that all of the apostles continued to see the
Temple in Jerusalem as the natural and obvious focal point in their
devotion to God, just like all other Jews. They had nothing against the
sacrifices in the Temple, but even participated in them. And this is the
way it continued, almost up to the destruction of the Temple. Jacob,
the brother of Jesus, who was the leader of the first Messianic community in Jerusalem, is even praised by the Jewish historian Josephus
as a *tzaddik*, a righteous man. Later, when Jacob was murdered by the
Saduccees, Josephus remarks that the rabbis were greatly upset over
his death.[3]

It was only a few years before the destruction of the Temple in 70
CE that the Saduccees, led by the High Priests, forced the Messianic

---

3 Josephus, *Antiquities* 20.197–201, Eusebius, *Ecclesiastical Histories* 2.23.4,10–
   18.

believers out of the Temple. According to the church father Origin, Josephus wrote that when they shed the innocent blood of Jesus' brother Jacob the *tzaddik*, the fate of Jerusalem was sealed. Nothing could stop its destruction.[4]

The Center of the First Generation of Disciples

The apostolic church was born in Jerusalem. Until shortly before the destruction of the Temple, the community of Jewish believers in Jerusalem was the self-evident headquarters for all the followers of Jesus. And since the believers in Jerusalem met daily in the Temple at Solomon's Portico, it is no exaggeration to say that the Temple was their physical headquarters, corresponding to what the Vatican and St. Peter's Basilica are for the Catholic Church today. Jesus' brother Jacob, the leader of the community in Jerusalem, practically corresponded to the Pope.

Jesus had told them in His final address, *"But you will receive power when the Holy Spirit has come upon you, and you will be my witnesses in Jerusalem and in all Judea and Samaria, and to the end of the earth."* (Ac 1:8) After Jerusalem and all Judea, Samaria was next to receive the gospel. When this was accomplished through Philip the Evangelist, the apostles in Jerusalem sent Peter and John there to give further guidance and instructions to the new believers.

> *"Now when the apostles at Jerusalem heard that Samaria had received the word of God, they sent to them Peter and John, who came down and prayed for them that they might receive the Holy Spirit, for he had not yet fallen on any of them, but they had only been baptized in the name of the*

---

4   *Origen and Josephus*, Wataru Mizugaki, in Louis H. Feldman, Gohei Hata (editors), *Josephus, Judaism and Christianity*, (Wayne State University Press, 1987), p. 329.

Lord Jesus. Then they laid their hands on them and they received the Holy Spirit." (8:14–17)

When the first Gentile, Cornelius, came to faith with his entire household, through the preaching of Peter, news about what had happened reached the leaders in Jerusalem. The people in Samaria were "half Jews," and Jesus had also ministered to them. But Cornelius was a pure Gentile, a Roman centurion, and this was a completely new development. Peter had to explain to them what had taken place, because some in the Jerusalem community objected to what he had done.

> *"Now the apostles and the brothers who were throughout Judea heard that the Gentiles also had received the word of God. So when Peter went up to Jerusalem, the circumcision party criticized him, saying, 'You went to uncircumcised men and ate with them.' But Peter began and explained it to them in order."* (11:1–4)

Peter ended his report by saying, *"'If then God gave the same gift to them as he gave to us when we believed in the Lord Jesus the Messiah, who was I that I could stand in God's way?' When they heard these things they fell silent. And they glorified God, saying, 'Then to the Gentiles also God has granted repentance that leads to life.'"* (11:17–18) The leaders in Jerusalem were satisfied. They recognized that a door had opened also for Gentiles to be saved.

When more Gentiles came to faith in Jesus in Antioch, the leaders in Jerusalem sent Barnabas there. The mother community in Jerusalem took responsibility for the developments in Antioch. Barnabas took charge and organized the work so that it would continue in a healthy way. He recruited Paul, and together they stayed in Antioch for a whole year, to establish all the believers.

*"But there were some of them, men of Cyprus and Cyrene, who on coming to Antioch spoke to the Hellenists also, preaching the Lord Jesus. And the hand of the Lord was with them, and a great number who believed turned to the Lord. **The report of this came to the ears of the church in Jerusalem, and they sent Barnabas to Antioch.** When he came and saw the grace of God, he was glad, and he exhorted them all to remain faithful to the Lord with steadfast purpose, for he was a good man, full of the Holy Spirit and of faith. And a great many people were added to the Lord. So **Barnabas went to Tarsus to look for Saul, and when he had found him, he brought him to Antioch.** For a whole year they met with the church and taught a great many people. And in Antioch the disciples were first called Christians."* (11:20–26)*

Eventually, Antioch became the outpost for missionary outreach to the Gentile world. Paul, or Saul of Tarsus, as he was also known, was the main instrument that God used. Paul, in fact, later on referred to himself as *"the apostle of the Gentiles,"* (Ro 11:13 KJV) Though Paul was originally from Tarsus, he was definitely a Jerusalemite, educated in Jerusalem under Gamaliel, the most well-known rabbi in the holy city at that time. Paul submitted his ministry and what he taught to the leaders in Jerusalem, *"to make sure I was not running or had not run in vain."* (Gal 2:2) The apostles in Jerusalem told Paul that he should continue to remember the poor among the saints in Jerusalem, which Paul said was *"the very thing I was eager to do."* (2:10) It was important that Paul, as the apostle to the Gentiles, taught the Gentile believers their special responsibility for the believers in Jerusalem. Paul wrote to the believers in Rome,

"At present, however, I am going to Jerusalem bringing aid to the saints. For Macedonia and Achaia have been pleased to make some contribution for the poor among the saints at

Jerusalem. They were pleased to do it, and indeed they owe it to them. For if the Gentiles have come to share in their spiritual blessings, they ought also to be of service to them in material blessings." (Ro 15:25–27)

The financial support for the believers in Jerusalem became a custom and tradition among all the Gentile churches, and continued for several generations, until the bishop of Rome finally abolished it for purely political reasons. He wanted the church in Rome, and not the one in Jerusalem, to be the leader among all the churches in the world. However, in the beginning and during the entire time period of the Book of Acts, the church in Jerusalem was the unchallenged center for all the believers.

When the controversy arose at Antioch, about whether or not Gentile believers had to be circumcised, they had to take the matter before the leaders in Jerusalem.

"But some men came down from Judea and were teaching the brothers, 'Unless you are circumcised according to the custom of Moses, you cannot be saved.' And after Paul and Barnabas had no small dissension and debate with them, Paul and Barnabas and some of the others were appointed to go up to Jerusalem to the apostles and the elders about this question." (Ac 15:1–2)

This decision by the elders in Jerusalem was then communicated to all the churches that Paul started. Luke wrote about Paul and Silas, *"As they went on their way through the cities, they delivered to them for observance the decisions that had been reached by the apostles and elders who were in Jerusalem. So the churches were strengthened in the faith, and they increased in numbers daily."* (16:4–5)

The Book of Hebrews

The Book of Hebrews was written to the Jewish Messianic community in Jerusalem that had been forced out of the Temple. Naturally, they were sorrowful that they had been expelled from the place that had been their natural home for decades. The author exhorted them to not lose hope. Even though they could not continue to worship in the Temple, the author encouraged them that they still had access to the Throne of Grace in the Holy of Holies in heaven.

> *"Since then we have a great high priest who has passed through the heavens, Jesus, the Son of God, let us hold fast our confession. For we do not have a high priest who is unable to sympathize with our weaknesses, but one who in every respect has been tempted as we are, yet without sin. Let us then with confidence draw near to the throne of grace, that we may receive mercy and find grace to help in time of need."* (Heb 4:14–16)

The author then summarized his message in the final chapter,

> *"So Jesus also suffered outside the gate in order to sanctify the people through his own blood. Therefore let us go to him outside the camp and bear the reproach he endured. For here we have no lasting city, but we seek the city that is to come. Through him then let us continually offer up a sacrifice of praise to God, that is, the fruit of lips that acknowledge his name. Do not neglect to do good and to share what you have, for such sacrifices are pleasing to God."* (Heb 13:12–16)

The author of the Book of Hebrews told the Messianic Jews to do three things, now that they could no longer participate in the Temple services:

1. Continue to offer the sacrifice of praise to God through Messiah;
2. Continue to do good deeds;
3. Continue to share with others—in other words, give alms to the poor.

This was written just a few years before the destruction of the Temple and the subsequent destruction of Jerusalem, when all Jews had to leave both the Temple and eventually, also, the city. At that time, after the Temple was gone, the Jewish rabbis had to rethink Jewish faith. It is very interesting that they eventually came up with the same three foundational obligations as the apostles, which have been the basis of Rabbinic Judaism to this very day: (1) the daily prayers, (2) doing good deeds by keeping the commandments, and (3) giving to the poor. The rabbis even quoted the same verse from Hosea that the author of Hebrews also referred to as support of the idea that prayer, or the sacrifice of praise, is a substitute for the sacrifices of animals.

> *"Take words with you, and return to the Lord. Say to Him, 'Take away all iniquity; receive us graciously, for we will offer the sacrifices of our lips.'"* (Hos 14:2 NKJV)

The Hebrew text literally says *"the bull calves of our lips,"* while the Septuagint, which the Book of Hebrews quotes, uses the words *"the fruit of our lips."*

Notice also that the text in Hebrews does not say, "For here we have no lasting city, but we look forward to going to heaven." It says rather, *"For here we have no lasting city, but we seek the city that is to come."* As we have pointed out, *"the city that is to come"* does not refer to heaven, but to the same city that Abraham looked forward to: the new Jerusalem that will one day come down from heaven with the glory of God, the restored Garden of Eden. Yes, to this day, *"present Jerusalem,"* as Paul expresses it in Galatians, is still in bondage with her children. *"But the Jerusalem above is free, and she is our mother."*

(Gal 4:26) This is the city that will soon manifest itself on earth in the Holy Land.

Many have perverted the message in the Epistle of Hebrews to mean, that if the Jewish believers that the letter is written to, began to sacrifice again in the Temple, they would *"then have fallen away, since they are crucifying once again the Son of God to their own harm and holding him up to contempt."* (Heb 6:6) Such a person would have *"trampled underfoot the Son of God, and has profaned the blood of the covenant by which he was sanctified, and has outraged the Spirit of grace."* (10:29)

That would be true, if they were to reject their faith in Jesus in order to sacrifice in the Temple. But sacrificing in the Temple—something that all the apostles and believers in Jerusalem **continued to do** for decades after the death and resurrection of Messiah—would, by itself, in no way constitute a rejection of their faith in Jesus.

But over the past two millennia, the anti–Jewishness that the later church fathers introduced into the church has deeply colored the way that most Christians view the Temple and the Temple Mount, the heart of the holy city. They see absolutely no value in it. When the Christian Byzantine Empire took over Jerusalem in the fourth century, the Emperor Constantine began to build his "New Jerusalem" around the Church of the Holy Sepulcher. The Temple Mount, the most holy place to God, represented something that was old, and gone forever. It was eventually even transformed into a garbage dump! The original gospel message of comfort to Jerusalem was perverted.

The story goes that when the Muslims conquered Jerusalem in the year 638, the Caliph Omar came to Jerusalem, and he wanted to know where the Jewish Temples had stood. When the Jews showed him the Temple Mount, he found a Christian woman, who had walked all the way from Bethlehem that morning, in order to throw her garbage there. When Omar asked her why, she answered that her priests had taught her that it brought good luck if one could throw one's garbage on the Temple Mount. That is how deeply the Christian community in the seventh century despised and resented the most holy place on earth in God's eyes—the very place He has reserved for His Son, from which He will rule forever, and about which it is written,

> *"the LORD loves the gates of Zion more than all the dwelling places of Jacob."* (Ps 87:2)

> *"For the LORD has chosen Zion; he has desired it for his dwelling place: 'This is my resting place forever; here I will dwell, for I have desired it.' ... There I will make a horn to sprout for David; I have prepared a lamp for my anointed."* (Ps 132:13–14,17)

> *"As for me, I have set my King on Zion, my holy hill."* (Ps 2:6)

Islam teaches that the people who control the Temple Mount hold the key to the entire world. The Muslims know the importance of this place, more than Christians do. The Muslim Brotherhood has stated that there will never be peace on earth as long as the Jewish people have any control over the Temple Mount.

Jesus said, *"Jerusalem will be trampled underfoot by the Gentiles, until the times of the Gentiles are fulfilled."* (Lk 21:24) In 1967, Jerusalem was once again reunited under Jewish sovereignty for the first time in over 2,000 years. Many preachers began to teach that Jesus must be coming soon, because the times of the Gentiles were now fulfilled. But that is not true. On the day after the Israeli Army conquered the Temple Mount in 1967, General Moshe Dayan handed back the key to the Muslim waqf on the Mount, and it has remained in their hands ever since. The most important part of Jerusalem is still trampled under foot by Gentiles.

Psalm 76 begins:

"In Judah God is known; his name is great in Israel. His abode has been established in Salem, his dwelling place in Zion." (Ps 76:1–2)

If Israel is the hour hand on God's big clock, showing us what time it is, then Jerusalem is the minute hand, showing us the minutes, and Zion—the Temple Mount—shows us the seconds, because when God builds up Zion, He will appear in His glory, as it is written in Psalm 102.

"But you, O LORD, are enthroned forever; you are remembered throughout all generations. You will arise and have pity on Zion; it is the time to favor her; the appointed time has come. For your servants hold her stones dear and have pity on her dust. Nations will fear the name of the LORD, and all the kings of the earth will fear your glory. For the LORD builds up Zion; he appears in his glory." (Ps 102:12–13,16)

The King James Version reads, *"When the Lord shall build up Zion, he shall appear in his glory."* (102:16)

The building up of Zion is the true sign of the appearing and coming of Messiah in glory. Psalm 102 gives us the reason behind the appointed time to restore Zion: *"For your servants hold her stones dear and have pity on her dust."* (102:14)

God is right now doing something extraordinary and historic in the hearts of the Jewish people. There is a deep longing to return to Zion. He is moving in their hearts, stirring up a passion for the stones and dust of the Temple Mount. It is a precursor to the coming of Messiah.

It is time for Christians to deeply repent of all contempt for the Temple and the Temple Mount, and for all complacency and lack of passion for God's holy hill. It is a matter of having a heart for the glory of Messiah and His throne in the earth. How can we say that we love Him, if we do not share His heart for the resting place of His glory?

The fear of everything "Jewish" runs deep in Christian thinking today. We have inherited it with the mother's milk of Christian tradition. It is far from the heart of the first disciples in Jerusalem, and it is far from the heart of David, the man after God's own heart, who said, *"I will not enter my house or get into my bed, I will not give sleep to my eyes or slumber to my eyelids, until I find a place for the LORD, a dwelling place for the Mighty One of Jacob."* (Ps 132:3–5)

It is time for reflection and repentance among the followers of Jesus.

9

WATCHING ON THE WALLS
OF JERUSALEM

"O Lord, according to all your righteous acts,
let your anger and your wrath turn away from your city
Jerusalem, your holy hill." —Daniel 9:16

The Calling to Be Watchmen

Isaiah 62 gives us a glimpse into the mystery of intercessory prayer. God begins by saying, *"For Zion's sake I will not keep silent, and for Jerusalem's sake I will not be quiet, until her righteousness goes forth as brightness, and her salvation as a burning torch."* God has promised that He will not be silent until His will comes to pass in Jerusalem. This is a wonderful promise!

The following verses then give us an outline of His future plans for the city,

> *"The nations shall see your righteousness, and all the kings your glory, and you shall be called by a new name that the mouth of the LORD will give."* (62:2)

The next verse continues,

"You shall be a crown of beauty in the hand of the LORD,
and a royal diadem in the hand of your God." (62:3)

The list goes on with glorious promises for God's own city, until it says:

"... On your walls, O Jerusalem, I have set watchmen; all the
day and all the night they shall never be silent. You who put
the LORD in remembrance, take no rest, and give him no rest
until he establishes Jerusalem and makes it a praise in the
earth." (62:6–7)

In Isaiah 62:1, God says that **He** will not be silent until Jerusalem is restored. But here in 62:6–7, He says that He has also placed watchmen on the walls of Jerusalem and **they** must never be silent day or night, but call out to Him and remind Him of His promises until He fulfills them.

Intercessory prayer is a holy work of cooperation with God, to implement His will on the earth. What an awesome privilege! But also, what a profound responsibility! Intercessory prayer is not a matter of praying whatever we want. We are not called to pray that our will is done. This is the largest hindrance to anyone being used in prayer. Intercessory prayer is a matter of praying for **God's will** to be done, and not giving up until it has come to pass. For this to work, we must be familiar with His plans and His program. We must know what God's will is. That is why we are called to be watchmen. We must watch in the Scriptures as well as in prayer, listening to Him and His voice until we know what His will is. Then we can pray.

The Apostle John explained it in this way, *"And this is the*
confidence that we have toward him, that if we ask anything
according to his will *he hears us. And if we know that he*
hears us in whatever we ask, we know that we have the re-
quests that we have asked of him." (1 Jn 5:14–15)

The key to intercession is that we must know what God's will is. When we do, we can count on God's answer to our prayers—whatever it is. Whether it is something small or something big, something personal, or something national—or even international, something physical and material, or something spiritual. That is not up to us. It is up to God. Then He will answer us, regardless of what it is, provided it is His will. Prayer is not trying to change God's will. It is when God's will is known that effective prayer and intercession really begin.

We see this vividly explained in the life of Daniel. In Daniel 9, we read that he found out from the Book of Jeremiah what God's will was for Jerusalem at that time.

> *"In the first year of Darius the son of Ahasuerus, by descent a Mede, who was made king over the realm of the Chaldeans—in the first year of his reign, I, **Daniel, perceived in the books** the number of years that, according to the word of the LORD to Jeremiah the prophet, must pass before the end of the desolations of Jerusalem, namely, seventy years."* (Dan 9:1–2)

Daniel was studying the Scriptures when he discovered that the captivity of Jerusalem would last seventy years. When Daniel read this, it was the first year of the reign of King Darius. Daniel had been deported from Jerusalem to Babylon by Nebuchadnezzar in 605 BCE, and Darius began to reign in 539 BCE. This means that Daniel had, by this time, been in captivity in Babylon for almost seventy years. What does the Bible say that Daniel did with the revelation from the Book of Jeremiah? Did he sit back and say to himself, "This is great! We are soon getting out of here. I need to start packing"?

No! The Bible tells us that Daniel began to pray very earnestly, with fasting in sackcloth and ashes, as if everything depended on him! That is how sincerely he took his responsibility to pray for God's will to be done. In fact, with great intensity, Daniel prayed as if God had said the very opposite, and he had to force God to change His mind.

> **"Then I turned my face to the Lord God, seeking him by prayer and pleas for mercy with fasting and sackcloth and ashes.** I prayed to the LORD my God and made confession, saying, 'O Lord, the great and awesome God, who keeps covenant and steadfast love with those who love him and keep his commandments, we have sinned and done wrong and acted wickedly and rebelled, turning aside from your commandments and rules ...
>
> "'O Lord, hear; O Lord, forgive. O Lord, pay attention and act. Delay not, for your own sake, O my God, because your city and your people are called by your name.'" (Dan 9:3–5,19)

This is how we also need to act regarding true prophetic revelations from the Scriptures! We need to take responsibility for their fulfillment in persevering, intercessory prayer.

Watching and Waiting for the Redemption of Jerusalem

> "The voice of your watchmen—they lift up their voice; together they sing for joy; for **eye to eye they see the return of the LORD to Zion.** Break forth together into singing, you waste places of Jerusalem, for the LORD has comforted his people; he has redeemed Jerusalem. The LORD has bared his holy arm before the eyes of all the nations, and all the ends of the earth shall see the salvation of our God." (Isa 52:8–10)

We are now living in the times of restoration spoken of by the prophets of Israel thousands of years ago. In the midst of pain and conflict, God is continuing to move history forward towards the goal of the Messianic kingdom from Jerusalem, at the return of Messiah. If we step back and look at the larger perspective over the past hundred years, we can see a steady progression of the LORD returning to Zion.

Even though replacement theology is still alive and well in the church today, the rebirth of the State of Israel in 1948 dealt a significant blow to this false doctrine. The reunification of Jerusalem in 1967 was another landmark event that brought redemption closer. During the time of our involvement in active ministry, spanning over close to fifty years now, we have witnessed a significant awakening, both in our own lives and among Christians in general, concerning God's redemptive plans for Israel and Jerusalem. The Spirit is truly at work preparing the Bride for the coming of Messiah!

Being a pastor's son and growing up in church, I remember the first time I listened to Derek Prince teach on Israel, and how it shook the eschatology I had grown up with, to the core. Questions ran around in my head, "Why is he so excited about Israel? We are going to heaven, what do we have to do with Israel? Israel is God's problem, not ours, etc." This experience, over forty years ago, actually led to me to reject all teaching on eschatology for almost five years, because I felt that the subject was too confusing to me. Of all the prophecy teachers I had listened to, no two of them seemed to agree, and I did not know who was right.

Then one day in 1977, God spoke to me to read the Bible for myself and find out what He says in His Word on this subject. One of the first discoveries I made was that God truly has a plan for His kingdom, right here on this planet. Our Master told us to pray, *"Your kingdom come, your will be done, on earth as it is in heaven."* (Mt 6:10) I came to understand that the Father really intends to answer this prayer very literally. His kingdom will be here, on this earth! The devil is not going to win. The Messiah will return and the devil is going to have to get out. Daniel prophesied about this glorious future:

> *"And in the days of those kings* **the God of heaven will set up** **a kingdom that shall never be destroyed,** *nor shall the kingdom be left to another people. It shall break in pieces all these kingdoms and bring them to an end, and it shall stand forever, just as you saw that a stone was cut from a mountain by no human hand, and that it broke in pieces the iron, the bronze, the clay, the silver, and the gold."* (Dan 2:44–45)

And the last book in the Bible contains this glorious proclamation:

> *"Then the seventh angel blew his trumpet, and there were loud voices in heaven, saying, '***The kingdom of the world has become the kingdom of our Lord and of his Messiah,** *and he shall reign forever and ever.'"* (Rev 11:15)

The second thing I discovered was that Israel holds the key to the physical breakthrough of this kingdom on earth. God's throne will be established in Jerusalem, specifically on the Temple Mount,[1] when the Messiah returns in power and great glory[2] and restores the kingdom to Israel.[3] All nations will come to Jerusalem and learn to walk in God's ways.[4] Jerusalem will become the praise of the earth.[5] The Messiah will rule all the nations in righteousness and peace.[6] What a glorious kingdom it will be![7]

However, before this kingdom is established, there will first be a final uproar against God led by the antichrist, or anti-messiah. He will

---

1   Eze 43:1–7.

2   Lk 21:27.

3   Ac 1:6.

4   Isa 2:1–4.

5   Isa 62:6–7.

6   Isa 2:1–4.

7   Isa 11:5–10.

establish a false "messianic" kingdom for a brief period of time, even from Jerusalem, as he takes his seat on the Temple Mount. Violence and lawlessness will abound. Sin will have the upper hand, it seems. Things will go from bad to worse for those who are waiting for the kingdom. But, it is exactly *"in the days of those kings"* ruling with the anti-messiah, that their end will come, and *"the God of heaven will set up a kingdom that shall never be destroyed."* During this difficult time period before the breakthrough of the kingdom of God, our faith will be tested severely. Will Messiah ever come? Peter wrote,

> *"... knowing this first of all, that scoffers will come in the last days with scoffing, following their own sinful desires. They will say, 'Where is the promise of his coming? For ever since the fathers fell asleep, all things are continuing as they were from the beginning of creation.'"* (2 Pe 3:3–4)

Pray and Never Give Up!

It is with this scenario in mind that Jesus told the parable to His disciples about the widow and the unrighteous judge in Luke 18, encouraging us to pray and never give up.

> *"And he told them a parable to the effect that they ought always to pray and not lose heart. He said, 'In a certain city there was a judge who neither feared God nor respected man. And there was a widow in that city who kept coming to him and saying, "Give me justice against my adversary." For a while he refused, but afterward he said to himself, "Though I neither fear God nor respect man, yet because this widow keeps bothering me, I will give her justice, so that she will not beat me down by her continual coming."' And the Lord said, 'Hear what the unrighteous judge says. And **will not God give justice to his elect, who cry to him day and night?***

*, Will he delay long over them? I tell you, he will give justice to them speedily. **Nevertheless, when the Son of Man comes, will he find faith on earth?**"* (Lk 18:1–8)

Of course, this parable teaches us an important principle about prayer in general. But, it is specifically a parable teaching us about praying for the redemption of Jerusalem. Remember what God says in Isaiah, "... **all the day and all the night they** [the watchmen] **shall never be silent ... take no rest, and give him no rest** *until he establishes Jerusalem and makes it a praise in the earth."* (Isa 62:6–7) Jesus is referring to this when He says, *"And will not God give justice to his elect,* **who cry to him day and night?"** (Lk 18:7) The parable is then summed up in the question, *"Nevertheless, when the Son of Man comes, will he find faith on earth?"* (Lk 18:8)

The widow in the parable is a picture of God's elect, longing and praying for justice through the return of Messiah to set up the kingdom of heaven, in fulfillment of all the promises in the Scriptures. He is the One who will establish justice in the earth. *"...a bruised reed he will not break, and a faintly burning wick he will not quench;* **he will faithfully bring forth justice.** *He will not grow faint or be discouraged* **till he has established justice in the earth**; *and the coastlands wait for his law."* (Isa 42:3–4) The widow's plea for justice is a prayer for the coming of Messiah.

Just like the heavenly Jerusalem is a picture of the Bride of Messiah,[8] the widow is a picture of Jerusalem in its present form, desolate and bereaved, waiting for the Redeemer. God says about Jerusalem,

"For your Maker is your husband, the LORD of hosts is his name; and the Holy One of Israel is your Redeemer, the God of the whole earth he is called. **For the LORD has called you**

---

8   Rev 21:9–10.

like a wife deserted and grieved in spirit, like a wife of youth when she is cast off, says your God." (Isa 54:5–6)

We are like the widow asking for justice. *"Give me justice against my adversary."* (Lk 18:3) The adversary is Satan. The devil is a usurper. He does not belong in Jerusalem. Jesus compares the unrighteous judge with whom the widow pleads, to God the Father. *"And the Lord said, 'Hear what the unrighteous judge says. And will not God give justice to his elect, who cry to him day and night? , Will he delay long over them? I tell you, he will give justice to them speedily.'"* (Lk 18:6–8)

Sometimes our faith is tested in prayer and it seems as if God is like an unrighteous judge and He is not fulfilling His promises. This is what it will look like in the end times. It will seem like the adversary will have the upper hand, controlling the situation. The encouragement that Jesus is wanting to give us in this parable is that even if God seems to be an unrighteous judge who is not fulfilling His promises, He will not put us off forever when we call out to Him day and night for the restoration of Jerusalem and the coming of Messiah. If even an unrighteous judge gave the widow her right, how much more will our loving, heavenly Father answer our prayers if we do not give up? Jesus' final sentence in the parable presents the ultimate challenge He wants to convey to us, *"I tell you, he will give justice to them speedily.* **Nevertheless, when the Son of Man comes, will he find faith on earth?"** (Lk 18:8)

What faith is our Master talking about? He is talking about the faith that the widow had, who would not give up, but kept asking the unrighteous judge, day and night, for justice until she received it. It is specifically referring to us praying and interceding, day and night, for the restoration of Jerusalem through the coming of Messiah. Will He find us eagerly waiting and watching for Him when He comes? *"It will be good for those servants whose master finds them watching when he comes. Truly I tell you, he will dress himself to serve, will have them recline at the table and will come and wait on them."* (Lk 12:37 NIV)

Peter said, *"Heaven must receive him until the time comes for God to restore everything, as he promised long ago through his holy prophets."* (Ac 3:21 NIV) Our task is to pray day and night as watchmen on the walls of Jerusalem for this promised restoration that will lead to His return. We need to be like the widow who kept coming to the unjust judge with her demand, *"Give me justice against my adversary."* (Lk 18:3) It is the application of the command in Isaiah, *"You who put the LORD in remembrance, **take no rest, and give him no rest until he establishes Jerusalem and makes it a praise in the earth.**"* (Isa 62:7)

The entire Bible ends with a prayer for Messiah's return: *"The Spirit and the Bride say, 'Come.' And let the one who hears say, 'Come.'...He who testifies to these things says, 'Surely I am coming soon.' **Amen. Come, Lord Jesus!**"* (Rev 22:17,20) When He comes, will the Son of Man find this faith and expectancy in us, expressing itself in a desperate prayer and longing for His return?

Our hearts and our eyes need to be focused on Jerusalem and the coming of Messiah in these last days! We need to fill our minds and our hearts with the words of the prophets and apostles about the coming kingdom, as fuel for fervent prayer and intercession. The Apostle Peter said that the words of the prophets are like a lamp shining in a dark place until the morning star rises in our hearts. *"And we have something more sure, the prophetic word, to which you will do well to pay attention as to a lamp shining in a dark place, until the day dawns and the morning star rises in your hearts."* (2 Pe 1:19 ESV–UK)

The morning star is the planet Venus that can sometimes be seen in the Middle East on the eastern horizon, just before dawn. At times, it is so bright that it can almost be confused with the actual sun. But the morning star heralds the new day, just before the sun rises. The sunrise is a picture of the coming of Messiah. The words of the prophets will give us the needed assurance in our hearts that the new day is near. If He tarries, we must not give up. We must be watching and waiting, praying for the restoration of Jerusalem, eagerly longing for Him.

*"The voice of your watchmen—they lift up their voice; together they sing for joy; for **eye to eye they see the return of the LORD to Zion**. Break forth together into singing, you waste places of Jerusalem, for the LORD has comforted his people; he has redeemed Jerusalem. **The LORD has bared his holy arm before the eyes of all the nations**, and all **the ends of the earth shall see the salvation of our God**."* (Isa 52:8–10)

"I wait for the LORD, my soul waits, and in his word I hope; my soul waits for the Lord more than watchmen for the morning, more than watchmen for the morning." (Ps 130:5–6)

Two Problems

There are two major problems that must be dealt with in our prayers concerning the breakthrough of the kingdom of God in the earth. The first problem is that many Christians are still lost concerning our future hope and destiny. They do not know what Jesus will do when He returns. He is not coming to take us away from here. He is coming to establish His kingdom here. The rapture is our transformation to be like Him, when He takes us up to meet Him, when He comes.

Jesus promised, *"And **this gospel of the kingdom** will be proclaimed throughout the whole world as a testimony to all nations, and then the end will come."* (Mt 24:14) The gospel of the kingdom is more than just the gospel of the forgiveness of sins. It is the good news about the coming kingdom of Messiah out of Jerusalem! We must pray that the eyes of Christians will be opened through the proclamation of the gospel of the kingdom. Many Christians are ignorant about the coming kingdom, and therefore they have no heart and no motivation to pray like Anna did, day and night, for the redemption of Jerusalem.

The second problem is that, just as lost as Christians are concerning our future hope and the mission of the Messiah, the Jewish people do not know who their Messiah is. They cannot see Him in Jesus of Nazareth. Part of this problem is a divine, partial (not complete!) hardening of their hearts, just as Paul wrote, *"Lest you be wise in your own sight, I do not want you to be unaware of this mystery, brothers: a **partial** hardening has come upon Israel, until the fullness of the Gentiles has come in."* (Ro 11:25)

Another part of this problem is that for centuries the church has largely presented a false, unscriptural picture of the Messiah, that the Jewish people cannot reconcile with the promised Messiah in their Scriptures. The church has, in a sense, hijacked the Messiah from the Jewish people and dressed Him up as a Gentile Jew–hater. This is a very serious problem that must be dealt with in prayer.

Daniel: Our Example

In Babylon, God raised up an intercessor and watchman on the walls of Jerusalem—Daniel. We read in Daniel 6 about his faithfulness to pray for Jerusalem, even in the face of death.

> *"All the high officials of the kingdom, the prefects and the satraps, the counselors and the governors are agreed that the king should establish an ordinance and enforce an injunction, that whoever makes petition to any god or man for thirty days, except to you, O king, shall be cast into the den of lions. Now, O king, establish the injunction and sign the document, so that it cannot be changed, according to the law of the Medes and the Persians, which cannot be revoked.'*
> *Therefore King Darius signed the document and injunction. When Daniel knew that the document had been signed, he went to his house where he had windows in his upper chamber open toward Jerusalem. He got down on his knees three*

times a day and prayed and gave thanks before his God, as he had done previously." (Dan 6:7–10)

Daniel's faithful ministry of prayer caused him to end up in the lions' den. But God honored his faithfulness and delivered him from death.

> *"Then, at break of day, the king arose and went in haste to the den of lions. As he came near to the den where Daniel was, he cried out in a tone of anguish. The king declared to Daniel, "O Daniel, servant of the living God, has **your God, whom you serve continually**, been able to deliver you from the lions?" Then Daniel said to the king, "O king, live forever! My God sent his angel and shut the lions' mouths, and they have not harmed me, because I was found blameless before him; and also before you, O king, I have done no harm."* (6:19–22)

Daniel truly is an example for all of us in praying continually for the restoration and peace of Jerusalem. The story of the lion's den coincides with the first year of the reign of Darius, when Daniel received his revelation that the desolation of Jerusalem would last seventy years, which encouraged him to pray for Jerusalem to the point that he did not even care if he was thrown to the lions.[9] He had the same dedication as Paul: *"I do not account my life of any value nor as precious to myself, if only I may finish my course and the ministry that I received from the Lord Jesus."* (Ac 20:24)

Once God's will is revealed, then powerful prayer can begin, as Jesus taught us, *"Pray then like this: 'Our Father in heaven, hallowed be*

---

9   The events of both Daniel 6 and 9 occurred during the first year of Darius' reign. It is also a possibility that Daniel received his revelation regarding the 70 years after the lion's den, as a reward for his faithfulness to prayer, even in the face of death.

your name. Your kingdom come, your will be done, on earth as it is in heaven." (Matt 6:9–10) This is why I have written this book about God's plans for Jerusalem. God is looking for people in our time who, like Daniel, will agree with His will in prayer until His will is done.

Daniel fasted and prayed, confessing before God his own, as well as his people's sins, crying out with all his might,

> *"O Lord, according to all your righteous acts, let your anger and your wrath turn away from your city Jerusalem, your holy hill, because for our sins, and for the iniquities of our fathers, Jerusalem and your people have become a byword among all who are around us. Now therefore, O our God, listen to the prayer of your servant and to his pleas for mercy, and for your own sake, O Lord, make your face to shine upon your sanctuary, which is desolate. O my God, incline your ear and hear. Open your eyes and see our desolations, and the city that is called by your name. For we do not present our pleas before you because of our righteousness, but because of your great mercy. O Lord, hear; O Lord, forgive. O Lord, pay attention and act. Delay not, for your own sake, O my God, because your city and your people are called by your name."* (Dan 9:16–19)

As a result of his prayer and fasting, an angel from heaven visited Daniel, revealing more of God's will for Jerusalem to him.

> *"While I was speaking and praying, confessing my sin and the sin of my people Israel, and presenting my plea before the LORD my God for the holy hill of my God, while I was speaking in prayer, the man Gabriel, whom I had seen in the vision at the first, came to me in swift flight at the time of the evening sacrifice. He made me understand, speaking with me and saying, 'O Daniel, I have now come out to give you insight and understanding. At the beginning of your*

pleas for mercy a word went out, and I have come to tell it to you, for you are greatly loved. Therefore consider the word and understand the vision.'" (9:20–23)

The vision had to do with the future and even God's end time purposes for Jerusalem. We are still waiting for the vision's complete fulfillment, and we have to pray just like Daniel did, continually, faithfully, even in the midst of much opposition, for Jerusalem—God's "holy hill." The prophecies of Isaiah, Jeremiah, Ezekiel, Daniel, and Zechariah are still waiting for their complete fulfillment.

But some might say, "Were they not all fulfilled when Jesus died and rose again? Or, when he ascended to heaven? Or, when he poured out the Holy Spirit? Have not all the promises of God found their 'Yes' in Christ?" Yes, but not all of them were fulfilled when He came the first time. Listen to what Peter said about Jesus:

"He must remain in heaven until the time comes for God to restore everything, as he promised long ago through his holy prophets." (Ac 3:21 NIV)

Here, we see it clearly! Many of the promises of the prophets are still waiting for their fulfillment. Jerusalem has not yet become a praise in the earth where the nations assemble to learn God's ways. We must pray today, like Daniel and others have done in past centuries as watchmen on the walls of Jerusalem, until this happens. We need to fast and weep like Nehemiah, over the desolation of Jerusalem. The prophetess Anna spent decades fasting and praying, day and night in the Temple, for the consolation of Jerusalem.

Jesus said, *"Jerusalem will be trampled underfoot by the Gentiles, until the times of the Gentiles are fulfilled."* (Lk 21:24) We are getting very near that time, and the ultimate battle lines are being drawn in the final climax between heaven and hell. Satan will make one last attempt to take God's place. It is written about Lucifer, *"You said in your heart, 'I will ascend to heaven; above the stars of God I will set my throne on high; I will sit on* **the mount of assembly in the far reaches of the north.***"* (Isa 14:13)

This is talking about the Temple Mount, which is *"in the far reaches of the north"* of biblical Jerusalem. It is Zion, God's holy hill where Jesus, the Messiah will reign. *"... beautiful in elevation, is the joy of all the earth, Mount Zion,* **in the far north,** *the city of the great King."* (Ps 48:2)

Watchmen On the Walls

We are now living in the sixth millennium, or the sixth day, from the creation of Adam, waiting for the seventh day, the Great Sabbath, that will begin when Jerusalem becomes the praise of the earth.

The biblical calendar and the feasts of the LORD, listed in Leviticus 23, provide a clear, prophetic outline of God's entire plan of redemption.

The month of Elul, which is the sixth month on God's calendar, is the month of preparation for the High Holy Days and the final feasts of the LORD, which all occur in the seventh month. Prophetically, we are now living in the sixth month on the biblical calendar, waiting for the final fall feasts to begin. No doubt, this is an intense season of watching and praying on the walls of Jerusalem.

The Feasts of Passover and Pentecost were both fulfilled when Jesus came the first time. We are now waiting for the next feast on God's calendar to be fulfilled, which is the Feast of Trumpets. It is the only feast that occurs on the new moon. In biblical days, it meant that even though people knew the approximate time, the exact day came without prior warning. The watchmen on the walls of Jerusalem were watching intently for the sign of the new moon to appear. The same day that it appeared, the feast began.

The sixth month is, therefore, a time of preparation. Every morning during this month, the shofar is blown in the synagogue, to wake people up in preparation for the final feasts. When the Feast of Trumpets, the first day of the seventh month, finally arrives, the last crescendo of shofar blasts resound throughout the entire day. How prophetic this is for the times that we live in, as we wait for the last shofar, the last trumpet, to sound from heaven!

> *"Behold! I tell you a mystery. We shall not all sleep, but we shall all be changed, in a moment, in the twinkling of an eye,* **at the last trumpet.** *For the trumpet will sound, and the dead will be raised imperishable, and we shall be changed."* (1 Cor 15:51–52)

> *"For the Lord himself will descend from heaven with a cry of command, with the voice of an archangel, and* **with the sound of the trumpet of God.** *And the dead in Messiah will rise first. Then we who are alive, who are left, will be caught up together with them in the clouds to meet the Lord in the air, and so we will always be with the Lord."* (1 Th 4:16–17)

We always need to prepare ourselves for *"the appearing of the glory of our great God and Savior Jesus the Messiah."* (Tit 2:13) Yet, we believe that the month of Elul is a special time on God's calendar for prophetic preparation and watchfulness in prayer! It is no coincidence that the Second Intifada broke out during the last week of Elul in 2000, or that the Twin Towers fell during this same week a year later, or that the Oslo Accords were signed in 1993, during the same week on the biblical calendar. This is a special time to watch and pray on the walls of Jerusalem.

Prophetically speaking, it is "in the last week of Elul," that the antichrist will take his seat in the Temple of God, proclaiming himself to be God. He will then be destroyed by the Messiah, through the splendor of His appearing on the Feast of Trumpets.

> *"Let no one deceive you in any way. For that day will not come, unless the rebellion comes first, and the man of lawlessness is revealed, the son of destruction, who opposes and*

exalts himself against every so–called god or object of wor-
ship, so that he takes his seat in the Temple of God, proclaim-
ing himself to be God ...

"And then the lawless one will be revealed, whom the Lord
Jesus will kill with the breath of his mouth and bring to
nothing by the appearance of his coming. The coming of the
lawless one is by the activity of Satan with all power and
false signs and wonders, and with all wicked deception for
those who are perishing, because they refused to love the
truth and so be saved. Therefore God sends them a strong
delusion, so that they may believe what is false." (2 Th 2:3–4,
8–11)

In John 1:49, Nathanael declared, *"Rabbi, you are the Son of God!*
You are the King of Israel!" Jesus is here declared to be three things: (1)
Rabbi, (2) Son of God, and (3) King of Israel. Are we ready to meet
Him?

Most Christians know Him as Son of God, but He is also the Jewish
rabbi, or Torah teacher, who will teach God's Torah to the nations
when He comes. *"many peoples shall come, and say: 'Come, let us go*
up to the mountain of the LORD, to the house of the God of Jacob, that
he may teach us his ways and that we may walk in his paths.' For out
of Zion shall go the law [Torah]*, and the word of the LORD from Jeru-*
salem." (Isa 2:3) Jesus is not only the Son of God, but He is also the
King of Israel, who will restore the kingdom to His nation. *"He shall*
judge between the nations, and shall decide disputes for many peoples;
and they shall beat their swords into plowshares." (Isa 2:4) He will take
His seat on the throne of David in Jerusalem, and judge the nations by
how they have treated His people Israel. How can we say that we love
Him if we care nothing for Israel? It is impossible!

Praying Together In Unity

> *"Again I say to you, if two of you agree on earth about any-*
> *thing they ask, it will be done for them by my Father in heav-*
> *en. For where two or three are gathered in my name, there*
> *am I among them."* (Mt 18:19–20)

James wrote in his epistle, *"The prayer of a righteous person has great power as it is working. Elijah was a man with a nature like ours, and he prayed fervently that it might not rain, and for three years and six months it did not rain on the earth. Then he prayed again, and heaven gave rain, and the earth bore its fruit."* (Jas 5:16–18)

Elijah is an outstanding example of what the prayers of just one righteous man can accomplish. Yet there is even more power available when we come together in unity, to pray. Watchman Nee compared the effectiveness of one person's prayers versus praying together in a group to the water that can be contained on a piece of flat glass, compared to the amount of water that a glass of water can hold. Jesus said,

> *"Truly, I say to you, whatever you bind on earth shall be*
> *bound in heaven, and whatever you loose on earth shall be*
> *loosed in heaven. Again I say to you, if two of you agree on*
> *earth about anything they ask, it will be done for them by*
> *my Father in heaven. For where two or three are gathered in*
> *my name, there am I among them."* (Mt 18:18–20)

Notice that this power is dependent on the amount of agreement or harmony that there is in the meeting, *"**if two of you agree** on earth about anything they ask, it will be done for them."* Jesus did not say, "If two or three hundred of you agree." He said, *"if two of you agree on earth about anything they ask, it will be done for them by my Father in heaven."* A small group that is united can accomplish a whole lot more in prayer than a large group that is divided. Try to find at least someone of like mind to pray with, in order to form a "prayer cell" that can come together regularly, to pray for Israel and Jerusalem.

The power of corporate prayer is based on the testimony of two or more witnesses. Let us read the entire context:

> *"If your brother sins against you, go and tell him his fault, between you and him alone. If he listens to you, you have gained your brother. But if he does not listen, take one or two others along with you,* **that every charge may be established by the evidence of two or three witnesses.** *If he refuses to listen to them, tell it to the church. And if he refuses to listen even to the church, let him be to you as a Gentile and a tax collector. Truly, I say to you, whatever you bind on earth shall be bound in heaven, and whatever you loose on earth shall be loosed in heaven. Again I say to you, if two of you agree on earth about anything they ask, it will be done for them by my Father in heaven. For where two or three are gathered in my name, there am I among them."* (Mt 18:15–20)

What is a witness? A witness is someone who can testify in court to what he has seen or heard. When two or more can testify what they have seen or heard from God, regarding a subject they pray for, true unity in prayer can be established based on these testimonies.

Paul wrote, *"For we know in part and we prophesy in part."* (1 Co 13:9) And, *"Let two or three prophets speak, and let the others weigh what is said ... For you can all prophesy one by one, so that all may learn and all be encouraged."* (1 Co 14:29,31)

Powerful, corporate, prophetic intercession in unity can be likened to laying a jigsaw puzzle. Each witness' testimony of what he or she has seen or heard from God represents one piece of the puzzle. Someone might have received a Scripture, another has seen a vision, a third person might have received a prophetic word, or a word of knowledge. When we put the pieces together, a picture emerges of how God wants us to pray and we can pray in true unity.

This prophetic intercession is what is needed in the nations now for Israel, and we encourage all of you to be a part of this movement of prayer cells. Learning how to pray together effectively takes commitment, practice, patience, and endurance. It is not always easy, but it is very powerful. When we have this kind of unity in prayer, through prophetic revelation, Jesus said, *"Truly, I say to you, whatever you bind on earth shall be bound in heaven, and whatever you loose on earth shall be loosed in heaven. Again I say to you, if two of you agree on earth about anything they ask, it will be done for them by my Father in heaven."* (Mt 18:18–19)

During World War II, Rees Howells devoted his entire Bible school in Wales to this kind of prophetic intercession until Hitler was defeated and the State of Israel had been established. He called the birth of the State of Israel in 1948 the greatest victory for the Holy Spirit in the past 2,000 years.[10]

Nehemiah and Ezra: Our Examples

While Daniel prayed for the return of the Jewish people from Babylon, Nehemiah fasted and prayed for Jerusalem after they had begun to return from the exile. Nehemiah cared deeply for the welfare of Jerusalem, just as we ought to do. The famous verse "Pray for the peace of Jerusalem!" could also be translated, "Inquire about the welfare of Jerusalem!"

> *"And I asked them concerning the Jews who escaped, who had survived the exile, and concerning Jerusalem. And they said to me, 'The remnant there in the province who had survived the exile is in great trouble and shame. The wall of Je-*

---

10 See Norman Grubb, *Rees Howells: Intercessor* (CLC Publications, 1988).

rusalem is broken down, and its gates are destroyed by fire.'"
(Neh 1:2–3)

The present state of Israel and Jerusalem is much the same. The people who have returned are in great trouble and disgrace today. We need to pray for Jerusalem like Nehemiah. *"As soon as I heard these words I sat down and wept and mourned for days, and I continued fasting and praying before the God of heaven."* (1:4)

Even though the people had come back from Babylon, they were in great distress, just like the people of Israel are today, under the yoke of the nations. *"Behold, we are slaves this day; in the land that you gave to our fathers to enjoy its fruit and its good gifts, behold, we are slaves. And its rich yield goes to the kings whom you have set over us because of our sins. They rule over our bodies and over our livestock as they please, and we are in great distress."* (Neh 9:36–37)

Later on, we read how Ezra prayed after he received news about the sins of the people who had returned. He gathered people *"who trembled at the words of the God of Israel."* (Ezr 9:4) This we also must do. Here is the record of Ezra's prayers:

> *"As soon as I heard this, I tore my garment and my cloak and pulled hair from my head and beard and sat appalled. Then all who trembled at the words of the God of Israel, because of the faithlessness of the returned exiles, gathered around me while I sat appalled until the evening sacrifice. And at the evening sacrifice I rose from my fasting, with my garment and my cloak torn, and fell upon my knees and spread out my hands to the LORD my God, saying:*

> *"'O my God, I am ashamed and blush to lift my face to you, my God, for our iniquities have risen higher than our heads, and our guilt has mounted up to the heavens. From the days of our fathers to this day we have been in great guilt. And for our iniquities we, our kings, and our priests have been*

given into the hand of the kings of the lands, to the sword, to captivity, to plundering, and to utter shame, as it is today. But now for a brief moment favor has been shown by the LORD our God, to leave us a remnant and to give us a secure hold within his holy place, that our God may brighten our eyes and grant us a little reviving in our slavery. For we are slaves. Yet our God has not forsaken us in our slavery, but has extended to us his steadfast love before the kings of Persia, to grant us some reviving to set up the house of our God, to repair its ruins, and to give us protection in Judea and Jerusalem.

"'And now, O our God, what shall we say after this? For we have forsaken your commandments, which you commanded by your servants the prophets, saying, 'The land that you are entering, to take possession of it, is a land impure with the impurity of the peoples of the lands, with their abominations that have filled it from end to end with their uncleanness. Therefore do not give your daughters to their sons, neither take their daughters for your sons, and never seek their peace or prosperity, that you may be strong and eat the good of the land and leave it for an inheritance to your children forever.' And after all that has come upon us for our evil deeds and for our great guilt, seeing that you, our God, have punished us less than our iniquities deserved and have given us such a remnant as this, shall we break your commandments again and intermarry with the peoples who practice these abominations? Would you not be angry with us until you consumed us, so that there should be no remnant, nor any to escape? O LORD the God of Israel, you are just, for we are left a remnant that has escaped, as it is today. Behold, we are before you in our guilt, for none can stand before you because of this.'" (Ezr 9:3–15)

The situation is much like this even today in Israel. The people have begun to return, just like Ezra prayed, *"But now for a brief moment favor has been shown by the LORD our God, to leave us a remnant and to give us a secure hold within his holy place, that our God may brighten our eyes and grant us a little reviving in our slavery."* (9:8) But the people have not yet turned to God with their whole hearts to seek Him. This is why we must pray until God fulfills His promises in Ezekiel:

> *"I will take you from the nations and gather you from all the countries and bring you into your own land. I will sprinkle clean water on you, and you shall be clean from all your uncleannesses, and from all your idols I will cleanse you. And I will give you a new heart, and a new spirit I will put within you. And I will remove the heart of stone from your flesh and give you a heart of flesh. And I will put my Spirit within you, and cause you to walk in my statutes and be careful to obey my rules. You shall dwell in the land that I gave to your fathers, and you shall be my people, and I will be your God."* (Eze 36:24–28)

Israel Has a Right to All of Palestine

Today, the nations want to deprive the Jewish people of their rightful inheritance on the mountains of Israel. God Almighty has given the Land of Israel to the Jewish people as an eternal inheritance. On a political level, this right was granted to the Jewish people in the Balfour Declaration, which was made into international law by the League of Nations in 1922, and then assumed by the United Nations in 1945 under article 80.[11] The Jewish people therefore have a legal

---

11   For a good overview, see the mini–documentary, *Give Peace a Chance*, (European Coalition For Israel, 2011), youtu.be/oVsjNzXojCM.

right, under international law, to settle in the so-called "West Bank," which is rightfully called Judea and Samaria, and where 80% of the mountains of Israel are located. Because of the greed for oil and rejection of Judeo-Christian values, the nations today are selling out Israel to their enemies by wanting to establish an Islamic, Palestinian state on the mountains of Israel, including in biblical Jerusalem.

In fact, already in the 1960s, the world's foremost superpower, the United States of America, promised Yasser Arafat a Palestinian state on the mountains of Israel, on the condition that Arafat would not target the United States with terror. Today, therefore, the UN and the international community wrongfully claim that Israel is occupying Judea and Samaria, and that the Jewish settlements there are illegal. This is a lie!

We can, however, take heart and remember that the situation was exactly the same during the time of Ezra. The Book of Ezra begins:

> *"In the first year of Cyrus king of Persia, that the word of the LORD by the mouth of Jeremiah might be fulfilled, the LORD stirred up the spirit of Cyrus king of Persia, so that he made a proclamation throughout all his kingdom and also put it in writing: 'Thus says Cyrus king of Persia: The LORD, the God of heaven, has given me all the kingdoms of the earth, and he has charged me to build him a house at Jerusalem, which is in Judah. Whoever is among you of all his people, may his God be with him, and let him go up to Jerusalem, which is in Judah, and rebuild the house of the LORD, the God of Israel—he is the God who is in Jerusalem. And let each survivor, in whatever place he sojourns, be assisted by the men of his place with silver and gold, with goods and with beasts, besides freewill offerings for the house of God that is in Jerusalem.'"* (Ezr 1:1–4)

This corresponds in our day to the unanimous decision by the League of Nations in July 1922, to recognize the Jewish people's historic right to restore their homeland in all of Palestine, a decision that also mandated Great Britain to supervise, and help make this right a reality.

We read in the Book of Ezra how the Jews—because of Cyrus' decree—returned to Judah and began to rebuild the Temple, beginning with the altar. But then the enemies of the Jewish people began to cause trouble. Eventually, they sent a letter to the Persian King Artexerxes with accusations against the Jews:

> *"... be it known to the king that the Jews who came up from you to us have gone to Jerusalem. They are rebuilding that rebellious and wicked city. They are finishing the walls and repairing the foundations. Now be it known to the king that if this city is rebuilt and the walls finished, they will not pay tribute, custom, or toll, and the royal revenue will be impaired."* (Ezr 4:12–13)

Because of the letter, the king of Persia ordered that all work to rebuild the city should be stopped.

> *"Therefore make a decree that these men be made to cease, and that this city be not rebuilt, until a decree is made by me. And take care not to be slack in this matter. Why should damage grow to the hurt of the king?' Then, when the copy of King Artaxerxes' letter was read before Rehum and Shimshai the scribe and their associates, they went in haste to the Jews at Jerusalem and by force and power made them cease. Then the work on the house of God that is in Jerusalem stopped, and it ceased until the second year of the reign of Darius king of Persia."* (4:21–24)

Then the prophets Haggai and Zechariah encouraged the leaders of Judah to continue building on the Temple anyway. Because of their prophetic words, the work on the Temple that had stopped eventually continued. When the enemies complained to the leaders of Judah and told them that they were not allowed to rebuild the Temple, the Jews referred to the first decree by Cyrus, that they were actually allowed to rebuild the Temple. A search was then made in the archives in Persia, where they indeed found Cyrus' decree. This caused King Darius to issue a new decree:

> *"In the first year of Cyrus the king, Cyrus the king issued a decree: Concerning the house of God at Jerusalem, let the house be rebuilt, the place where sacrifices were offered, and let its foundations be retained. Its height shall be sixty cubits and its breadth sixty cubits ... Now therefore, Tattenai, governor of the province Beyond the River, Shethar-bozenai, and your associates the governors who are in the province Beyond the River, keep away. Let the work on this house of God alone. Let the governor of the Jews and the elders of the Jews rebuild this house of God on its site ... May the God who has caused his name to dwell there overthrow any king or people who shall put out a hand to alter this, or to destroy this house of God that is in Jerusalem. I Darius make a decree; let it be done with all diligence."* (Ezr 6:3; 6:6–7,12)

Ezra continued to record what happened:

> *"And the elders of the Jews built and prospered through the prophesying of Haggai the prophet and Zechariah the son of Iddo. They finished their building by decree of the God of Israel and by decree of Cyrus and Darius and Artaxerxes king of Persia; and this house was finished on the third day of the month of Adar, in the sixth year of the reign of Darius the king."* (6:14–15)

Today, through faithful, prophetic intercession, we need to reverse the illegal decree to establish a Palestinian state on the mountains of Israel. We need to pray that just like it happened in the time of Ezra, the leaders of Israel will begin to refer to the League of Nations decision in 1922, a decision that was confirmed by the United Nations in 1945, that the Jewish people have the right to live in Judea and Samaria, and also establish the Jewish state there.

Simeon and Anna

When the time finally came for God to send the Messiah, we find two faithful intercessors in Jerusalem preparing the way. God had promised to send the people salvation and deliverance from their sins. And so we read in Luke 2 about the righteous Simeon and the prophetess Anna fasting and praying for the "consolation of Israel" and the "redemption of Jerusalem."

> *"Now there was a man in Jerusalem, whose name was Simeon, and this man was righteous and devout, waiting for the consolation of Israel, and the Holy Spirit was upon him. And it had been revealed to him by the Holy Spirit that he would not see death before he had seen the Lord's Messiah ...*

> *"And there was a prophetess, Anna, the daughter of Phanuel, of the tribe of Asher. She was advanced in years, having lived with her husband seven years from when she was a virgin, and then as a widow until she was eighty–four. She did not depart from the Temple, worshiping with fasting and prayer night and day. And coming up at that very hour **she began to give thanks to God and to speak of him to all who were waiting for the redemption of Jerusalem.***" (Lk 2:25–26, 36–38)

This is now where we are, once again. We need to speak about the Messiah to all who are looking for the redemption of Jerusalem, but also fast and pray for His speedy return to comfort Jerusalem. We need to prepare the way for Him, as watchmen on the walls of Jerusalem, praying for the outpouring of the spirit of grace and supplication until Jerusalem will cry out, "Blessed is He who comes in the name of the Lord! We bless you from the house of the Lord!"

> *"And I will pour out on the house of David and the inhabitants of Jerusalem a spirit of grace and pleas for mercy, so that, when they look on me, on him whom they have pierced, they shall mourn for him, as one mourns for an only child, and weep bitterly over him, as one weeps over a firstborn."* (Zec 12:10)

Jesus the Messiah is the only consolation of Israel and redemption for Jerusalem. Let's prepare the way for Him as watchmen on the walls of Jerusalem, like Daniel, Nehemiah, Ezra, Simeon, Anna, John the Baptist, and others before us. Psalm 137 says,

> *"If I forget you, O Jerusalem, let my right hand forget its skill! Let my tongue stick to the roof of my mouth, if I do not remember you, if I do not set Jerusalem above my highest joy!"* (Ps 137:5–6)

> *"Restore our fortunes, O LORD, like streams in the Negeb! Those who sow in tears shall reap with shouts of joy! He who goes out weeping, bearing the seed for sowing, shall come home with shouts of joy, bringing his sheaves with him."* (Ps 126:4–6)

If we sow our prayers in tears, we will one day reap with shouts of joy!

"'Shall I bring to the point of birth and not cause to bring forth?' says the LORD; 'shall I, who cause to bring forth, shut the womb?' says your God. 'Rejoice with Jerusalem, and be glad for her, all you who love her; rejoice with her in joy, all you who mourn over her; that you may nurse and be satisfied from her consoling breast; that you may drink deeply with delight from her glorious abundance.' For thus says the LORD: 'Behold, I will extend peace to her like a river, and the glory of the nations like an overflowing stream; and you shall nurse, you shall be carried upon her hip, and bounced upon her knees. As one whom his mother comforts, so I will comfort you; you shall be comforted in Jerusalem. You shall see, and your heart shall rejoice; your bones shall flourish like the grass; and the hand of the LORD shall be known to his servants, and he shall show his indignation against his enemies." (Isa 66:9–14)

10

GOD'S HOLY MOUNTAIN

"Then David said, 'Here shall be the house of the LORD God
and here the altar of burnt offering for Israel.'"
—*1 Chronicles 22:1*

I t is quite common for Christian ministers to speak with enthusiasm about the Tabernacle in the wilderness, and to use its furnishings as illustrations of important spiritual truths. This is indeed praiseworthy. It is a powerful testimony of God's eternal truths and His unchanging ways.

The Holy Temples that stood on Mount Moriah have, however, generally been treated with less admiration by Christian ministers. And the fact that God will once again have a Holy Temple in this place—as explained in detail in, for instance, the Book of Ezekiel—is at best met with silence.

The early church condemned Marcion in Rome as a heretic for preaching that the God of the Old Testament was different from the God of the New Testament. But his ideas have unfortunately remained in much of Christian thinking. Not so long ago, a well-known prosperity preacher said in a conference, "Giving will change your life. Look what happened to God after He gave His only begotten Son!" In the Old Testament, God was hard and judgmental. In the New, He is kind and loving. That is sort of an unspoken understanding among many Christians. This false theology brings with it devastating consequences. The Scriptures are clear that God never changes. He has never changed, and He will never change. He is eternally the same.

Many Christians are aware that Moses ordered the Tabernacle to be built according to the vision of the heavenly Tabernacle that he saw on Mount Sinai, as it says in the Book of Hebrews, *"For when Moses was about to erect the tent, he was instructed by God, saying, 'See that you make everything according to the pattern that was shown you on the mountain.'"* (Heb 8:5) However, when it comes to the Holy Temple, fewer Christians are aware of the fact that it was also built in obedience to precise instructions of the Holy Spirit, given to David.

> *"Then David gave his son Solomon the plans for the portico of the Temple, its buildings, its storerooms, its upper parts, its inner rooms and the place of atonement. **He gave him the plans of all that the Spirit had put in his mind for the courts of the Temple of the Lord** and all the surrounding rooms, for the treasuries of the Temple of God and for the treasuries for the dedicated things. He gave him instructions for the divisions of the priests and Levites, and for all the work of serving in the Temple of the Lord, as well as for all the articles to be used in its service ...*
>
> *He also gave him the plan for the chariot, that is, the cherubim of gold that spread their wings and overshadow the ark of the covenant of the Lord. '**All this,' David said, 'I have in writing as a result of the Lord's hand on me**, and he enabled me to understand all the details of the plan.'"* (1 Ch 28:11–13,18–19 NIV)

Paul wrote, *"... he raised up David to be their king, of whom he testified and said, 'I have found in David the son of Jesse a man after my heart, who will do all my will.'"* (Ac 13:22) God instructed King David exactly how the Temple should be built. David was a prophet, *"the sweet psalmist of Israel"* (2 Sa 23:1), and the Holy Spirit also revealed to him how the worship service in the Temple was to be organized. He wrote most of the Psalms that were used in the different services in the Temple. Finally, he also divided the priests and Levites into divisions, appointing some of the Levites as singers and others to play on different kinds of instruments. And most importantly, God crowned the completion of the Temple by manifesting His presence there. The Book of Second Chronicles details what happened when King Solomon dedicated the First Temple.

> *"And now arise, O LORD God, and go to your resting place, you and the ark of your might. Let your priests, O LORD God, be clothed with salvation, and let your saints rejoice in your goodness. O LORD God, do not turn away the face of your anointed one! Remember your steadfast love for David your servant.' As soon as Solomon finished his prayer, **fire came down from heaven and consumed the burnt offering and the sacrifices, and the glory of the LORD filled the Temple**. And the priests could not enter the house of the LORD, because the glory of the LORD filled the LORD's house. When all the people of Israel saw the fire come down and the glory of the LORD on the Temple, they bowed down with their faces to the ground on the pavement and worshiped and gave thanks to the LORD, saying, 'For he is good, for his steadfast love endures forever.'"* (2 Ch 6:41–7:3)

The fire fell from heaven and God filled the Temple with His glory. Just like it happened with the Tabernacle in the wilderness, the priests could not enter the house of the LORD, because His glory filled the Temple. And God said, *"I have chosen and consecrated this house that my name may be there forever. My eyes and my heart will be there for all time."* (2 Ch 7:16) Ever since that moment, the Temple Mount has unquestionably been the most holy place on earth for the Jewish people, as it also truly is, not only for Jews, but for all mankind. It is the place where God chose to put His holy name forever.

The Babylonians destroyed the First Temple primarily because idolatry had crept in among God's people. After seventy years, a Second Temple was rebuilt in the same place. Eventually, King Herod greatly beautified this Temple, which existed in the time of Jesus, who called it *"my Father's house."* (Lk 2:49, Jn 2:16)

In the year 70, Rome destroyed the Second Holy Temple. The rabbis say that the reason for this judgment from heaven was *sinat chinam*, which means "baseless hatred" among brothers. This certainly was true about Messiah, who was sentenced to death by his kinsmen. Jesus said, *"But the word that is written in their Law must be fulfilled: 'They hated me without a cause.'"* (Jn 15:25) According to the church father Origin, Josephus wrote that when Jacob the brother of Jesus was killed, the cup of iniquity was full, and the judgment was inevitable.[1]

The Second Temple is where the Holy Spirit fell on the disciples, on the day of Pentecost. It became the home and center of the apostolic church, which came together every day in the Temple. This is where they worshiped God while the priests offered animal sacrifices on the altar. No church since has ever been able to rival their spiritual power.

> *"Now many signs and wonders were regularly done among the people by the hands of the apostles. And they were all together in Solomon's Portico. None of the rest dared join them, but the people held them in high esteem. And more than ever believers were added to the Lord, multitudes of both men and women, so that they even carried out the sick into the streets and laid them on cots and mats, that as Peter came by at least his shadow might fall on some of them. The people also gathered from the towns around Jerusalem,*

---

1   *Origen and Josephus*, Wataru Mizugaki, in Louis H. Feldman, Gohei Hata (editors), *Josephus, Judaism and Christianity* (Wayne State University Press, 1987), p. 329.

bringing the sick and those afflicted with unclean spirits, and they were all healed." (Ac 5:12–16)

Less than 30 years later, Jacob told Paul when he came to Jerusalem, *"You see, brother, how many thousands there are among the Jews of those who have believed."* (Ac 21:20) The Greek word *myriads* that is used in this verse literally means "tens of thousands." It is estimated that the population of Jerusalem at this time was between 60,000–100,000.[2] This means that between one half and one third of the population in Jerusalem had come to faith in Jesus as their Messiah at this time.

When Rome destroyed the Temple ten years later, the believers in Jerusalem were scattered. Within one generation, a large part of the Roman world had heard the gospel, and it has continued to spread all over the world. For this, we are forever grateful. But we have yet to see the same glory that we read about the apostolic church that worshiped in the Temple in Jerusalem.

The Temple Mount Over the Past 2,000 Years

After the Second Holy Temple was destroyed in 70 CE, the Jewish people did not abandon the Temple Mount.[3] They continued to visit the site, and historical sources say that Jews even continued to offer sacrifices there on a temporary altar.[4] Very soon, all Jews everywhere

---

2   The Israel Museum places the estimate between 50,000–80,000. "Second Temple Model" (© The Israel Museum, Jerusalem, 1995–2014), http://goo.gl/57zdQK.

3   This section draws from F.M. Loewenberg's article "Did Jews Abandon the Temple Mount?" (*Middle East Quarterly: Summer 2013*), pp. 37–48, http://goo.gl/FQr1IJ.

4   m.*Eduyot* 8.6; Maimonides, *Hilkhot Bet Ha–bechira* 6.15; *Ha'emek Davar* commentary on Leviticus 26:31.

began to pray three times a day for the rebuilding of the Temple, a custom that has continued among the Jewish people, to this day.

Already in the second century, the Roman Emperor Hadrian originally granted permission for the Jewish people to rebuild the Holy Temple, but he went back on his word. After a second Jewish revolt against Rome, led by Bar Kochba, during which time the Jewish people again attempted to rebuild the Temple, Hadrian forbade Jews to even visit Jerusalem.

These strict laws were soon relaxed, and the Jews once again began to pray on the Temple Mount. The Christian Byzantine Empire, however, made it harder for the Jews, and Constantine restricted Jewish prayer on the Temple Mount to one time a year only: on the ninth of Av, the anniversary of the destruction of both Holy Temples. But the Jews never forgot their holy place. A sixth–century Jewish work, *Midrash Shir Hashirim Rabba*, includes an instruction for Jews everywhere to face in the direction of the Temple Mount when praying, adding that "and those who pray on the Temple Mount should turn to the Holy of Holies."[5] This shows that Jews were still finding ways to pray on the Mount and that the exact place where the Holy Temples had stood was known 500 years after the destruction of the Second Temple.

Byzantine Period (300–618 CE)

The Christian Byzantine Empire controlled the area for over 300 years. This period reveals historical Christendom's appalling attitude towards Jews and the Temple Mount.

In 361 CE, the first Christian emperor, Constantine, was succeeded by his nephew, Julian, who was not Christian. He reversed the ban on Jews living in Jerusalem and even promised to rebuild the Temple. Jews around the world greeted the news with great enthusiasm and preparations for the rebuilding began. Emperor Julian made large sums of money available and the foundation began to be cleared.

---

5   *Midrash Shir Hashirim Rabba* 4.

The Christians of Jerusalem were greatly alarmed and vigorously opposed the Jewish effort. Many gathered in the Church of the Holy Sepulcher to pray against the rebuilding of the Temple. They got what they wished for. Emperor Julian died on the battlefront, and as soon as a Christian emperor regained power, he cancelled all Temple-rebuilding efforts.

In the year 401 CE, a tolerant ruler again appeared in the Byzantine Empire, the Empress Eudocia. When the rabbis requested permission to ascend the Temple Mount, Eudocia immediately agreed.

> "Great excitement gripped the local Jewish leaders who sent letters to other communities throughout the world informing them of the good news and asking them to come on pilgrimage to Jerusalem for the coming Sukkot festival. More than 100,000 Jews came to Jerusalem that year, but once again, Jerusalem's Christians launched a violent protest and blocked access to the mountain. For almost two centuries after this incident, Jews were forbidden to live in Jerusalem."[6]

The Temple Mount began to be deliberately ignored in Byzantine Jerusalem. Detailed maps of Jerusalem's holy sites made by Christian pilgrims from the fourth to the sixth centuries, omit the Mount entirely. The attitude progressed from neglect, to shunning, to outright desecration. The Temple Mount became the local garbage dump, in order to somehow help fulfill the already fulfilled words of Jesus, "Not one stone here will be left upon another."

So ended the legacy of nominally "Christian" rule in Jerusalem, except for a brief period during the Crusades. That later period (1099–1187 CE), was, if anything, worse. The Crusaders almost completely

---

6   Loewenberg, "Did Jews Abandon the Temple Mount?" pp. 37–48, http://goo.gl/FQr1lJ.

massacred the Jewish and Muslim residents of Jerusalem, and all non-Christians were strictly banned from the Temple Mount.

Early Muslim Rule (638–1099 CE)

When Islam conquered Jerusalem in 638 CE, the Muslims eventually built a Mosque facing Mecca on the southern edge of the Temple Mount. For political reasons, in order to magnify the importance of Jerusalem over Mecca, the mosque was named the Al-Aqsa Mosque after a story about Mohammed, found in the Koran. Caliph Omar, who conquered Jerusalem, had a Jewish adviser who had converted to Islam, and in the beginning, the relationship between the Muslims and the Jews in Jerusalem was good. Former Chief Rabbi of the IDF and Israel, Shlomo Goren, wrote in his famous book, *The Temple Mount,* that the original Dome of the Rock was actually built for the Jewish people, as a place of prayer for them.

> "The Al-Aksa Mosque [at the southern end of the Mount, opposite the Dome of the Rock] was built as a Muslim house of prayer outside the boundaries of the original Temple Mount, and therefore it points southward towards Mecca. And at the request of the Jews, Omar built the Dome of the Rock sanctuary to serve as a house of prayer for the Jews. This was after the Jews showed him the site where the Holy Temple had stood—and it does not point to Mecca."[7]

This is amazing. It seems that the golden dome that today stands on the Temple Mount as a symbol of Islamic sovereignty over this place, was originally built at the request of the Jewish people as a house of prayer! The very name Dome of the Rock indicates that it is built on top of the Foundation Stone, the rock where the Ark of the

---

7   Shlomo Goren, *The Temple Mount* (Jerusalem: HaIdra Rabba Publications, 2005, 2nd ed.), p. 327 [Hebrew].

Covenant stood in Solomon's Temple, as well as the place of the Holy of Holies in the Second Temple.

Crusader Kingdom of Jerusalem (1099–1187 CE)

The Crusaders later transformed this building into a church and called it "The Temple of God." They built an altar on the Foundation Stone, thereby making some changes on the surface of the rock. They even cut away pieces of the rock and sold it for the price of its weight in gold. It is interesting that they had two paintings in this church. One of the paintings showed the old Simeon receiving the baby Jesus in his arms when He came to the Temple. The other painting pictured Jacob dreaming about the ladder reaching up to heaven, which indicates that the church embraced the Jewish tradition that Jacob had his dream on Mount Moriah.

Muslim Reconquest (1187 CE)

When the Kurdish general Saladin conquered Jerusalem, he originally allowed both Jews and Christians to pray on the Temple Mount, but with time, it became harder for all non-Muslims to pray there. When the Turks took control of the city in the sixteenth century, they prevented all non-Muslims from praying on the Mount. Suleiman the Great allowed Jews to pray at the Western Wall, on the condition that they agreed to stay completely away from the Temple Mount.

This clear degradation of being removed from the actual Temple Mount was, however, partly supported by some of the Jewish rabbis themselves. They had begun to forbid Jews to ascend the Temple Mount, out of fear that they might desecrate the holiness of the place, since it was no longer possible to rid oneself of ritual impurity through the ashes of a red heifer.[8] This is how the Western Wall became the most famous place of prayer for the Jewish people—a situation that

---

8 The ceremony of the red heifer (cow) is described in Num 19. This ceremony is the basis for the entire Levitical purity system and a requirement for entering the holy precincts.

now has continued for more than 300 years. But before the 16th century, Jewish rabbis always tried to ascend the Mount itself, to pray. It was only when Jews were not allowed to do so, that they prayed either on the Mount of Olives where they could see the Mount, or at the Western Wall, where they were as close as possible to the Holy of Holies in the Temple.

Modern Era

In 1948, when the State of Israel was reborn, Jerusalem became a divided city. The Kingdom of Jordan occupied the Old City of Jerusalem and forced every Jew out of the Jewish Quarter. For the first time in centuries, and in contradiction of signed agreements by the Kingdom of Jordan to allow freedom of worship, Jews could not even pray at the Western Wall. This tragic situation remained for 19 years, until the liberation of Jerusalem during the Six Day War in 1967.

On June 7, 1967, Israeli paratroopers entered the Lion's Gate in Jerusalem's Old City and quickly made their way to the Temple Mount. Colonel Mordechai Gur, the brigade's commander, soon broadcast the historic message to the Israeli nation, "The Temple Mount is in our hands." For the first time in almost 2,000 years, the Temple Mount was under the control of a sovereign Jewish people. It was an overwhelming and almost surreal moment.

Israeli paratroopers climbed to the top of the Dome of the Rock and put up an Israeli flag. Rabbi Shlomo Goren, the IDF's chief rabbi at that time, was among the first soldiers to appear on the Temple Mount and he described what happened next:

> "When we arrived on the Temple Mount, I blew the shofar, fell on the ground and prostrated myself in the direction of the Holy of Holies, as was customary in the days when the Temple still stood. ... I found General Moti Gur sitting in front of the Omar Mosque. He asked me if I wanted to enter, and I answered him that today I had issued a ruling permitting all soldiers to enter because soldiers are obligated to do

so on the day when they conquer the Temple Mount in order to clear it of enemy soldiers and to make certain that no
booby traps were left behind. ... I took along a Torah scroll
and a shofar and we entered the building. I think that this
was the first time since the destruction of the Temple almost 2,000 years ago that a Torah scroll had been brought
into the holy site which is where the Temple was located.
Inside I read Psalm 49, blew the shofar, and encircled the
Foundation Stone with a Torah in my hand. Then we
exited."[9]

It soon became obvious that the secular Israeli leadership was not
prepared for, or capable of, handling the new situation on the holy
hill of the LORD. After only four hours, Defense Minister Moshe Dayan ordered that the Israeli flag over the Dome of the Rock be taken
down. He then commanded the company of Israeli paratroopers that
had conquered the site to leave the Temple Mount.

Dayan handed the keys of the Jewish people's most holy place
back to the Muslim religious authorities on the Mount. At the same
time, however, he declared that there would be unrestricted access
for Jews to the Temple Mount, except for prayer. The subsequent decades have proven that Dayan's thinking was tragically flawed. It is
impossible to combine Islamic control over the Temple Mount and
freedom of Jewish access to the place. Dayan should have known better. At the burial place of the Jewish patriarchs in Hebron, the situation was solved in a better way, by dividing the place between Jews
and Muslims, and granting access for both to pray.

Right after the Six Day War, Rabbi Goren tried to establish a synagogue and study hall on the Temple Mount, but was quickly removed
from the place by the order of General Dayan. The Israeli government

---

9   Shlomo Goren, "Selection from Personal Diary on the Conquest of Jerusalem,"
     cited in *Shabbaton* no. 422, May 29, 2009.

then prevented him from any further activities on the Mount, and this is the situation that has remained ever since.

Islamic Revisionism of History

For the past 2,000 years, there has been an overwhelming consensus among the Jewish religious leadership, as to where the Holy Temples stood. Until recently, this has, in fact, also been the case among Muslim authorities. They have always believed that the Dome of the Rock stands in the place where the Jewish Temples stood. A brochure published by the Supreme Muslim Council in 1925 was handed out to tourists visiting the Temple Mount and the Al-Aqsa Mosque. It stated clearly that the Dome of the Rock's "identity with the site of Solomon's Temple is beyond dispute. This, too, is the spot, according to universal belief, on which 'David built there an altar unto the Lord, and offered burnt offerings and peace offerings.'"[10]

This has, however, changed over the past decades, since 1967. During the Camp David peace negotiations between Israel and the Palestinians, in the summer of 2000, President Clinton brought up the issue of what should be done about the Temple Mount. Yasser Arafat shocked the American president by shouting in anger, "What Temple Mount? There have never been any Jewish Temples in Jerusalem!"

Arafat then stormed out of the meeting and told the journalists outside of the meeting that from now on, they are not allowed any more to refer to the site as the Temple Mount, but as *al-Haram al-Sharif*, the Noble Sanctuary. For several years, the international press obeyed this order quite strictly.

Yasser Arafat claimed that the Jewish Temples had stood in Samaria. In September 2000, shortly after he told President Clinton

---

10   *A Brief Guide to al-Haram al-Sharif* (Jerusalem: The Supreme Muslim Council, 1925). This reference was completely expunged from editions published after 1948.

that there had never been any Jewish Temples in Jerusalem, he launched the Al-Aqsa Intifada, a wave of terrorism. For three years, the Temple Mount remained closed to all non-Muslims.

Today, the Palestinian leaders have gone even further than Arafat, and claim that there have never been any Jewish Temples in "Palestine," period—not even in Samaria. On February 17, 2014, the former Chief Justice of PA Religious Court, Sheikh Tayseer Al-Tamimi, stated that Jews have no right to pray anywhere around the Al-Aqsa Mosque—not even at the Western Wall. He said:

> "Allah decreed that the blessed Al-Aqsa Mosque is Islamic and belongs to Muslims alone ... It is part of the religious belief of a billion and a half Muslims, and the Jews have no right to it. No party, no matter how much power and international support it has, can change this established fact by giving the Jews any right to it, or the right to pray in any part of it. The Al-Aqsa Mosque includes all its courtyards ... and specifically, its western wall."[11]

Then on March 26, 2014, the highest religious authority in the PA, PA Mufti Muhammad Hussein, said:

> "The plazas, walls, buildings, courtyards, domes, colonnades and stone benches of the Al-Aqsa Mosque, everything underneath the Al-Aqsa Mosque and everything above it, are *waqf* [an inalienable religious endowment in Islamic law] until Judgment Day, and the Palestinians have an exclusive right to them, which they share with no one."[12]

Mahmoud Abbas, who wrote his doctoral thesis denying the truth about the Holocaust, has stated that Jewish history in Jerusalem is

---

11   *Al-Hayyat Al-Jadida*, Feb. 17, 2014.

12   Ibid. March 26, 2014.

Israel's "delusional myth." He has also declared that taking Jerusalem from Israel is an Islamic obligation of the highest level, a *fard ayn*—a personal Islamic commandment incumbent on every Muslim:

> "I say to the leaders of our Arab nation and to its peoples: Jerusalem and its environs are a trust that Allah entrusted to us. Saving it from the settlement monster and the danger of Judaization and [land] confiscation is a personal [Islamic] commandment incumbent on all of us."[13]

Daniel prophesied about the coming antichrist, called "the little horn," that *"it will throw truth to the ground."* (Dan 8:12) Abbas' historical revisionism is shocking. The truth is that for the past 3,000 years, Jerusalem has—except during the artificial, short-lived Crusader Kingdom—never been the capital of any nation other than Israel.

During almost 1,300 years of Muslim rule, Jerusalem was never the capital of any Islamic dynasty. Adriaan Reland, a Dutch geographer, cartographer, and well-known philologist, visited Jerusalem in 1695. He later wrote in his book *Palestina* that the city had approximately 5,000 inhabitants, most of them Jews and some Christians.[14]

By the 19th century, Jerusalem had been so neglected by Islamic rulers that French writer Gustav Flaubert, who visited Jerusalem in 1850, wrote that he found "ruins everywhere" in Islam's third holiest city. Mark Twain, who came to Jerusalem seventeen years later, wrote that Jerusalem had "become a pauper village." Aerial photographs of Jerusalem from 100 years ago confirm Twain's observations.

Indeed, Jerusalem's importance in the Islamic world only appears evident when non-Muslims like the Crusaders, the British, or the Jews, control or capture the city. Only at those points in history do

---

13   *Al-Jazeera TV*, March 27, 2010.

14   Adriaan Reland, *Palaestina ex monumentis veteribus illustrata* (Trajecti Batavorum: Ex libraria Guilielmi Broedelet, 1714) [Latin], http://goo.gl/CQYXw7.

Islamic leaders claim Jerusalem as their third most holy city, after Mecca and Medina. It is significant that the PLO's National Covenant, written in 1964, never mentioned Jerusalem. Only after Israel regained control of the entire city did the PLO 'update' its Covenant to include Jerusalem. Now that the Jews govern Jerusalem, the Palestinians suddenly speak of Jerusalem as their own "eternal capital."

The Temple Mount Today

It is no accident that Yasser Arafat called the Second Intifada (uprising) against Israel, the "Al-Aqsa Intifada." During Palestinian demonstrations against Israel around the world, people do not just shout, "Free Palestine," they also scream *"Allahu akhbar"* (Allah is greater). It is a religiously motivated conflict. During the Gaza War in 2014, Hamas spokesperson Sami Abu Zuhri said, "The time has come for us to say that the true war is not aimed at opening border crossings [around Gaza]. Our true war is aimed at the liberation of Jerusalem, Allah willing."[15]

The battle for Jerusalem is primarily centered on the Temple Mount. Today, access to the Temple Mount has become severely restricted for Jews, limited, at best, to only certain hours a day. Orthodox Jews are usually harassed by angry Muslim mobs whenever they enter the compound. These mobs are paid by Qatar and Islamic foundations around the globe to do just that. The funds are transferred as donations to the Northern Branch of the Islamic Movement in Israel. This movement, headed by the "Al-Aqsa Sheikh" Raed Salah, then pays thousands of shekels per month to hundreds of men and women, who are members of the "Murbitat" (the male and female holders of the holy places on Earth).

The Murbitat is supposedly an innocent study group dedicated to learning Islamic scripture. In reality, it is something very different.

---

15 Tova Dvorin, *Israel National News*, 8/26/2014, "Hamas: Our War is For Liberating Jerusalem, Not Lifting Blockade," http://goo.gl/gezlaK.

They are primarily bands of agitators who bombard Jewish groups that ascend the Mount with chants of "Allahu Akhbar" (Allah is greater), yelling and cursing at them. And it does not stop with screams and curses. Frequently, riots are started where rocks, wooden beams, Molotov cocktails, metal rods, and fireworks are directed at both Israeli policemen and Jewish visitors on the Temple Mount. Hamas flags, and even ISIS flags, are waved today on God's holy hill, to shouts of "Death to the Jews!"

Psalm 74 accurately describes the situation today on the Temple Mount:

> *"O God, why do you cast us off forever? Why does your anger smoke against the sheep of your pasture? Remember your congregation, which you have purchased of old, which you have redeemed to be the tribe of your heritage! Remember Mount Zion, where you have dwelt. Direct your steps to the perpetual ruins; the enemy has destroyed everything in the sanctuary! Your foes have roared in the midst of your meeting place; they set up their own signs for signs ... How long, O God, is the foe to scoff? Is the enemy to revile your name forever? Why do you hold back your hand, your right hand? Take it from the fold of your garment and destroy them!"* (Ps 74:1–4,10–11)

International leaders of the Muslim Brotherhood, who founded Al-Qaida, Hamas and other terrorist organizations, have declared that there will never be peace in the earth, as long as Jews have any rights or presence on the Temple Mount. The goal of ISIS is to set up a Muslim caliphate that will take over the world, from the Temple Mount in Jerusalem.

Psalm 125, however, states about Zion, *"The scepter of the wicked will not remain over the land allotted to the righteous."* (Ps 125:3) There is coming a time when God will restore Zion. *"You will arise and have pity on Zion; it is the time to favor her; the appointed time has come. For your servants hold her stones dear and have pity on her dust."* (Ps 102:13–14)

Three things have changed in recent years on the Jewish side, regarding the Temple Mount. First of all, the exact locations of the holy areas on the Temple Mount, where Jews are not allowed to go without being ritually purified with the ashes of a red heifer, have been determined today with great consensus among Jewish rabbis. This is making the long-held rabbinic ban on Jews entering the Temple Mount increasingly outdated. More and more rabbis are now in favor of Jews entering the "safe" areas of the Temple Mount. There is still a sign from the Chief Rabbinate of Israel at the entrance of the Mount, stating in English that entering the Temple Mount is strictly forbidden for everyone, due to the holiness of the site. However, Orthodox Jews are today offered guided tours to the Mount which adhere to Jewish purity laws. This is a change of historic proportions.

Secondly, there is a remarkable groundswell of longing among Orthodox Jews today, to pray on the Temple Mount, and it is steadily growing. Despite the enormous opposition and harassment that they face when they visit the Temple Mount, their desire to do so is increasing every day.

Thirdly, more and more secular Jews also want to ascend the Mount today. Some do it out of curiosity, but many also out of a sense that it is unfair and unjust that Jews should not be able to visit the most historically important place for the Jewish people, and they see it as an infringement on Israel's sovereignty. In 2014, a bill was jointly formulated in the Knesset by a right wing, religious Knesset member as well as a secular left wing politician, demanding freedom for Jews to pray on the Temple Mount.

All of these factors point to the fact that something of historical and even prophetic significance is taking place. Psalm 102 explains that it is time for God to restore Zion when the Jewish people begin to fall in love with the stones and the dust of the place. This is indeed happening today.

The Exact Location of the Temple

The Dome of the Rock is now standing where most Jewish people believe that the Third Temple will be rebuilt one day. In recent years, however, different theories have been proposed, that the Jewish Temples might have been located in other places than where the Dome of the Rock stands. Some believe that this would make it easier to solve this issue without a head on confrontation with one and a half billion Muslims around the world.

In 2004, Asher Selig Kaufman, a Jewish physicist at the Hebrew University in Jerusalem, as well as an Orthodox Jew, published his research on this matter in a book called *The Temple Mount: Where Is the Holy of Holies?* Based on his understanding of Ezekiel 8:16, Kaufman concluded that the Holy Temples must have stood north of the Dome of the Rock. As early as 1980, he sent a copy of his research to Israeli Prime Minister Menachem Begin, encouraging him to look into the matter, in order to hopefully solve the question of the Temple Mount peacefully with the Muslim world. Kaufman suggested to Begin that Jews and Muslims could share the Temple Mount. The Muslims would be able to keep the Al-Aqsa Mosque as well as the Dome of the Rock, even if the Jews rebuilt the Temple on their ancient site. Many found Kaufman's idea interesting.

In 1994, Ernest L. Martin published a book called *The Temples That Jerusalem Forgot*. He suggested that the Holy Temples stood south of the Temple Mount, in what is today called the City of David. Recently, an American Christian adventurer, Robert Cornuke, has come out with a book titled *Temple: Amazing New Discoveries that Change Everything About the Location of Solomon's Temple*. His sensational theory, which is becoming very popular, is built on Martin's original idea that the Temples stood south of the entire Temple Mount.

The one who has solved the case of where the Temples stood in the most compelling scientific way is, without a doubt, the Dutch archeological architect, Dr. Leen Ritmeyer. His book, *The Quest: Reveal-*

ing the Temple Mount in Jerusalem, is truly a fascinating study. Leen Ritmeyer, originally from Holland, has been involved in all of Jerusalem's major excavations. He was chief architect of the Temple Mount excavations directed by the late Prof. Benjamin Mazar, and of the Jewish Quarter excavations in the Old City of Jerusalem directed by the late Prof. Nahman Avigad, both of the Hebrew University. His work has been published in many journals, magazines, and books about biblical archaeology, and has been shown in eminent museums, including the Israel Museum. Ritmeyer is not a Jew, but his work is highly acclaimed, also among Orthodox Jews.

Dr. Ritmeyer began his research of where the Temples stood by first studying the outer walls of the Temple Mount, trying to line up what he found with the available historical accounts on the subject, primarily the Jewish historian Josephus and a chapter called *Middot* in a rabbinic book, the *Mishnah*. Ritmeyer was eventually able to solve the biggest problem that has faced archeologists and researchers before him, namely how to reconcile a seeming contradiction between Josephus and the *Mishnah*. The *Mishnah* states that the Temple Mount platform was a 500 cubit square, while Josephus describes the platform as a rectangle, which is, of course, the way the platform looks today.

Several archeologists before Ritmeyer had suggested different solutions to this problem. Ritmeyer eventually came to realize that what the *Mishnah* describes is the original, square Temple Mount platform from the First Temple period of King Hezekiah. The Jewish sages never gave any sacred recognition to extensions of **that original holy platform**, whereas Josephus described the extended platform that Herod had made. When Ritmeyer was able to locate where the original Solomonic square platform was on the Temple Mount, a huge problem was solved, as to where the Temples must have stood, since the *Mishnah* contains very detailed and exact measurements of the Second Temple. In scientific circles, the original square Temple platform was named the Ritmeyer Square, in his honor.

All archeologists before Ritmeyer, who tried to find out where the Temples stood, started by theorizing about where the Holy of Holies was located on the Mount, and then attempting to reconcile their theories with the facts on the ground. This led to several different suggestions among scholars.

Ritmeyer, however, did the complete opposite. He started from the outside, by carefully identifying the different walls around the Temple Mount and then working his way in. When he finally studied the rock itself under the golden Dome of the Rock, he found traces of the foundations to the ancient walls of the Holy of Holies that fit exactly with the biblical and mishnaic measurements. Being a calm scientist, he still wrote "... the thrill of discovery was electrifying."[16] The crowning moment came when he was able to verify that the very place where the Ark of the Covenant must have stood in the First Temple fit exactly with a rectangular depression in the rock, in the exact size of the Ark of the Covenant. Ritmeyer also verified the precise location of the Holy of Holies in both Temples by studying the topography of the Temple Mount, comparing this data with the records in the *Mishnah*, of the different steps on the Temple Mount and their exact heights.

Today there is, in other words, a complete agreement between scientific scholarship and Jewish religious tradition about where both the First and Second Holy Temples stood, on the Temple Mount.

For those who believe in the testimony of the Holy Scriptures— both Jews as well as Christians—that a Third Temple will one day be rebuilt on this site, and that the glorious throne of Messiah will be on Mount Zion, this is not only very interesting, but also highly important information. The prophetic word is coming alive, and we know more exactly what it is that we are looking forward to and praying for. Both Simeon and Anna were watching in the Temple for the coming of Messiah.

---

16 Leen Ritmeyer, *The Quest:Revealing the Temple Mount in Jerusalem* (Jerusalem: Carta, 2006), p. 246.

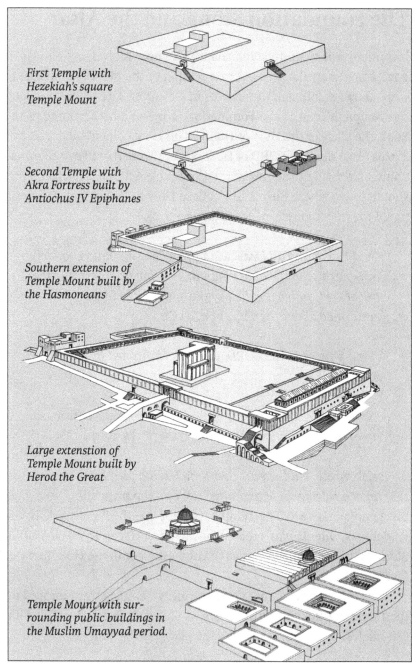

First Temple with
Hezekiah's square
Temple Mount

Second Temple with
Akra Fortress built by
Antiochus IV Epiphanes

Southern extension of
Temple Mount built by
the Hasmoneans

Large extenstion of
Temple Mount built by
Herod the Great

Temple Mount with sur-
rounding public buildings in
the Muslim Umayyad period.

The Temple Mount through history, showing the Ritmeyer Square (top).

The Foundation Stone and the Altar

It is important to understand that the Temple Mount, even today, is not a completely flat area. A cross section of the Mount, from east to west, shows significant differences in elevation. The highest peak on the Temple Mount is the Foundation Stone under the Dome of the Rock, the place of the Holy of Holies. This is no coincidence, as it was in this place that the LORD of Hosts sat enthroned between the cherubim, on the lid of the Ark of the Covenant. Actually, this fact alone should prove where the location of the Holy of Holies was. It was on top of the holy mountain, on its highest peak.

> *"And David and all Israel went up to Baalah, that is, to Kiriath–jearim that belongs to Judah, to bring up from there the ark of God, which is called by the name of the LORD who sits enthroned above the cherubim."* (1 Ch 13:6)

> *"Sing praises to the LORD, who sits enthroned in Zion!"* (Ps 9:11)

> *"The LORD reigns; let the peoples tremble! He sits enthroned upon the cherubim; let the earth quake!"* (Ps 99:1)

Isaiah wrote, *"In the year that King Uzziah died I saw the Lord sitting upon a throne, high and lifted up; and the train of his robe filled the Temple."* (Isa 6:1) The Temple was not like the Tabernacle in the wilderness, which was erected on a flat surface. The Foundation Stone in the Holy of Holies was the highest place in the Holy Temples on Mount Zion.

We know, however, also that the Holy Temples were located on the threshing floor of Ornan, as it is stated in the account in First Chronicles, when David selected the place for the Temple:

"So David paid Ornan 600 shekels of gold by weight for the
site. And David built there an altar to the LORD and presented burnt offerings and peace offerings and called on the
LORD, and the LORD answered him with fire from heaven
upon the altar of burnt offering. Then the LORD commanded the angel, and he put his sword back into its sheath. At
that time, when David saw that the LORD had answered
him at the threshing floor of Ornan the Jebusite, he sacrificed there ... Then David said, 'Here shall be the house of the
LORD God and here the altar of burnt offering for Israel.'" (1
Ch 21:25–28; 2:1)

Threshing floors were, however, never located at the top of a
mountain, but slightly lower, so that the wind would only carry away
the lighter chaff, but not the heavier grain. Since most of the heavy
winds in Jerusalem come from the west, the threshing floor should be
slightly east of the peak, or in other words east of the Foundation
Stone. Notice what David said when he stood at the altar that he had
built on the threshing floor of Ornan, *"Here shall be the house of the
LORD God **and here the altar of burnt offering for Israel**."* (1 Ch 2:1)

If we read earlier in the text, we will notice where the angel stood:

"And God sent the angel to Jerusalem to destroy it, but as he
was about to destroy it, the LORD saw, and he relented from
the calamity. And he said to the angel who was working destruction, "It is enough; now stay your hand." And **the angel
of the LORD was standing by the threshing floor** of Ornan
the Jebusite. **And David lifted his eyes and saw the angel of
the LORD standing between earth and heaven**, and in his
hand a drawn sword stretched out over Jerusalem. Then David and the elders, clothed in sackcloth, fell upon their faces." (1 Ch 21:15–16)

David looked up and saw the angel standing *"between earth and heaven."* The text indicates, in other words, that the angel of the LORD stood higher than Daniel. The only higher place than the threshing floor would be the Foundation Stone, the place for the Holy of Holies and the throne of the LORD, truly a fitting place for the revelation of the angel of the LORD.

We know that the angel of the LORD also spoke to Abraham in this place. Jewish tradition holds that Abraham built his altar in the exact same place on Mount Moriah that David later built his altar. This truly makes sense, even if it cannot be conclusively proven from the biblical text. After all, Abraham built his altar in Moriah, in a place that God had pointed out to him, as we mentioned in Chapter 2. It was a specifically chosen place.

The Scriptural pattern is that all sacrifices were always offered before the LORD. In the Hebrew language, the word for "before" also means "east of." Both in the Tabernacle and in the Temple, the altars were always east of the Holy of Holies. The people were facing west. The fact that the angel of the LORD appeared to David west of the altar follows this Scriptural pattern. We read about Abraham when he built his altar in the same place:

> *"Then Abraham reached out his hand and took the knife to slaughter his son. But the angel of the LORD called to him from heaven and said, 'Abraham, Abraham!' And he said, 'Here am I.' He said, 'Do not lay your hand on the boy or do anything to him, for now I know that you fear God, seeing you have not withheld your son, your only son, from me.' And Abraham lifted up his eyes and looked, and behold, behind him was a ram, caught in a thicket by his horns. And Abraham went and took the ram and offered it up as a burnt offering instead of his son. So Abraham called the name of that place, 'The LORD will provide'; as it is said to this day, 'On the mount of the LORD it shall be provided.'"* (Gen 22:10–14)

Most likely, Abraham was also facing west when he drew his knife to slaughter Isaac, and the angel of the LORD spoke to him standing on the Foundation Stone, the place that would later be the Holy of Holies and the throne of the LORD. When Abraham discovered the ram that took Isaac's place, just as Abraham had prophesied to Isaac, *"God will provide for himself the lamb for a burnt offering, my son"* (Gen 22:8), it says, *"Abraham lifted up his eyes and looked, and behold, **behind him was a ram**, caught in a thicket by his horns. And Abraham went and took the ram and offered it up as a burnt offering instead of his son."* (22:13)

The ram that took Isaac's place is, of course, pointing to the sacrifice of Messiah on the tree crowned with thorns. If Abraham looked up and saw the ram behind him, he must then have been looking to the east. East of Moriah is the Mount of Olives, the place where many believe that Jesus gave His life on Golgotha, in our stead. "The LORD will provide" can also be translated "The LORD will be seen." The Mount of Olives can be seen everywhere in Jerusalem. And this is also where He will be seen when He comes, and will stand with His feet to make His entrance into Jerusalem from the east.

One more important note about the Temple Mount: after David had selected the place for the Temple, and made all the preparations for it, he appointed his son Solomon to be the heir after him, to sit on his throne. He told Bathsheba, *"As the LORD lives, who has redeemed my soul out of every adversity, as I swore to you by the LORD, the God of Israel, saying, 'Solomon your son shall reign after me, and he shall sit on my throne in my place,' even so will I do this day."* (1 Ki 1:29–30)

After Solomon had finished building the Temple, he built his own palace just south of the Temple. The LORD sat enthroned on the cherubim in the Holy of Holies, facing east. This means that Solomon, the son of David and the prophetic shadow of Messiah, was sitting at His right hand. The Scriptures state that Solomon not only sat on the throne of his father David, but also that he sat on the throne of the LORD:

*"Then **Solomon sat on the throne of the LORD** as king in place of David his father. And he prospered, and all Israel obeyed him."* (1 Ch 29:23)

This is also what Messiah will do on the Temple Mount in the new Jerusalem when He returns, as it is stated in the last chapter in the Bible:

*"Then the angel showed me the river of the water of life, bright as crystal, **flowing from the throne of God and of the Lamb** through the middle of the street of the city; also, on either side of the river, the tree of life with its twelve kinds of fruit, yielding its fruit each month. The leaves of the tree were for the healing of the nations. No longer will there be anything accursed, but **the throne of God and of the Lamb will be in it**, and his servants will worship him. They will see his face, and his name will be on their foreheads. And night will be no more. They will need no light of lamp or sun, for the Lord God will be their light, and they will reign forever and ever."* (Rev 22:1–5)

Then the words of Gabriel to Mary will be fulfilled:

*"Do not be afraid, Mary, for you have found favor with God. And behold, you will conceive in your womb and bear a son, and you shall call his name Jesus. He will be great and will be called the Son of the Most High. And the Lord God will give to him **the throne of his father David**, and he will reign over the house of Jacob forever, and of his kingdom there will be no end."* (Lk 1:30–33)

What About the "Temple of Antichrist"?

Some Christians say that if a Jewish Temple is rebuilt on the Temple Mount in Jerusalem, it will only be for the purpose of revealing the antichrist. They call this Temple "the antichrist temple," saying that it is certainly not anything that Christians should be involved in or be excited about.

But let us look at what the Scriptures really say about this. First, we have the statement by Jesus in His eschatological speech on the Mount of Olives. He said,

> *"So when you see the abomination of desolation spoken of by the prophet Daniel, standing in the holy place (let the reader understand), then let those who are in Judea flee to the mountains ... Pray that your flight may not be in winter or on a Sabbath."* (Mt 24:15–16,20)

Bible scholars see this as referring to an image or idol that will one day be placed in the Temple in Jerusalem by the antichrist. It might also refer to antichrist himself. Daniel prophesied several times about this, and the prophecy was fulfilled the first time, during the reign of Antiochus Epiphanes in 167 BCE. The name Epiphanes, which he chose for himself, means "[God] manifest"—a clear picture of the antichrist.

Antiochus hated the Jewish people and placed a statue of Zeus, with an image of his own face on it, in the Holy Temple in Jerusalem. He then unleashed a cruel persecution of all God-fearing Jews in the land. Thousands of them were brutally murdered. It was an exact fulfillment of Daniel's prophecy about *"the abomination of desolation."*

But Jesus said that there would also be a fulfillment of this prophecy in the future. Something similar did indeed happen when Titus destroyed the Temple in Jerusalem in 70 CE. The Roman Tenth Legion set up their idolatrous standards in the Temple. The Temple was not only defiled, but also destroyed, and thousands upon thousands of Jews were killed.

However, it also seems like there is yet a future, final fulfillment of Daniel's prophecy in the end times as well. Scholars believe the Gospel of Matthew was composed between 80–90 CE, with a range of possibility between 70–110 CE. At that time, the second fulfillment of Daniel's prophecy had already happened, and still Matthew added the words, *"let the reader understand,"* showing the importance of Jesus' words also for future generations who would read His words.

The context also clearly points to a future fulfillment right before the return of Jesus. Matthew describes the result of the appearance of the abomination of desolation: *"For then there will be great tribulation, such as has not been from the beginning of the world until now, no, and never will be."* (Mt 24:21) Then Matthew adds:

> **"Immediately after the tribulation of those days** *the sun will be darkened, and the moon will not give its light, and the stars will fall from heaven, and the powers of the heavens will be shaken. Then will appear in heaven the sign of the Son of Man, and then all the tribes of the earth will mourn, and they will see the Son of Man coming on the clouds of heaven with power and great glory."* (24:29–30)

The context clearly points to an end time fulfillment of the prophecy of Daniel about the abomination of desolation.

The point, though, that we want to make here about this prophecy of the abomination of desolation, is that Jesus said that "it," or "he," will stand *"in the holy place."* This is important to note. The abomination will not stand in a wicked or unholy place. He will stand in a place that is holy. Paul also wrote about this:

> *"Let no one deceive you in any way. For that day will not come, unless the rebellion comes first, and the man of lawlessness is revealed, the son of destruction, who opposes and*

exalts himself against every so–called god or object of wor-
ship, so that he takes his seat in the Temple of God, proclaim-
ing himself to be God." (2 Th 2:3–4)

Once again, the text does not say that the antichrist will take his seat in "his temple," meaning the temple of antichrist, or in *"a wicked, unholy temple,"* but in *"the Temple of God."* The Temple is not called the "Temple of Antichrist" or "The Temple of the Man of Lawlessness." Even though the antichrist will take his seat in this Temple and desecrate it, it is still the Temple of God. The Temple is also described by Jesus Himself as *"the holy place."*

In other words, it is a Holy Temple of God, on the Temple Mount, in Jerusalem, that the antichrist will desecrate! This is a very important observation. The antichrist does not belong in this Temple, and Jesus will certainly cleanse it when He returns, just as the Temple that Antiochus Epiphanes desecrated was restored and rededicated to God. Messiah will restore and rebuild it, in line with what Ezekiel describes in the final chapters of his book, and it will be filled with the glory of God.

It is important also to add that the end time Holy Temple that antichrist will take his seat in might not be a very elaborate construction. The most important part of the Holy Temple is the altar where the sacrifices are made. That is what the God-fearing Jews who returned from Babylon began to rebuild, when they restored the Temple. The altar is more important than the Temple itself.

We need to bear in mind that Jesus even described the Temple that the wicked, cruel murderer Herod had essentially built, as "my Father's house." This is also where the first disciples met every day to worship God (see Lk 24:53).

It is the location and the purpose of the Temple that makes it holy to God, not necessarily the hands who built it or its magnificent construction. Let it be clear that the Bible nowhere talks about an antichrist temple. There is no such thing in the Scriptures.

The Bible says, *"You shall keep my Sabbaths and reverence my sanctuary: I am the LORD."* (Lev 19:30) The commandment to reverence the Temple is an important commandment for everyone, both Jew and Gentile, since the Temple is to be a house of prayer for all nations and *"all the nations shall flow to it"* (Isa 2:2) and *"the earth will be filled with the knowledge of the glory of the LORD as the waters cover the sea."* (Hab 2:14)

Let us end by joining Daniel in his prayer for God's holy hill, where He has appointed the Messiah to rule forever upon the throne of His father David:

> *"Then I turned my face to the Lord God, seeking him by prayer and pleas for mercy with fasting and sackcloth and ashes. ... 'O Lord, according to all your righteous acts, let your anger and your wrath turn away from your city Jerusalem, your holy hill, because for our sins, and for the iniquities of our fathers, Jerusalem and your people have become a byword among all who are around us. Now therefore, O our God, listen to the prayer of your servant and to his pleas for mercy, and for your own sake, O Lord, make your face to shine upon your sanctuary, which is desolate. O my God, incline your ear and hear. Open your eyes and see our desolations, and the city that is called by your name. For we do not present our pleas before you because of our righteousness, but because of your great mercy. O Lord, hear; O Lord, forgive. O Lord, pay attention and act. Delay not, for your own sake, O my God, because your city and your people are called by your name.'"* (Dan 9:16–19)

The holy hill of the LORD is the throne of God on earth, and the final answer to Daniel's prayer will soon make Jerusalem **the joy of the whole earth.**

*"The LORD will roar from Zion and thunder from Jerusa-
lem; the earth and the sky will tremble. But the LORD will be
a refuge for his people, a stronghold for the people of Israel.
Then you will know that I, the LORD your God, dwell in Zion,
my holy hill."* (Joel 3:16–17 NIV)

EPILOGUE

In the beginning of this book, we mentioned that during the first hundred years, the followers of Jesus kept the same biblical hope for the future that the Jewish people have always held. It is a hope centered on the restoration and rebuilding of Jerusalem, under Messiah.

Eventually, this hope was lost in the church. After the First Church Council in Nicaea, Emperor Constantine commanded all the bishops to "have nothing in common with the most hostile mob of the Jews ... that the purity of your minds may not be affected by a conformity in any thing with the customs of the vilest of mankind."[1] When the connection with the Jewish people was cut, the original biblical hope for the future was rejected as "childish, unspiritual, and Jewish." In its place came a hope tainted by Greek philosophy and a pagan worldview. The hope of a future, glorious Messianic kingdom out of Jerusalem was lost, and the kingdom of God became equal to the church, headed by the pope in Rome.

The loss of the original, biblical hope has produced a seriously flawed, unscriptural eschatology, especially in evangelical circles. The Jewish people, just like the early believers, look forward to the

---

1   Daniel Gruber, *The Church and the Jews: The Biblical Relationship* (Hagerstown, MD: Serenity Books, 1997), pp. 33–35.

restoration and renewal of all things (see Ac 3:21, Mt 19:28 and Ro 8:20–21, in Hebrew referred to as *tikkun olam*), and to the coming of the Messiah. In contrast, Christians, in general, are waiting for the **destruction** of all things and an **escape** from the world, with the Messiah.

Some time back, I read a blog on an Israeli website that illustrates this. The humorous article was entitled *Signs that the Redemption is near?* by Tuvia Brodie. Brodie commented on an American magazine column, called "Signs of the Apocalypse," by saying, "That magazine comes from America. We live in Israel, which follows a different religious and spiritual orientation. So if someone in America thinks about Christian-inspired world Destruction, perhaps we can think about something different—a Jewish-inspired New-world Redemption."[2]

This is an example of how Christians are looking for destruction and the end of the world, while the Jewish people are focused on redemption and the beginning of a new world. Even though there certainly is an element of truth to the way Christians think, we suggest that the Jewish thinking reflects a more healthy and biblical mindset. It is a positive mindset, versus a negative mindset. It is true that judgment is coming, but the focus is off. The gospel and the coming of Messiah are supposed to be good news, not bad news. It is difficult to get people excited about a message that everything is going to burn, and we must get out of here.

The Jewish people also believe that it will be a difficult time in the end, before the Messiah comes. They call it the "birth pains of Messiah." This is similar to the language Jesus used when He spoke about the end. He said, *"All these are but the beginning of the birth pains."* (Mt 24:8) But when a mother is pregnant she is not focused on the coming birth pains. Together with her husband, she looks forward to a new child being born. That is their focus. They feel the baby kicking

---

2   *Israel National News*, 12/30/2013, http://goo.gl/dQOKKm.

and moving around in the stomach of the mother and they are excited.

In the same way, we should not be focused on the antichrist, all the difficulties of the end times, or that everything is going to burn. We should be excited about the fact that the whole world will soon be born again into the kingdom of God, and we should watch for signs of redemption with joy-filled anticipation, just like parents are excited about the kicking of a baby in the womb. The problem, however, is that many Christians don't know what they are supposed to look forward to, because we have lost the biblical hope.

Randy Alcorn, in his book *Heaven*, quotes a famous British nobleman who said that when he was growing up, he decided that he would rather go to hell than to heaven. Why? Because being dragged to church as a child, he had heard the preacher announce the death of so-and-so, by saying that the deceased had now joined the choir in heaven, which, day and night, is worshiping God around His throne. From this, he imagined heaven as a never-ending Sunday morning church service, and it seemed to him that even hell must be better than that.[3]

How do the Jewish people picture the world to come, and how do they celebrate their holy day of the week, the Sabbath? They do so with a festive meal and the whole family gathered around a table full of delicacies, as the Sabbath begins. It is a weekly reminder of the great feast in the kingdom of God. The kingdom of Heaven is, more than anything else, described as a huge banquet feast. Is this something that a young boy is able to get excited about, more than a Sunday morning church service? You better believe it!

It is time for Christians to rediscover their biblical hope, and begin to present to a dying world a more biblically accurate gospel that is truly good news. The Messiah is coming soon to Jerusalem, and Paradise will be restored again—here on this planet—in a world filled with righteousness, peace, and joy. Satan and his followers will be de-

---

3   Randy Alcorn, *Heaven* (Tyndale House Publishers, 2004), p. 65.

stroyed, and sin and death will be no more. That truly is good news! Does that not motivate you to repent from all sin and receive the Messiah as King of kings and Lord of lords, in order to be a part of that kingdom? You do not want to miss the feast that is coming!

Lars Enarson
Israel, 2015

APPENDIX A:
THE ESCHATOLOGY OF
JERUSALEM

We felt a brief look on the eschatology of Jerusalem, as presented in this book, was needed. In the Jewish worldview, which is present in the New Testament writings of the apostles, the history of the universe is divided into "this age" (*olam ha-zeh*) and the "age to come" (*olam ha-ba*). For example: *"Truly, I say to you, there is no one who has left house or wife or brothers or parents or children, for the sake of the kingdom of God, who will not receive many times more in **this time, and in the age to come** eternal life."* (Lk 18:29–30)

A third expression, closely connected with these, is, the "days of Messiah," or the Messianic Era. The Messianic Era is seen as a transitional stage between this age and the age to come. It is not always clear in biblical or Jewish sources, which age the transitional period of the Messianic Era belongs to, this age or the age to come?

- This Age
- Messianic Era
- Age to Come

The theology of the apostles seems to place the Messianic Era in this present age.

Final Chapters of Revelation

In broad strokes, one could say that Chapter 20 of Revelation describes the Messianic Era (the thousand year reign of Messiah) as well as the final judgment (often seen as the concrete end of this age). Revelation Chapters 21–22 begin a new section describing the renewed heaven and earth with the glorious, renewed garden city of Jerusalem coming down to earth.

- Chapter 20A: Messianic Era (thousand year reign of Messiah)
- Chapter 20B: Final judgment before the great white throne
- Chapter 21–22: Renewed heaven and earth, renewed Jerusalem, paradise.

This Book

This book presents the view that the gloriously renewed creation and Jerusalem is part of the thousand year, Messianic Era, and not of the later age to come (or, the "eternal state").[1] In this way, Chapters 21–22 do not follow Chapter 20 in chronological, linear order, but instead are a more Hebraic, cyclical description. In other words, Chapters 21–22 back up to look more in detail at the Messianic Era described in Chapter 20.

This cyclical pattern is common enough in the Bible. The Jewish rabbis have a saying, "The Torah is not chronological," meaning that the Bible is often times more interested in looking at a certain topic

---

1   Both Paul (in Ro 8:18–25) and Peter (in 2 Pe 3:10–13) seem to connect the regeneration of the world immediately with the coming of Messiah, and not the age to come.

than in always presenting a strict, chronological story. One pertinent example of this would be the Genesis account of Creation. Genesis 1 describes Creation. After a summary statement, Genesis 2 "rewinds," so to speak, to look more in detail at the creation of man already described in Genesis 1. This could very well be the case of the final three chapters of Revelation.

Common View

However, the description above is not the most common view among those who have a similar, Jewish, eschatological hope as presented in this book. The more common view is that Revelation 20 describes the Messianic Era and the end of this age at the final judgment. Chapters 21–22 then present the age to come, or "eternal state."

Both views have strengths and weaknesses.

The common view is supported by several points. (1) The chronological order seems to suggest that Chapter 20 is the thousand year reign, the end of the age, and the final judgment, whereas Chapter 21 immediately begins with the description of a "new heaven and earth." (2) The measurements of Jerusalem seem different from Ezekiel's description. Therefore, Ezekiel's description belongs to the Messianic Era, and Chapter 21 must be the age to come. (3) The Apostle John reports that he did not see a "temple" in the renewed Jerusalem. Since the prophets, especially Ezekiel, describe a restored Messianic Temple, that Temple must be part of Chapter 20, and Chapters 21–22 must be a description of the world to come.

Those who see the end of Revelation in this more conventional way, may at the same time often look at the end time descriptions in the prophets about the kingdom of God, as a description of the Messianic Age. The maxim of the Jewish sages was—roughly paraphrased—"All the prophets prophesied of nothing but the Days of Messiah"—that is, they spoke of the Messianic Era and not of the world to come, which no eye has seen, nor ear has heard much of.

This book, and the more common held view, find common ground on this point: the prophets generally seem to describe the Messianic Era, and not the world to come.[2] And yet, Revelation 21–22 find their clearest parallels in the descriptions of the prophets!

This book has highlighted many of these parallels between the prophets and Revelation. For example:

- the husband, wife, and bride motifs;
- kings walking in the light of Jerusalem, bringing the wealth of the nations into it;
- the river of life and the tree of life;
- the foundations of precious stones;
- God providing the light instead of the sun and moon.

Therefore, this book takes the view that what Isaiah, Ezekiel and all the prophets described is the same thing which John the Apostle describes in the final two chapters of Revelation. If our understanding of Justin Martyr is correct, this was the view of the the early church as well.[3]

Those who take the more common approach, maintain that new Jerusalem of Revelation 21–22 belongs to the age to come, yet at the same time, hold that the apparently same new Jerusalem found in the prophets, belongs to this age and the Messianic Era. This is indeed a difficulty.

As for the other common objections to our approach, the book's first chapter shows that there need not be a contradiction between Ezekiel and Revelation as it regards the measurements of the city or the Temple buildings.

---

2   For example, that someone who dies at a hundred, dies young, hardly fits in an age without death (Isa 65:20).

3   Justin Martyr, *Dialogue with Trypho*, Ch. 80–81.

Our Common Hope

The outline of end time events described in this book is not meant to be taken as dogma in all its details. It certainly represent our best understanding, yet, we all "see in part" and we respect those of different positions.

Regardless at exactly which stage we shall see it, we all look forward with the greatest eagerness to the fulfillment of all of God's promises—the return of our precious Messiah to rule and reign on earth from Jerusalem, the resurrection of the dead, the restoration of the kingdom to Israel, the regeneration of all creation, God dwelling with us, and all of us worshipping Him in the paradise-city of Jerusalem.

> *"Behold, the dwelling place of God is with man. He will dwell with them, and they will be his people, and God himself will be with them as their God. He will wipe away every tear from their eyes, and death shall be no more, neither shall there be mourning, nor crying, nor pain anymore, for the former things have passed away." (Rev 21:3–4)*

APPENDIX B:
THE HISTORICAL PERIODS
OF JERUSALEM

*"Thus says the Lord GOD: This is Jerusalem. I have set her
in the center of the nations, with countries all around her"
... "the center of the earth." —Ezekiel 5:5; 38:12*

1. Canaanite Period: Until 1400 BCE

*"This is what the Sovereign LORD says to Jerusalem: Your ancestry
and birth were in the land of the Canaanites; your father was an
Amorite and your mother a Hittite." (Eze 16:3 NIV)*

4000 BCE	Creation of Adam
3500 BCE	First known settlement on the Eastern Hill
2974 BCE	Noah is born
2500 BCE	Earliest mention comes from the Ebla Tablets
2374 BCE	The flood occurs
2081 BCE	Abraham is born
2000 BCE	Abraham meets Melchizedek (approx.)
19th century BCE	Jerusalem mentioned in Egyptian Execration Texts

1981 BCE	Isaac is born
1950 BCE	The Binding of Isaac on Mt Moriah (approx.)
1922 BCE	Jacob is born
1906 BCE	Avraham dies
1871 BCE	Noah's son Shem dies 600 years old. (Isaac is 111 years old and Jacob 51 years old.)
1791 BCE	Jacob arrives in Egypt
14th century BCE	Jerusalem is mentioned in the El Amarna Letters, six of which were written by Jerusalem's Canaanite king, Abdi-Hepa. Jerusalem is a Jebusite city called Jebus.

2. Israelite Period: 1400–586 BCE

"You have led in your steadfast love the people whom you have redeemed; you have guided them by your strength to your holy abode. (Ex 15:13,17–18)

1581 BCE	The exodus from Egypt (rabbinical counting after 210 years, cf Gal 3:17)
1541 BCE	The conquest of Canaan under Joshua (rabbinical counting)
1000 BC	David captures "the fortress of Zion, the City of David" and makes Jerusalem the capital of Israel (2 Sam 5:6-12, 1 Chr 11:4–9).
	"The LORD swore an oath to David, a sure oath that he will not revoke: 'One of your own descendants I will place on your throne—if your sons keep my covenant and the statutes I teach them, then their sons will sit on your throne for ever and ever.' For the LORD has chosen Zion, he has desired it for his dwelling: 'This is my resting place for ever and ever; here I will sit enthroned, for I have desired it.'" (Ps 132:11–14 NIV)

960 BCE   The First Temple is built
"In this Temple and in Jerusalem, which I have
chosen out of all the tribes of Israel, I will put my
Name forever." (2 Ki 21:7 NIV)

3. Babylonian Period: 586–536 BCE

"Jerusalem will be trampled on by the Gentiles until the times of
the Gentiles are fulfilled." (Lk 21:24 NIV)

586 BCE   Jerusalem and the First Temple are destroyed
The times of the Gentiles (when there is no heir
reigning on the throne of David) begin
Foreigners move into the southern part of the Land
Jerusalem and northern Judah remain empty

4. Persian Period: 536–332 BCE

536 BCE   Jews return from Babylon
516 BCE   The Temple sacrifices are restored and the Second
Temple is soon after dedicated

5. Hellenistic Period: 332–63 BCE

332–312 BCE   Alexander the Great
312–198 BCE   Ptolemies (Egypt)
198–167 BCE   Seleucids (Syria)
167 BCE   The Maccabean Revolt
167–63 BCE   The Hasmoneans
Jerusalem begins to expand to the Western Hill and

is surrounded by the First Wall
Development of the Pharisees and Sadducees

6. Roman Period: 63 BCE–324 CE

40 BCE–70 CE   The Herodian Period
Jerusalem expands northward, surrounded first by
the Second Wall and then the Third Wall after
Messiah's death and resurrection.

70 CE   The Second Temple is destroyed

135 CE   Jerusalem is rebuilt as a Roman city and named Aelia
Capitolina (*Aelia* is the family name of Hadrian.
Capitolina refers to the three capitoline gods: Jupiter,
Juno and Minerva)
The name of Israel and Judeah is changed to Pales-
tina
Christianity begins to spread
From 70 CE until the end of the third century, the
city remained without a wall, even during the times
it was being built up

7. First Byzantine Period: 324–614 CE

324 CE   Christianity becomes the official religion of the
Roman Empire under Constantine
The building of many churches in Jerusalem over
Christian holy sites

527–565 CE Jerusalem reached the peak of its Byzantine development during the reign of Emperor Justinian

8. Persian Period: 614–629 CE

The churches in Jerusalem are destroyed
Jews are allowed to return

9. Second Byzantine Period: 629–638 CE

Jews are once again banished

10. First Muslim Period: 638–1099 CE

638–750 CE Umayyad rule out of Ramlah and Damascus
Jerusalem is rebuilt
The Temple Mount is turned into a Muslim holy site
The Dome of the Rock is built
Jews are permitted to return to Jerusalem and
became caretakers of the Temple Mount
750–877 CE Abbisid rule out of Bagdad
The al-Aqsa Mosque built
Jews were forbidden to enter the Temple Mount
Jerusalem suffers decline
877–1071 CE   Fatimid rule out of Cairo
The Church of the Holy Sepulchre destroyed
Large influx of Karaite Jews until they equaled the
number of other Jews in the city
1071–1099 CE   Seljuk Turk rule out of Bagdad
Wide-spread mistreatment of Christians
Desecration of churches

11. The Crusader Period: 1099–1187

1099   Jerusalem becomes the capital of the Latin Kingdom
of Jerusalem
Rebuilding of the churches
Jerusalem enters a period of prosperity
The Jewish community is destroyed and ceased to
exist
The Greek holy places are confiscated by Latins

12. Second Muslim Period: 1187-1517

1187	Salahdin captures Jerusalem
1187–1250	Ayyubid rule out of Damascus and Cairo
	Walls of Jerusalem fortified but later demolished in 1219
	Jews permitted to return to the city
	Overall population decreases due to fear of living in unfortified city
	Construction and renovation carried out on the Temple Mount
	Interrupted by the short Second Crusader Period (1229–1244) during which time the Jews were again expelled
1243–1244	The city was invaded by the Khwarizmians who massacred the Christians and destroyed church buildings
1250–1517	Mameluke rule out of Egypt
	Development of religious institutions but Jerusalem remains politically and economically insignificant
	Many Pilgrimages
	The Citadel of David was reinforced in 1310 but otherwise Jerusalem remained an unwalled city
	Jewish community begins to grow
	(a) Initially in the area of modern Mount Zion
	(b) Later in the 14th century, it spread to the present Jewish Quarter

13. Ottoman Turkish Period: 1517–1917

	Jerusalem is ruled out of Istanbul
1535–1542	The present walls of Jerusalem are built by Suleiman the Magnificient
	Jerusalem is turned into a typical oriental town

Reached the height of its development during the
rule of Suleiman the Magnificent and, thereafter, it
went into constant decline with no new buildings or
constructions

19th century   New, Jewish neighborhoods began outside
the walls and the population began to grow again

1860 (or 1841)   The Jews were the majority population of
Jerusalem
Local government was centered on key families
whose authority was passed down dynastically,
father to son
(a) The Nashashibis
(b) The Husseins
(c) The Alamis
(d) The Khalidis

1831–1840   An interruption of Turkey's rule during with the
Egyptian conquest of Palestine which spurred the
19th century growth and which continued when the
Turks began
(a) New construction inside the Jewish Quarter
and Jewish neighborhoods outside the wall
(b) New buildings and churches in the Christian
Quarter and along the Via Dolorosa
(c) Christian group also began to spread outside
the city wall with places like the Russian
Compound, the American Colony, the Ger-
many Colony and buildings opposite the New
Gate
(d) Muslims begin building north of the Old City
opposite the Damascus and Herod Gates
(e) Protestants begin to get a foothold, starting
with the Anglican Christ Church inside the
Jaffa Gate

14. British Mandate Period: 1917–1948

(1) Jerusalem grew and expanded
(2) Establishment of garden neighborhoods such as Talpiot, Rahavia, the German Colony, the Greek Colony, the American Colony and Romema
(3) Period of Jewish and Arab tensions

15. Israeli-Jordanian Period (Divided City): 1948–1967

(1) New City becomes the capital of Israel
(2) Development of the New City
 (a) The Jewish city expands westward since, on all the other sides, it was surrounded by Jordan
 (b) The Arab city expands primarily northward but also somewhat eastward
(3) Construction of many public buildings on both sides of the border

16. Israeli Period (Unified City): 1967–Present

(1) Jewish Quarter rebuilt
(2) Municipal boundaries expanded
(3) There has been a massive increase in the building of new neighborhoods
 (a) *First phase: 1968–1970*, Surrounding Arab Sheich Jarrah
  i. Sanhedria Hamurheret
  ii. Ramot Eshkol
  iii. Maalot Dafna
  iv. Givat Hamivtar
  v. Givat Shapira (French Hill)
 (b) *Second Phase: 1970–1980*, North and South
  i. Neve Yaakov - North

   ii. Ramot Allon - North

   iii. East Talpiot - South

   iv. Gilo – South

 (c) *Third Phase: 1980–Present*

   i. Pisgat Zeev: To close the gap between Neve Yaakov and French Hill

   ii. Har Nof: A new religious suburb

(4) New public buildings built in eastern Jerusalem

 (a) The Government Office Complex

 (b) Israel Police Force Headquarters

(5) Commercial Center Development

(6) Cultural Centers

(7) New neighborhoods connected with new wide roads

(8) Since the Intifada began in 1987, there has been continuous tension between Jews and Arabs

(9) There has been a gradual increase in the religious Jewish population.

THE CITY THROUGH TIME

BACKGROUND ILLUSTRATIONS: RITMEYER ARCHAEOLOGICAL DESIGN. USED WITH PERMISSION.

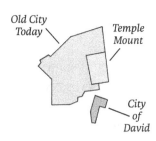

Old City Today — *Temple Mount* — *City of David*

JEBUSITE / DAVID

SOLOMON

HEZEKIAH / ZEDEKIAH

NEHEMIAH

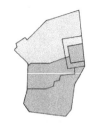

HASMONEAN

HEROD THE GREAT

PRE-ROMAN DESTRUCTION

BYZANTINE

THE TOPOGRAPHY OF JERUSALEM

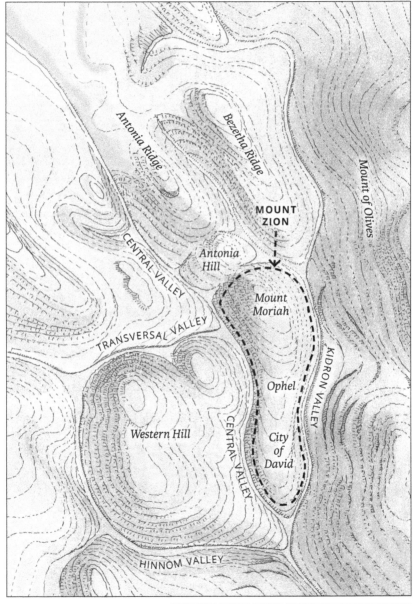

BACKGROUND: RITMEYER ARCHAEOLOGICAL DESIGN. USED WITH PERMISSION.

SELECTED BIBLIOGRAPHY

Alcorn, Randy, *Heaven*, Tyndale House Publishers, 2004.

Justin Martyr, *Dialogue with Trypho*.

Edersheim, Alfred, *The Life and Times of Jesus the Messiah, Vol. 1*, Bellingham, WA: Logos Bible Software, 1896.

Freedman, Shalom, *Rabbi Shlomo Goren: Torah Sage and General*, Urim Publications, 2006.

Give Peace a Chance, European Coalition For Israel, 2011, youtu.be/oVsjNzXojCM.

Goren, Shlomo, *The Temple Mount,* Jerusalem: HaIdra Rabba Publications, 2005, 2nd ed., [Hebrew].

Grubb, Norman, *Rees Howells: Intercessor*, CLC Publications, 1988.

Gruber, Daniel, *The Church and the Jews: The Biblical Relationship*, Hagerstown, MD: Serenity Books, 1997.

Gruber, Daniel, *The Separation of Church & Faith, Vol. 1: Copernicus and the Jews*, Hanover, NH: Elijah Publishing, 2005.

Horovitz, Ahron, and Meiron, Eyal, ed. *City of David: The Story of Ancient Jerusalem*, Lambda Publishers, Inc., 2009.

Laird, H., Archer Jr., G., and Waltke, B., eds. *Theological Wordbook of the Old Testament*, Chicago: Moody Press, 1999.

Larson, Frederick A., bethlehemstar.net.

Loewenberg, F.M., "Did Jews Abandon the Temple Mount?" *Middle East Quarterly: Summer 2013*, pp. 37–48, http://goo.gl/FQr1IJ.

Ritmeyer, Leen, *The Quest: Revealing the Temple Mount in Jerusalem,* Jerusalem: Carta, 2012.

Ritmeyer, Leen, *Jerusalem: The Temple Mount – A Carta Guide Book,* Jerusalem: Carta, 2015.

Scherman, Nosson, *Artscroll Series: Chumash Stone Edition Travel Size (Ashkenaz),* Brooklyn, NY: Mesorah Publications Ltd., 1998.

Steinmann, Andrew, "When Did Herod the Great Reign?" *Novum Testamentum,* Vol. 51, Number 1, 2009, pp. 1–29.

The Complete Jewish Bible with Rashi Commentary, © 1993–2015 Chabad–Lubavitch Media Center, http://goo.gl/1zQwNR.

Warner, Tim, "The 'New Jerusalem' is Jerusalem Restored," © answersinrevelation.org, http://goo.gl/641xzO.